MW01296063

Warranty Void If Seal Is Broken

Jon Bush

authorHOUSE®

AuthorHouse™
1663 Liberty Drive
Bloomington, IN 47403
www.authorhouse.com
Phone: 1-800-839-8640

First published by AuthorHouse 4/25/2011

ISBN: 978-1-4567-6483-8 (e)
ISBN: 978-1-4567-6482-1 (dj)
ISBN: 978-1-4567-6481-4 (sc)

Library of Congress Control Number: 2011906298

Printed in the United States of America

This book is printed on acid-free paper.

This book is based on a true story. While the entire book is based on true events, some parts of this book are fiction, while some remain fact. Neither Jon Bush, Author House Publishing, nor any retailer who stocks this book are responsible for the accuracy of the content within.

To protect the cowards, all names and identifying features of individuals in this book have been changed. If changed because of true innocence, I've taken the time to say so.

Dedicated to: My Mom, Paula Bush

Recognition To: Sammy, da puddy cat

Special Recognition To:
(In no particular order)
Nissa Chester, Lauren Smith Simms, Lyndee and Marc Phillips

Special thanks to Aaron Tennyson for photo,
Web and cover work!
http://jonbushbooks.com

Sincerest Appreciation To:
(In no particular order)
Nancy Horn, Debbie and Randy Jacobs, Bill Campbell, Phyllis Hickey, Louise Stephens (Grandma), and David Downs

Contents

"Therefore, I urge you, brothers, in view of God's mercy, to offer your bodies as living sacrifices, holy and pleasing to God--this is your spiritual act of worship. Do not conform any longer to the pattern of this world, but be transformed by the renewing of your mind. Then you will be able to test and approve what God's will is--his good, pleasing and perfect will. For by the grace given me I say to every one of you: Do not think of yourself more highly than you ought, but rather think of yourself with sober judgment, in accordance with the measure of faith God has given you."

Romans 12:1-3

Chapter 1

Best Friends.

You know your friends well to call them friends. But your best friends, you know them better than anyone. You know how they think, what they eat and you can finish most of their sentences. Many would lay their life down to protect a best friend. Trust is never questioned; it is taken for granted with a best friend. Your best friend is there to help you, console you and protect you on your worst day. Your best friend is there to get wasted with you in the happiest celebratory moments in your life. Your best friend is there to love you.

My best friend did all those things. He was amazing in every way. You could not ask for a better best friend. My best friend was Gage Tate. He was attractive, funny, sensitive, loyal and implausibly honest with me when I needed it the most. In fact, honesty was an important virtue for Gage. He took that seriously. And he didn't accept many apologies from those who lied to him. Honesty and loyalty were the anchors of his cruise ship in life. He thought of everyone first and himself last. No matter what he felt like, if I needed him, he was there for me. He would stay up late when he was tired or miss dinner when he was hungry to help me with anything I ever needed. He would give me the last dollar in his pocket to help me out if I really needed it. I loved Gage Tate. He was my very best friend in the world.

Betrayal is difficult to process. It is difficult to understand, even on the most basic level. As people, we understand and accept the possibility of betrayal from people we don't know or people we know casually. In a dog eat dog world, it is too often that the choice is him or you. And in my experience, more often than not, he will choose himself over you. Best friends, however, tend to be different. For someone you grace with that title, you'd sacrifice many things for their well-being. And betrayal? Well you don't even think about betrayal when it comes to your best friend. After all, if there is anyone in the world you can trust, it is your best friend, right?

Well that's what I thought too. My name is Brayden Cooper and Gage Tate betrayed me. As I considered how he took advantage of my trust, I began to realize that our friendship was based on lies and betrayal. And of the two of us, I was the only one who didn't know. I can only compare the betrayal of my best friend to having the love of my life break it off and completely not see it coming. It is shocking, unbelievable and nearly unbearable. This is my story of lies, betrayal and turmoil. Pray that you cannot relate to my story.

Chapter 2

EIGHTEEN MONTHS EARLIER.

11:31 PM Saturday night and it is hot and humid outside. I have to work tonight some time, but I can go later. Or tomorrow. As I scrolled through my black Motorola cell phone, I found the entry I was looking for. "Gage-Cell" as it read on my screen. I decided if he couldn't, or didn't want to do anything, I would just go to work. Little did I know that decision would set into motion a series of events that would change my life forever.

After several rings, I heard the call connect. No one said anything for a few seconds. Finally, Gage spoke.

"Yea," he grumbled. He sounded funny, like maybe he was asleep.

"Hey, what's up? Did I wake you?"

After another pause Gage said, "Who is this?"

"Uh... it's Brayden. Brayden Cooper, remember me?"

"Oh, hey. I'm awake."

"You sound odd, what are you doing?"

"Hanging out with Jack," he said.

"Yeah?" I paused, trying to figure out who Jack was. Then, just like a light bulb flipped on, it was all clear. He was with Jack

Daniels, drinking. Drunk, no doubt. Gage was, by the way, under age. "Are you drunk?" I asked.

"Little bit," he said.

I was hearing something in the background that sounded like music. Almost a slow hip hop type of sound, not something Gage would normally listen to. I asked him, "So, where are you?"

"I'm at the house my parents live in."

So, I'm thinking, what the hell? Gage did live at home with his mother and stepfather. He didn't so much get along with his mother, though they didn't have a bad habit of fighting a great deal. She was just never there; really more of a strained relationship based on omission of a relationship. She liked to drink too much and his stepfather and her loved to smoke pot. He hated his stepfather. He was overall very unhappy at home and with his family situation. Still, I was thinking a much less dramatic answer could have been "I'm home."

"Is everything ok?" I asked him.

"Just peachy," he snapped. The sarcasm was too obvious to ignore.

I sighed and, with a bit of my own sarcasm said, "And funny, though I don't take you for a liar, I don't believe you when you say that. What's up?"

"Goodbye, Brayden," he said.

"Wait, I was just kidding..." He hung up. I sat there for a few minutes just staring at the phone. This was very unusual, even for the sometimes completely unpredictable Gage Tate. I contemplated calling him back and I didn't know if I should. Maybe he just wanted to be alone and not to talk to anyone. Maybe he was just really drunk. Maybe I didn't have a clue.

I knew for sure that this was not normal for Gage Tate. I was worried about him and decided to call him back. About ten minutes had passed and I picked up my phone.

The phone rang four or five times and when he finally picked up, I was almost surprised.

"Gage?" I said, "Are you there?"

"What?" He said hatefully.

"I'm your best friend and you just hung up on me, that's what. You've never done that before. What's wrong with you?"

"Everything," he said, "Everything is wrong. I don't need to be... anywhere, anymore."

"What is that supposed to mean?" I asked.

"I guess it means whatever you want it to mean," he said.

"C'mon Gage, stop talking all crazy. This is getting stupid. I'm serious, what's going on?"

"Maybe I am crazy."

"You are not crazy!" I screamed, "Look, you're freaking me out, I'm coming over."

"Whatever," he said. Then he hung up, again. His tone of voice almost had a tone of disbelief. It is like he didn't believe I would actually come to his house. This was all very strange to me.

I told Mom I was going out and may work before I came home. I left the apartment and drove to Gage Tate's house. Well, the house his parents live in.

As I pulled up to his house, I noticed his car was the only one there. It wasn't unusual for his mom to be gone. It was a Saturday night and she was a waitress, so she was at work. His step father, however, drew a disability check from a back injury and didn't work. He was usually home. I picked up my phone and called him to let him know that I was there, as was normal for us.

He answered and said, "Yeah?"

"Hey, I'm here."

"Well, I'm sure you can find my room." He hung up again. The attitude was intense. I thought about just leaving, but I couldn't. I had to see what was going on. I had to try and help him.

I got out of my car and went to the front door. The door was unlocked, which was strange. With no one there and Gage in his room, anyone could walk in the house without him knowing it. I went up the stairs just inside the front door. When I came to his door, I knocked twice and pushed the door open slowly.

I stepped inside his room and stopped. I wasn't sure what I was looking at, but what I saw I wasn't comfortable with. His room was rather clean, which is not all that normal for Gage. He was sitting on the floor leaning against the night table behind him. His radio was on and two large candles lit the room from the table behind him. In his lap was a bottle of Jack Daniels®, less than half full, with no top. He was sitting Indian style and in front of him laid the one thing that me uneasy.

Lying on the floor, horizontally in front of him was a rifle. It seemed bigger than the first time I remember seeing it, several months ago after his father bought it for him.

After what seemed like forever, I managed to peal my eyes off the gun and look at Gage. His head was down, looking toward the whiskey. Gage picked up the bottle from his lap and took another drink.

I finally broke the silence with, "Gage, what's going on?"

"I assume you interrupted me for a reason, what do you want?"

"I want to help you. I want you to tell me what's going on so I can help you."

"Is that it?" He asked, "Is that the only reason you came over?"

"Dude, you know, or you should know, that I'm here for whatever you need."

"Is that right, Brayden?" He said, "Is that all you're really here for?"

I nodded. I didn't know what else to say. That was all I was there for. Something was very wrong. I couldn't imagine a drunken

Gage with a rifle. Something was hurting him so bad and I just wanted to ease that pain for him.

He looked up at me for the first time and we made eye contact. He had tears in his eyes. He took his right hand off the whisky bottle and moved it to the floor. He raised it up, and in it was a handgun. I had not seen this before now. He raised the gun and pointed it at me. I stood there, frozen. I didn't know what to do or what Gage was going to do.

He said, "Are you scared?"

I didn't say anything and I didn't move. I was scared of the gun, but I wasn't scared of Gage. What reason would Gage have to hurt me? We were best friends.

He said, "You should go now."

Again, I said nothing and I didn't move.

He began yelling, "Hey! Are you listening to me? If you haven't noticed, I'm pointing a gun at you! Now, I think you should do as you're told and get the hell out!"

"Or what, Gage? Are you going to shoot me?" I asked softly.

He didn't respond and the look on his face made it clear that he didn't expect that response. Though, right then, he did appear to consider shooting me.

I spoke again and said, "Or what if I leave? Then what, Gage? You gonna kill yourself?"

His hand was shaking, causing the gun to move around some. I knew he was scared but I couldn't figure out what had sparked all this.

"Fine!" he yelled, "You don't want to leave, then stay!"

He pulled the gun back and pointed it at his own head.

"Gage!" I screamed, "What are you doing? Put it down! Put the gun away!"

"Brayden," he said very calm, "just go away."

"Fuck you Gage Tate! I'm not going to stand here while you do this! I mean, shit dude. Just talk to me, for God's sake. What is so wrong that it has come to this?"

"Everything," he said, "Everything is wrong."

"Well fucking talk to me about it! What is it? Talk to me damnit!"

"I CAN'T!" he screamed, "I can't tell you! I can't tell anyone."

"Look," I said, "Whatever it is I can help you. Or I can at least try to help you. But either way, you have to talk to me. I can't help with a problem when I don't know the problem."

"You can't help me, Brayden, it's over."

"What are you talking about, Gage? Nothing is over!"

I took a step forward and without thinking, I grabbed the barrel of the gun. I jerked it away from his head and with his hand still on the trigger, I point the gun at my own head.

"Fine then," I said, "Then save me the trouble and just shoot me first. I love you Gage. You are my best friend and I'm not going to be able to live with myself if I stand here and let you kill yourself."

"Why are you doing this?" he asked.

"Why are *you* doing this, Gage?"

"You don't understand."

"No, Gage, I don't understand. I can't understand if you don't talk to me. Just put the gun down and talk to me, please."

I felt the weight of the gun increase as he let go of it. I set the gun on the table behind me. It was about this time when my heart resumed beating.

"I can't," he said, "I can't tell you."

He started crying and sat up on his bed. I sat on the bed next to him. He leaned over and hugged me tighter than he ever had before. I could feel his body shake and jerk. I couldn't imagine what could have happened to my friend to make him suffer this much.

We talked for a long time and covered an array of usual subjects. As far as the root of his big problem at that very moment, that's about all we *didn't* talk about. We did talk about trust and he assured me if he wanted or needed to talk about it, I'd be person he'd come to. I wasn't sure that was a good thing, but I felt better knowing he would talk to me about it eventually. It was unlike Gage to keep secrets from me, especially secrets that made him this upset.

He did confess that his therapy wasn't working and, as for his therapist, "I'm going to have to get a new one," he said.

"Thank you for being here tonight," he said.

"Any time, Gage. Really, I mean any time you need anything you can always call."

He made eye contact with me and there was an awkward pause.

He grinned at me and said, "You love me, don't you?"

"Yes," I said, "I do. Don't forget that."

With a light chuckle he said, "You are in love with me, aren't you?"

Truthfully, I didn't know if I was in love with Gage. Looking back from today, I'd have to say that, in that moment, I wanted to be in love with him. It would have pleased me to know we could be together and be happy. But there was a big difference, even then, in *wanting* to be in love with him and being in love with him. I think I was just so blindsided by that question that, beyond not knowing how to answer it, I wasn't sure what the answer was.

"Why... what are you asking me exactly?" I asked.

"You know you are, just say it. I want you to say it," he said.

"Even if it is true, why are you bringing it up now?"

"Do you want to have sex with me? If I said right now, let's have sex. This minute, on my bed right now, would you say yes? Would you do me?"

"Gage..."

"Just answer. Yes or no?"

"...No, Gage, right now, this minute, I would not have sex with you. I love you. You are my best friend. But you are not gay and you wouldn't want this to happen. What you are is drunk and out there a bit right now. Tomorrow you'll be sober and I don't want you to regret something I can put a stop to."

He was literally laughing at me. "So, if I wasn't drunk, you'd have sex with me right now?"

"I don't know, Gage. You don't really want to have sex with me, so if you weren't drunk it wouldn't come up."

He leaned over to me and was so close I could hear him breathing. He said, "Go ahead, Brayden. Make a move on me."

"Gage, you're drunk," I said as I moved away from him.

"I'm horny," he said.

I reached down and picked up the bottle of whiskey, which was about a third full. I picked up the handgun and wrapped the two in a towel from the bed.

"I'm gonna go, dude," I said to him, "And I'm taking these with me. You don't need either of them tonight."

He smiled and said, "I'll remind you tomorrow how you had the chance to fuck me tonight. Pop my gay cherry. You'd like that, wouldn't you?"

"Tomorrow you'll thank me, Gage. Call me when your hangover is getting better."

And the next day he did thank me. His drinking had become worse over time but it seems this had opened his eyes a bit. After that night, we were closer than ever. He began to really open up to me and talk about things he never had. I was really getting to know him well, or so I thought.

Over the next few months, I learned many things about the way Gage truly felt about areas in his life that needed improvement. He had spent years trying to talk his mom and stepfather out of smoking pot and drinking as much as they did. He recognized, from the time he was a young teen, that these behaviors were destructive. I respected his efforts, though ultimately they were made in vain. After so long of trying to convince them what they were doing was hurting him, he decided to take a more radical approach. He began drinking heavily and smoking pot, and not even attempting to hide it.

If they could see what it was like to watch someone they love destroying themselves, perhaps they could then see his point and stop their own destruction. But two things happened that ruined that plan. First, Gage's mom didn't seem to be as upset with his drinking and drug use as he was with hers so the impact of getting caught turned out to be minimal. And secondly, something Gage hadn't counted on, he began to become heavily addicted to both the alcohol and the marijuana.

Gage is a control freak of sorts when it comes to other people but when it comes to himself, he feels he has the ultimate self-control. It was hard for him to handle an addiction that at least partially seized that control. He was in denial about the addictions and that made it harder to help him. However, as it turns out, the demons in Gage's closet went far beyond a bottle of vodka and joint. As he began declining, we all fell for the troubled addict issues as the only source of demonic secret to plague him. And through that decline, it all seemed to just make sense...

Chapter 3

Gage's Decline.

"C'mon Gordy, you know he does stuff no one else wants to do. He's the only one that does all his side work and never complains about it. He actually does care about the job, which is more than you can say for a few people here," I said to Gordy, the general manager of O'Charley's.

"Yea, all that may be true," he said, "When he comes to work. I am not going to keep dealing with this every day. I used to could rely on him."

This was a similar conversation to many I had with Gordy. Gordy and I had worked together in the past. We had been friends for a long time. We had a mutual respect for each other. Gordy would talk straight to me, though. He never wore kid gloves because we were friends and that is what made him a good manager. If I needed correcting, Gordy didn't have a problem being direct.

It wasn't any different with Gage Tate. Just because we were friends didn't mean he wasn't going to do what was best for the restaurant. And Gordy didn't like Gage, not at the end, anyway. Gage's work ethic changed. He began coming to work late and his attitude was, at times, unbearable. Gage had become a bit of an ass and Gordy began to care less about his personal issues. He only cared that it was beginning to affect his store. And that was unacceptable. Gordy told me a few times that if Gage didn't straighten himself out, he was going to get fired. Many conversations started, "If Gage blankity blank blanks one more time..."

I tried talking to Gage on many occasions. Early on, it was more just being a few minutes late than anything. And a few minutes could be dealt with. Though annoying, he had been there for a while and wasn't going to get fired over a few minutes. But then, there was the first really bad day. I mean, a day that had us all freaked out.

It was around 11PM and I remember being sleepy. My phone rang and I remember it jolting me because I was dozing off a bit.

"Hello?"

"What's up?" It was Gage and he sounded down.

"Not much, what's going on?"

"I dunno, I just need to talk," he said.

"Yea dude, everything ok?"

"Yea, everything is fine actually. I don't know why, I am just really depressed."

"Well that's not good, did something happen?"

"No," he said, "I was just laying here thinking, and drinking a bit, and I just... I don't know dude. I am just so sad."

Honestly, I didn't know what to say. Gage had seemed a bit distant lately but nothing really seemed to have happened.

"Hmm... What were you thinking about when you started feeling sad?"

"Just random stuff. I dunno dude, what am I really doing with life? Am I just gonna be a host forever? Make $10 an hour forever?"

"Is there something else you had in mind, specifically?" I asked

"No, that's just it; I'm not really good at anything."

After a short pause, I asked, "How much have you had to drink, Gage?"

"Not that much, maybe taken eight shots," he said.

"That is a lot, dude. Look, Gage, you are good at a lot of things. I thought you were going back to school this fall? Maybe you can find something you really enjoy there?"

"Yea, maybe I will, I dunno. Sorry I called so late... look I'm going to get off here. I took a few sleeping pills, I'm getting sleepy now. I'm gonna crash."

"Shit, dude, you aren't supposed to take those together... the pills and the alcohol. Ugh, get some rest buddy. See you in the morning," I said.

But that morning is when it would all begin. Gage's decline was really brought to the surface for all to see. No more hiding in the shadows.

I was the opening host, got there at about 10:30 in the morning. Gage was scheduled at 11:30. Leala, I remember, was the opening manager.

"Leala! I love when you open!"

"Aw, I'm glad to see you too. Would have enjoyed it more a few hours later, but what can ya do?"

"Mornings do come early," I said. And Leala would have been there hours before me. The opening managers usually arrived around 7am.

We did our usual opening tasks, had our morning meeting and got ready for the lunch rush. We opened at 11AM and 11:30 approached quickly.

At about 11:35, Leala came to the front of the store. "Where's Gage?" she asked.

"I don't know, but I'm sure he'll be here. Want me to call him?"

"Give him a few minutes and we'll see," she said.

So that's what we did. We gave him a few minutes and few more. At almost noon, she decided to call him. He didn't answer.

"I'm kind of worried about him, Leala," I said.

"Well it is weird that he's late..."

"No," I interrupted. "I am actually worried. Last night he called me. He wasn't acting like himself. He was depressed. He had been drinking and took some sleeping pills. He might not be ok, I dunno, it is just not like him to not answer the phone like this."

"That's no good. But not sure what else we can do at this point. We are getting busy, just let me know if you need help up here and I will keep trying to call him."

Leala is great at this. She has an efficient process. Gather information, evaluate the situation, determine a course of action and, most of all, STAY CALM! She is one of the few people I know who can keep a bunch of servers calm when things get crazy. And she is definitely in the rare group of people that could keep *me* calm when shit hit the fan.

We did get busy. People were pouring in and I was working fast. At about 12:30 or so, I came back to the host stand to seat the next table and there stood Gage.

"Who's next?" he asked.

"Oh you do work today? Nice of you to join us," I said sarcastically. "Table 31, two top."

He grabbed the menus and silverware and off to table 31 he went. It wasn't until after we slowed down that I got to tell him how he worried the bageezus out of me.

"After last night, I..."

"It's cool. I just overslept. Sorry," he said.

Gage went back to talk to Leala, to whom he apologized for being late. And this was not a pattern, yet, so even though it wasn't a popular move, he wasn't in too much trouble.

Leala respected what Gage did as a host. He generally did everything that was asked of him. Behavior like this, showing up more than an hour late, was uncharacteristic of Gage. Leala knew that but since we had talked a few times about how Gage had a drinking problem, she was still a bit worried about him.

By this point, Leala and I had become great friends. We hit

it off from the beginning. We have similar personalities and we love to laugh. It was laughter that brought us together more often than not. We also shared a genuine concern for the people around us. I knew Gage had been drinking more and more. And he was underage, so it was especially important to try to intervene.

I never drank much, but loved going out with those who did. Naomi, the O'Charley's bartender at the time, Leala and I went out often. And often times it was with a larger group. That's what servers do, they go out. It took a while for me to get used to that pattern. You don't have to drink a ton or do crazy things, but if you take the time to just go out and have a good time, it can help you as a server. I quickly learned the value of expanding inter-restaurant relationships to improve my daily job. Serving is not fun, but you have to put on a good face every day just the same, if you want to be good at it. Even on your worst days, when you can't stand the thought of smiling or being around people, those days you still have to smile and be friendly. If you're not, you don't make money. By going out with the group, you build relationships that can spill over into the work day and make working as a team run even smoother.

When drama gets in the way, it can make the team vulnerable to collapse as well. Gage Tate, during this time, had become the center of much drama. "Gage takes his job too seriously" had become a common dialog around O'Chux.

During my time serving, at one point Leala needed a host for a shift after someone called in. She asked me if I would consider filling in. I had not really hosted there, but how hard could it be? Turns out, it wasn't hard. I had a great time and people enjoyed having me host. I understood things hosting that sometimes other hosts, ones who had never served, didn't understand. I understood the concept of a rotation, which seemed to get lost sometimes with other hosts. And the servers knew, because we were all friends that I wasn't going to screw anyone. If the rotation was altered because some nice couple decided they would tell me which table they wanted instead of accepting my suggestion, I went straight to the servers involved and explained the situation. That usually went over reasonably smoothly simply because I communicated with them. Ultimately, there was nothing I could do. If people ask to sit somewhere other than where I take them, I wasn't supposed to say no.

This is one problem Gage had. He usually sat guests wherever they requested, if they did. But he didn't communicate with servers. And when approached, it wasn't always a friendly conversation. A server would ask why they were skipped in a rotation and Gage would tell them not to come yelling at him. "Don't tell me how to do my job, I know what I'm doing" he would say. The problem is servers took that very personally. Servers are paid with and completely rely on tips. No tables, no tips. So when a host skips them in rotation, it is like taking money from them. It was no wonder they questioned a host who skipped them. And it was no wonder they were mad when the host was defensive.

So after my first hosting experience, it became more frequent. Leala knew I didn't enjoy serving. Immaturity played a big role in my dislike of serving. I was a decent server. Guests loved me, I got orders right most all the time and all was good as long as I wasn't very busy. The problem I had was getting too many tables. I could never get down how to handle a hundred things at once. I either tried to do too much and I screwed it up or I would do things in the wrong order and people would be unhappy. Either way, it wasn't good for me and it wasn't good for my managers.

The more I hosted, the more I was liked at the host stand. The managers liked me, the servers liked me and most of all the guests liked me. I am naturally a people person and I very much enjoyed seeing all the different people that would come through the door.

While all seemed rather perfect, what I didn't see was Gage's attitude boiling at my success. He had developed this attitude that I was trying to make him look bad. He thought I was talking about him behind his back, that I was playing cards just right to push him out completely and take over the job of head host that he so dearly coveted. Of course, that was not at all my intentions. In fact, I largely defended Gage's attitude to servers and managers alike. I always made excuses for why today he was in a bad mood.

And when I did talk "behind his back" about him, I did it out of concern, not ulterior motives. When Gage was in a good mood, I loved working with him. He was my best friend and I didn't even think along the lines of him ever not being there.

I remember talking to Leala and Naomi on a few occasions about his drinking and taking pills. I was concerned for his health and I was looking for ideas to keep him from doing these things. Despite my intentions, however, Gage and I drifted apart a bit. I began to get tired of his attitude and the way he treated people. I stopped defending him and we seemed to argue more and more.

One day, Gage came to work on his day off. He was driving a new car, 2005 gold Toyota Camry. I was having lunch and he came up to the lounge to sit with me.

"So, why did you get a new car? I didn't know you were looking," I said to Gage.

"I liked it. My Honda was costing so much money in repairs; I had to get something new."

"That's cool. It looks nice; I bet the monthly payment is a beast, huh?"

"It might have been, but I paid cash, so I dunno."

"Cash? As in, you bought it outright from the dealer?"

"Yup," he said casually, as if everyone knew he had millions of dollars stashed away.

"Whoa, you must have a lot of savings!"

"Yeah, I have some. You know I don't spend much money," he said.

And that was true. Gage was extremely stingy with his money. I don't mean that in a bad way, but it was true. One thing that stuck out in my mind was that only about three months prior to this he had paid cash for a new laptop. He came and asked me to help him pick one out that fit his needs. His main concerns were fast wireless internet and to have a reliable computer for school. Oddly, I remember he went to the ATM machine a couple of nights in a row to draw out enough cash to pay for the laptop. I remember telling him that he could much more easily just use his debit card for the purchase. He insisted, however, that he pay cash money for it. At the time, it didn't mean much.

I talked with my mom, Leala and Naomi about how he could afford these things. We knew he didn't have many bills. He paid for his cell phone, which was mostly used at night, so he didn't need many minutes. His dad paid for insurance for his car and he didn't pay rent. So, he made a full time wage and had no bills. It was commendable that he had saved so much, though not so surprising with such few financial responsibilities.

The idea had also come up that he could be dealing drugs on some low level. His brother had been involved with some drug dealers in Lexington. Perhaps he was involved with them and making some money on the side. Or, perhaps he was lying and he didn't pay cash for the car. Maybe he paid part and his parents paid part. It was curious, but not a huge deal at the time.

As Gage's decline continued, he began having more run-ins with management. It was one thing to have some angry servers that didn't like you, but when you want to keep your job, having managers upset with you is not good.

I remember this one encounter Gage had with Corey Jones, another manager at O'Charley's. Gage was supposed to be in at 11:30 to host and I was the opening host, just like it was many times. I remember Corey greeting me shortly after I got there that morning.

"How late is your buddy going to be today?" he asked.

"Well he still has an hour; I'd give him a little while before I started bitching about it."

"We'll see. If he's late today, I might need you to stay. I'm going to send him home. Could you stay if he's late?"

"Yeah, I can stay, but he will probably be here."

Corey and I didn't always get along. He was the kitchen manager, so we didn't have a great deal of direct contact anyway. Corey had a bad habit of getting irritated about small things and not saying anything. He would let it build up and BOOM, everyone would know he was mad. The situation with Gage wasn't much different. He would make snide comments about Gage's indiscretions at work, but not really to Gage other than in a joking manner. Part of this is because the other manager on duty usually took care of the "Gage situation" as it was commonly called. I think on this morning Corey was ready to unleash all his frustrations on Gage and just needed the smallest of triggers.

I called Gage around 11AM, just to remind him he needed to be at work in thirty minutes. I didn't want Corey to send him home and I didn't want to stay in his place. He, of course, didn't answer. And, of course, Corey was right. His 11:30 start time came and went. No Gage.

Somewhere around 12:45, he called. I answered the phone and he said he overslept but was on his way right now. He said he'd be there in less than five minutes.

"Gage," I said, "I don't think it will matter. You are too late; Corey is saying he will send you home if you come in."

"Who else is there?" he asked.

"Manager wise, no one, Corey is by himself. Host wise, just me."

"I'll talk to Corey when I get there, he'll let me stay."

"Ok, Gage. Hope so, talk to you later."

I went and told Corey that Gage had just called.

"Ok, I'll be up there in a minute, he is not staying," Corey said.

Corey had just arrived at the host stand about the time Gage entered the front door. He began waving at Gage as he was walking in, as if to wave goodbye.

"Bye, Gage. Go back home, you're too late."

"I just overslept; can we talk for a minute?" Gage asked.

"No, Gage. It is always something, just go."

And, though Corey and I didn't always see eye to eye, he was totally right. It was always something. That is a hard thing to deal with in the restaurant business. You need to know you have people there that were scheduled to be there. I remember Corey bought my lunch that day because I had to stay late. That's how this worked. If you can't do the job, someone else can and will do it for you. One man's failures will result in another man's benefits.

This decline of Gage Tate had become a steady, snowball like decline. He had alienated many people around him who had, at least at one point, cared greatly for him. I still did care for Gage. I still considered him my best friend. I just knew my best friend had some substance abuse issues. And I knew we had to get those fixed, somehow.

Chapter 4

FEBRUARY 22, 2006. 1:30 P.M. THE ARREST.

"Brayden!" Chris, a manager at O'Charley's yelled. "Hey, can you go to Office Depot™ for me?"

"Sure, what do you need?"

"We need a bulletin board that is half dry erase and half wooden, like for thumb tacks. I don't want two separate ones; see if you can find a big one that is split into two sections."

"Ok, you want me to go now?" I asked.

"If you don't mind," Chris said.

I didn't mind, so I left. I searched all over Office Depot™ for that stupid bulletin board and couldn't find it. I had decided to call back and ask Chris what he wanted me to do.

"Thank you for calling O'Charley's, this is Ashley, how can I help you?"

"Hey Ashley, it's Brayden. I can't find this bulletin board; can you let me talk to Chris?"

"Yeah, hey you won't believe what just happened!"

"What happened?"

"The cops were just here. They came in looking for Gage.

They wanted to know if he was here or when he might be back. Chris told them that he wasn't here, but was scheduled to work tonight."

"What?! That's crazy, why are they looking for him?"

"I don't know, you still want to talk to Chris?"

"Yes," I said. I wondered while on hold what on earth the police could ever want with Gage.

"Hey, Brayden, no luck?" Chris asked.

"Nope, didn't find it here. Hey what's going on with the cops looking for Gage? What did they want?"

"I don't know; they just left. Just come on back, we may need you here if Gage doesn't come in to work."

"Ok, I can do that."

I was upset for Gage. I couldn't imagine what he could have done. As soon as I hung up, I called Gage on his cell phone.

"Hello?" He answered.

"Hey dude, what's going on? I just talked to Ashley at O'Charley's and she said the cops were looking for you."

"Yeah," he said, "I just heard. Naomi called me."

"You have any idea what they want?"

"Yeah, I have a good idea. Listen I am on my way home, I will have to talk to you later."

"Uh... ok, well, what do they want?"

"I'll call you later dude."

"Um... ok dude. I will talk to you soon. Let me know what's up."

I remember thinking he was freakishly calm about this. He knew almost for sure what they wanted. It was almost like he had been expecting it. This was all very bizarre and I felt like I had missed something along the way.

I returned to O'Charley's around 2. Everyone was speculating about what the police could have wanted. "What did your buddy do, Brayden?" everyone asked. Suddenly he was nothing more than the butt of every joke to everyone else. He was "my buddy" and everyone looked to me for answers. I felt like I was his agent or some sort of representative or spokesperson. I was in the dark as much as the people asking me. All I could say is I didn't know.

Around 3pm, two Lexington Police Detectives returned to O'Charley's. They spoke with Leala and, as I found out later, asked her about who Gage was close with and had informed her of his charges and that he had been taken into custody. Obviously, I was brought up as a close friend to Gage.

Hand stuck out in front of him, the short and heavier detective said, "Hi Brayden. My name is Detective Hailey. I'd like to ask you a few questions if that's ok."

As I shook his hand I said, "Sure, is this about Gage? Is he in trouble?"

"What if I told you," he started, "that Gage Tate had hundreds of images of child pornography on his laptop?"

"I'd say you must be mistaken," I said.

"Have a seat, Brayden," he instructed. "Your friend is a pedophile who likes to masturbate to pictures of naked children. If there is anything you know about this, or anything that could help us with this, now would be the time to speak up."

I didn't immediately respond.

"I know it is not an easy thing to hear," the taller detective said. "Listen, no one wants to hear that about a friend, but we are just gathering information. I take it this is a bit of a shock to you?"

"No, not a bit shocking. Totally shocking. I don't know if I believe you."

"We have proof, Brayden. Solid proof. He's going to prison," said Detective Hailey. "Let me give you my card, and if you think of anything you want to share, just let me know, ok?"

"Um... ok..."

I remember feeling like I got shot right in the stomach. As they walked away, Leala said something to me. I didn't really hear her and I didn't respond.

"Brayden? Are you ok?" she asked.

I didn't really answer. I started to say something but I couldn't make the sounds into an audible word. I was shaking and I stood up, half way pointing towards the kitchen. I guess Leala knew what I meant because she just nodded.

I went through the kitchen and out the back door of the restaurant. Leala followed me and told me to just take some time. I was crying by then just trying to digest what had been said to me. There was a chair outside for people to sit on during smoke breaks and that is where I first sat. I replayed the conversation with Detective Hailey in my head seven or eight times.

It didn't hit me full force until I thought back to the conversation with Gage on the way back to O'Charley's. He was so calm, he must have known. I was so sick to my stomach at the thought of what had been told to me. I paced a couple of short steps until I leaned over the door of the dumpster and vomited inside. I was physically sick at the thought this could be true.

I somewhat composed myself and I pulled out my cell phone. I called my mom at work. I lost it again as soon as she answered the phone. I could barely play back in my head what the detectives had said to me, let alone repeat the words to anyone else. After about twenty minutes, I finally managed to spit it all out. My mom was quite shocked as well and she didn't know what to say.

After I hung up with her, I sat back down in the chairs outside. Chris, a manager and also a good friend of Gage's, came out and sat beside me. We sat for a few minutes and didn't say anything. I was still crying steadily.

"I don't know what to say, Brayden," Chris said. "This is so unbelievably screwed up."

"It's real, isn't it?" I asked.

"Yea, I'm sorry, Brayden. It is too real. Man, it feels so strange man."

"He was my best friend," I choked out. "My family knows him, I know him... this is just so unreal."

"Yea I know what you mean. He was just at my house for Halloween. With my kids, God man, he was in the house at the party with my kids and a bunch of other kids."

"You think they could be wrong?" I asked.

"I don't know, Brayden. These guys looked pretty confident."

There was another lengthy pause.

Chris finally broke the silence and said, "Listen, we have no one at the door right now, especially since Gage won't be in. Take your time, get yourself together. You think you can come back up front in a little bit?"

"I dunno," I said. And I didn't know. I couldn't imagine doing anything but crying and screaming and puking.

"I'm going to put a sign on the door so people won't come out here. When you're ready, just let me know."

And he did put a sign on the door. It read something like "If you go outside, you're fired." I'm pretty sure people believed it too, because no one came out that door.

Eventually I did go back up front and work for about another thirty minutes. After that, I told Leala and Chris that I just couldn't do it any longer. I knew I had to just go home.

I did go home, though I do not remember getting there. I remember my mom came home early that night and was there before the 5 o'clock news started.

As the news began, the first thing we saw was Gage's picture. He was the top story. "UK Student arrested on child pornography charges" was the top headline. This in itself was odd because Gage went to a community college in town, not to UK. Ironically, his father worked at UK. The entire story lasted about ninety seconds. I remember thinking Gage looked so scared. He just looked so out of place in jail, on the news, or anywhere that people were saying bad things about him. He was a nice kid, a good kid. He was not the "top story on the news" type.

As the story concluded, my phone began to ring. And it didn't stop ringing for several hours. I had to tell the same vague, boring, unspecific story over and over again.

The thing is Gage and I did most everything together. Most of my good friends knew Gage too and this was a huge shock to the entire group. I spent the most time talking another one of my very best friends, Jacob Gibbs. I can't tell you about the awkwardness in that call. We didn't know what to say to each other. We couldn't figure out if what we were hearing was just a big mistake, lies or the truth. We couldn't help but feel sort of duped. I think we both reserved some comments waiting for the alarm to go off and wake up thinking "what the hell did I eat last night to make have an f'd up dream like?" As time went on, however, clearly we were not going to wake up.

In fact, as I lay down to go to sleep that Wednesday night, I did everything but sleep. No alarm would go off waking me from this nightmare and I wouldn't need an alarm to wake from the sleep I wasn't getting. Although, waiting for that alarm to eventually go off and end all this horror wouldn't cease for some years.

So the day ended much differently than I had planned. I woke up complaining about having to work and went to bed in agony over a debacle that made me wish work was the worst thing that had happened that day. My best friend got arrested and I lay in bed dizzy from the spinning in my head. What could possibly happen tomorrow?

Chapter 5

February 23 – March 1, 2006. The Week.

A silhouette of my body droned through this week. Many of my memories are distorted thinking back to the end of February. Some memories have completely escaped me and some are still clear as a bell in my head. In my continued research for this book, I discussed this week with several close friends and family. I suppose in the interest of accuracy, I must say some details may be recalled slightly different in this account of that week than what others may remember. What I can say for sure, the main focuses I will discuss are accurate. This week was truly the worst week of my life, up to this point.

You might say this situation reminded me of high school and the feeling of betrayal I felt in a crossroads of my life then. I was 16 years old and, like most boys my age, was just discovering who I really was as a man. I made friends quickly and became close with a few people quicker than I should. I fell in love with every girl or guy who smiled at me. Typical 16 year old boy stuff, we all do it at some point.

One friend I became especially close with was Jason Lynn. We started out being friends and we grew close very fast. We spent as much time together as we could, talked on the phone constantly and tried to keep our closeness a big secret. Jason was gay and his parents did not know. His father was extremely prejudiced against gays and Jason was scared to talk to him about this issue. His reluctance to talk to his parents drove us closer together in his need to deal with his "demons."

I knew Jason had some issues at home and he had a hard time coming to terms with being gay. Eventually though, he decided to tell his parents. He knew he couldn't continue to hide who he was and even with no place else to go, he knew he had to just get it out so he could be himself. His father, as we suspected, went through the roof. They got in a huge fight and he beat Jason up pretty bad that night.

Jason called me and told me what happened. We talked for a while, but it was quite different that the previous times we talked. He was crying some, but he was oddly calm. He continued to tell me it was going to be ok. I didn't have to worry about him, he told me. But I was worried about him. What a horrible thing he had just gone through, how could he deal with it on his own?

The day before Valentine's Day my junior year of high school, I got the terrible news. He had been killed in a car accident on the interstate. I was crushed at the thought. How could this happen to him now? As bad as his life was getting at the time, it was like he just literally plummeted off a cliff. The next day more details were revealed. He had been killed by a semi-truck after a head-on collision. The truck driver, they said, had been drinking.

A drunk driver? Really, how terrible of a way to lose someone is that? It is the most senseless and preventable act of "accidental" deaths. The truck driver was physically ok and had been taken to the hospital as a precaution. He would later be charged with murder for Jason's death.

After about a week or so passed, even more devastating news came out. His parents surfaced publically with a suicide note that had been left behind. The specifics in that note left no doubt that this was no accident. Jason meant to collide with a semi-truck head-on and end his life. He had committed suicide. On that day, I lost a part of me that died forever. And I had lost Jason.

I felt incredible guilt for his death and still do to this day. Why had he not talked to me before he did something so stupid? Why had I not realized that this situation was much more serious? I felt that something could have been done to prevent this and whatever that something was, I didn't do it. I had failed him as a friend.

This same feeling surfaced in me the day after Gage Tate was arrested. I was guilt ridden, in shock and had an overwhelming feeling of responsibility. Had I really ignored all these warning signs or had there even been any? I had once again failed my best friend.

Ironically, when Jason committed suicide, it was then I became so close to Gage Tate. And it was now that I felt I had let Gage Tate down in the same way I had let Jason down. I couldn't think straight and I was literally running on cruise control.

02/23/2006. As the morning after his arrest began, I remember dreading the day at work. Everyone kept asking me questions like I was supposed to know more than they did about what was going on. I had no idea what was going on and I was very much in the dark like everyone else.

I did go to work that morning, though. I remember seeing on the noon news from a TV in the lounge that Gage had made bond. They reported that his bond was made by his father and it had been a $10,000 property bond. His father was a level headed guy with a good education and a good job. I couldn't imagine what he must have been thinking about all this.

I got off work in the early afternoon. When I checked my phone, I had a missed call from Gage. My stomach churned when I read the name. I wasn't sure if I should call him back. I wasn't sure about much of anything at this point. He had, however, been my best friend for a long time. I felt that I owed him at least the common courtesy of giving me his side of the story. I owed him the chance to defend himself or to at least explain himself.

I walked outside and sat in the car. I thought about driving home first, but I couldn't wait. I was dying to know what was going on. I was dying to know if he was ok, or at least as ok as he could be all considering.

The phone rang only once. "Hello," Gage said with a sigh in his voice.

"Gage, it's me. How are you doing?"

"I've been better. I can't talk long now. I just wanted to let you know I was out of jail."

"Gage, what they're saying about you..."

"I know, I know, Brayden. Would you wanna meet me somewhere later?"

"Uh, yea, I guess. When?"

"Like later tonight, after dark, maybe ten or eleven. At our spot?"

Next door to the school we both attended high school there was a small park and a large wooded area that separated school grounds from a residential area. There was a small playground and a few benches that went largely unused. It was a good neighborhood though, just mostly an older population. It was quiet at night, mostly flat ground, well lit and wide sidewalks, all of which made for a good place for a night time walk. Gage and I frequently enjoyed taking such a walk, just to get away from the hustle and bustle of everyday life. The entrance of this park had years earlier been dubbed by us "our spot." No one else knew that we commonly met there and it was sort of our getaway.

"Ok, I can do that," I said.

"Come alone," Gage quickly added.

"I usually do... I will be alone."

"Ok," he said, "I'll see you then."

"Ok later."

Almost the instant I hung up the phone I began to have this feeling of fear. In retrospect of the last couple of days, I had just agreed to meet someone who apparently had kept a ton of really bad things from me for a long time. I didn't feel like I knew Gage as well anymore. It was like he was a different person than I knew. It was similar to the awkward feeling of being around an ex-lover after a breakup. Even if it wasn't a bad breakup, you still have that feeling like you're missing something about them. I simply didn't know if I trusted Gage.

I went home and continued the process of returning the many calls I kept receiving. By looking at my phone, you might have guessed I was the one on the news instead of Gage. After being home for a couple of hours, I decided to return to O'Charley's and meet Leala as she was getting off work.

Leala, Naomi and I, along with a few others went to O'Neil's Irish Pub to have a drink. Boy did I need a stiff drink! I must say, I completely blocked out this middle part of the night prior to my meeting with Gage. After talking with Leala and Naomi, they most clearly remembered that in between time. In fact, it seems as though I was strange enough that they were both a bit freaked out that night.

According to them, we left O'Neil's, which was about three blocks from the park Gage and I would meet at later, and we walked to the park. After talking with Gage, I can only guess I was a bit in fear for my life. My goal was to take them up to this park to identify where I'd be later with Gage. I told them if anything were to happen to me they should send police here to investigate and to tell them that I was meeting with Gage. We also agreed that about twenty minutes after I was supposed to meet Gage, if she hadn't heard from me via call or text, Leala would try to get in touch with me. If I remember correctly, we had some sort of "code" phrase if I was in trouble, but I do not remember what it was.

Leala and Naomi seemed to be deeply impacted by this little trip. I don't believe either of them was quite fond of the idea of this meeting anyway. And I'm sure taking them on a walk to explain where to find my dead body if I was missing didn't exactly help with their reservations. I was distant and rattling. I would ramble some and not always make the most since. I didn't listen and comprehend well either, which was uncharacteristic of me. Short answers or no answers seemed to become a common trend.

We went back to the bar and I drove home. I decided after I got home that I would just walk to the park instead of drive there. My thought process was scary to think back on now, but it was simple. If I went to that park, and things went terribly wrong, at least my car would be at home for my mom to take care of and a couple of people would likely know what happened. Though the risk seemed possibly high, the possibility of nothing happening kept me from telling my mom where I was going. She didn't know I was meeting Gage Tate and she certainly didn't know I was going to the park that night.

There are two entrances to this park. I had not spoken with Gage since earlier in the day when we set the time for our meeting. I wasn't sure which entrance he would choose. When I came to the entrance of the park that we most frequented, I hung around outside the opening. It was hard to see anything more than five feet in front of you. There are no lights and it was pitch black dark outside.

I remember seeing what looked like a person in the shadows at the base of the entrance but I couldn't tell for sure. I stared at it for a minute to see if it moved and I didn't see any movement. Oddly, I didn't want to call out his name. I sat on the bench just outside that entrance and decided to wait there. After five minutes or so, I heard someone clear their throat as if to bring attention to their presence. When I looked up, I saw the same figure I had thought was a person once before but had disregarded. It was Gage; he had apparently been there the whole time.

This didn't set my mind at ease. Why wouldn't he have spoken up when he first saw me? As I got closer, he appeared to side step me a bit. As I got to within about ten feet of him, he told me to stop. I could still barely see him because he was wearing solid black pants, a black hoodie with the hood up and dark sun glasses.

"You wearing a wire?" he asked.

"A what?"

"A wire, you know a recording wire, don't play dumb. Are you wearing one?"

"No, dude."

"Let me check you, ok? I can't be too careful right now."

I reluctantly agreed and he frisked me up and down rather thoroughly. Perhaps a new trick he learned at the Fayette County Detention Center.

When he got finished I said, "Maybe I should check you for a wire, ha ha. Why would I wear a wire dude?"

"It doesn't matter, you aren't. I just need to be out of public eye right now. I can't let anyone see or hear from me right now. That's why I'm dressed like this. That's why I'm acting funny."

"Yea, I get it. So, they are saying some crazy stuff about you on TV. Is it true, Gage?"

"Look I can't go into great detail right now, but I will say it is not like they are saying. Some of it is true, some not. None of it is quite like they are saying."

"So what does that mean?"

"Brayden, listen man, I really can't go into it in great detail right now. Please, I just need someone I can trust right now. I don't know what to do, Brayden. I am in major trouble."

"Ok, Gage. I guess I just don't know what to think right now. You have always been able to trust me and it's no different now. I'm right here, nothing has changed with me."

Gage stepped in and gave me a hug. I thought he might be trying to kill me as tight as he hugged me. He was shaking and scared to death. He had already received some death threats and really felt like he wasn't safe anywhere he went. I was more confused than I have ever been. I didn't know who or what to believe. But Gage Tate was my best friend and as much as I had perhaps already failed him, I couldn't bear the thought of abandoning him now when he needed me the most.

"So what happens now?" I asked.

"Well I had my arraignment this morning and my dad posted bond with the house. Now I just wait to be indicted. My lawyer says it usually takes about sixty days."

"So you got to meet with your lawyer already?"

"Yes. We met today briefly and we have more thorough meeting Friday."

Gage caught me staring at him, in the moment of silence.

"I know this is fucked up, Brayden. It's just not what it looks like right now."

"I hope not, Gage, because right now it looks pretty crazy."

About that time, Leala sent me a text. I responded and told her I was with Gage and I was just fine. Gage and I walked for about thirty minutes to help him clear his head. He wanted to talk about anything but what was going on. I remember asking him what he wanted me to tell people who continue to ask what is going on. He told me I could tell them whatever I wanted. He seemed disconnected with the entire world one minute and deeply concerned about it the next.

What stood out to me the most is something I didn't process quite right at the time. I realized later that Gage was scared of people and the death threats because he had been caught and he knew there was a reason to be scared. After I appeared to "be ok" with this situation, he seemed to mellow out considerably and start acting like his old self. That was odd in itself. It was almost like he thought if I was ok with it at this point, at least for a while he had someone to kill time with while he worried about the case. I don't believe he cared if I was lying in that moment about supporting him, as long as I didn't tell him. But I wasn't lying, I was prepared to believe him when he said things weren't quite as the news people said.

02/24/2006. As day two started, I began to recognize people coming into O'Chux who knew I had been there for a while. They had seen the news and they wanted all the grimy details. I was told by management that, if anyone asked, O'Charley's and all of its employees had no comment. It was this day that managers began telling all the employees that we were not to talk to the press about this. I think many people feared that cameras would set up right outside the restaurant. Fortunately, that never really happened.

As the day crawled along, I began to remember how I really

did hate people. Let me make this very clear; Gage Tate was no innocent victim and couldn't possibly expect to make friends or collect fans of endearment showing up on the news for the reason he did. Everyone hates him on this day, I get it. He is a no good sleazebag baby rapist. Again, I do get it. But the day before, really not even twenty four hours before, he was my best friend. He was someone I knew well, or thought I knew well, and most of all someone I trusted. Even faced with the most extreme of circumstances, I didn't immediately think to throw Gage under the bus. Nearly everyone else, however, did just exactly that.

I had some people that just thought I might know some of the more gory details and they wanted to know. These people would usually ask me how bad it really was or they wanted to know what the cops said to me. They wanted to know about what Gage said after he made bail because, yes, everyone knew by this point that we met. And then there were those people who wanted the gory details but took the sympathy approach. They could see how upset I was and thought they could get more information by asking how Gage was or how I was, only as a lead in to the gory details questions.

Another group was the group of loud, vocally energized haters that wanted to broadcast separation from the guy they just had lunch with the day before. They wanted to make sure everyone knew that they hated Gage Tate and anyone who likes him. And yes, that includes me. Because I wasn't ready to kill him on the way out of the jail, I was somehow some kind of reprehensible freak. Gage didn't deserve a chance to answer for his actions. That was the underlying theme from the very people that if accused of something so minor as eating a French fry from a customer's plate would want a jury trial to prove their innocence.

The other most popular group wasn't vindictive or mean, but they were just as hard for me to take. They were the very small group of supporters. "How are you today" or "Are you ok" were common questions. I was bad and I was not ok. I wanted to burst into tears and run away crying every time someone asked me those questions. Of course, no one really knew what to say. Without talking to everyone that knew us, I'd say it is highly likely this was a first for most everyone involved. That didn't make it easier to answer those questions and it didn't stop me from feeling like I had it worse than all of them. Like I knew Gage the best and this was hurting me the most. And in all fairness, I did know Gage better than anyone else that worked with us. I often felt like Gage was somewhat misunderstood and that I really got him. I understood who the *real* Gage Tate was.

After work, I had a text from Gage asking if I wanted to get a bite to eat. I didn't immediately answer. I didn't know what to think about this and I didn't know how much contact I wanted with Gage until I knew more. I decided to talk to Naomi about it.

"I get it," Naomi said. "So, what are you leaning towards doing?"

"I don't know. Is this crazy to be meeting with him at all?"

"No, I don't think so. We don't really know anything yet, you should support him. He is your friend."

"What would you think about going with us?"

"Yea, I could do that," she said.

In looking back, that meant more to me than I could really process at the time. I mean, really, she was willing to go out in public with a guy who was just on the news for possessing child porn and the one person left supporting him. I must say, she didn't make the most popular decision. In retrospect, Naomi would make a bad politician. She sucks at lying and is way too loyal. On that day, however, there was no empty public office. There was just me and I felt so unbelievably empty.

We decided to go to Ruby Tuesdays, which was not a regular spot of mine, Naomi or Gage. I don't remember how we selected there, but perhaps for that very reason. We met for a late dinner, around nine or ten.

We all drove separate and I remember arriving about the same time as Naomi. Gage was a few minutes later. We talked about how we were both a bit nervous. It wasn't like a "this is dangerous" type of nervous. I'm not sure what it was, but we knew this might be crazy as we awaited his arrival.

When Gage came in he was wearing another collection of black and all long sleeves. He had a hoodie and a baseball cap on, but he left out the sunglasses this time. I remember it was a bit awkward to find him a seat in the booth. He wanted to sit on the inside and I quickly got the feeling that Naomi wasn't comfortable sitting next to him. She never said anything, but it seemed like the best idea to sit him on my side, just in case. We conversed about little stuff, mostly small talk for the first few minutes.

A few minutes in, Naomi asked Gage, "So, can you tell us anything about what's going on?"

"I really can't," Gage said. "I can't talk about the case at all. My lawyer told me not to say anything."

"Yea, I understand. Are you doing ok, all considering?"

"I guess, yea. Kind of spooked, hence my get-up here," Gage chuckled.

"I can imagine," Naomi said.

It seemed a little tense so I changed the subject to food. We all decided what we were going to eat and placed our order. Shortly after, I went to the restroom. Normally this wouldn't be a talking point but this trip to the restroom would be less about a potty break and more a frenzy of activity. As I entered the bathroom, I noticed hanging directly above the urinal was a glass case with a copy of the local newspaper hanging to be read. Right on the front page was the story about Gage and his picture.

All I could think was "man I gotta get rid of this" and that's what I did. The case has a cheap little lock that could be wiggled loose. When I got the case opened up, I snatched the newspaper down and tore it up. I threw away the pieces and moved to the sink to wash my hands.

"Shit," I said to myself. There was another copy on the sink. Just like the other paper, I tore it up and threw it away. The last thing we wanted was someone to see his picture and recognize him in the restaurant. As I was throwing that one away, someone came in the restroom. I quickly finished stuffing it the can and I left.

As I got back to the table, Gage announced he too needed to go to the restroom. As he left, I took a big sigh.

"You won't believe what was in there," I said to Naomi.

"What?" she asked.

"They had *two* copies of today's newspaper in there with Gage's picture on it!"

"Holy crap! Gage is going in there right now."

"I know! I threw it away though and thank goodness because he's going right now too. That was crazy!"

Gage came back and we finished our meal without any other eventful activities or surprises. When we left, we all drove our own ways and Naomi and I decided we didn't know much more than we knew before meeting him that night. This entire situation was so bizarre in every way.

02/25/2006. Saturdays are always busy in the restaurant business. I had to close this Saturday. I was scheduled to be off, but Gage was supposed to close. I was filling in for his open shift. About 11am that morning, my cell phone rang from a private number.

"Hello?"

"Yes, is this Brayden Cooper?" an unfamiliar voice asked.

"Yes it is. Who is this?"

"Brayden, this is Detective Donald Hailey with the Lexington Police Department, Crimes Against Children Unit. We spoke at O'Charley's a few days ago when your friend Gage Tate was arrested."

"I remember."

"Ok, I was wondering if you could come down to the station and talk to us for a few minutes before you went to work tonight."

"I guess; what do you want to talk to me about?"

"Just routine stuff really. We are just gathering some information. It would really help out."

"Ok, I guess. What time?"

"You can come whenever you are ready, Brayden. I will be here all afternoon."

We decided on 1pm for a meeting time. I had to be at work by 5pm, so I dressed for work before I went down to the station. I planned on leaving and going straight to O'Charley's to get some food before I started my shift.

I parked in the police parking garage and went in the front door just off Main Street. As he had instructed me, I told the officers at the front desk I was there to see Detective Hailey. They made a phone call and told me to have a seat. After a few minutes, Detective Hailey came through a big metal door and invited me to come with him. The building was big and old. The hallway we walked down on our way to his office was long and there were many doors on either side. It smelled like a storage room that hadn't been bothered for a few years. Musty and all, everyone seemed to still be chipper. Everyone except for me, that is.

Detective Hailey directed me to an elevator where we rode up a few floors. When we got to the floor where his office was located, we exited the elevator and I followed him down another long, narrow hallway. This was a bit nicer than the downstairs. It didn't smell bad anyway and the floor was carpeted. He opened a door to an extremely small room and told me to have a seat. The room had a desk that was cut in a way that you would sit in the chair with the back to the door to work on it and, clearly, the other small, ugly, uncomfortable chair was for people who were "visiting." I sat down as he fetched a folder from his desk.

He returned with the folder and sat down in his chair. He didn't say anything for a few minutes. When he finally looked up, he looked me up and down and smiled.

"Dress up for me?" he asked.

"No, I dressed up for work. I have to be there by 4 this afternoon."

"No problem, we won't be that long. I just want to ask you a few routine questions. Just to be clear, your full name is Brayden Courtney Cooper, right?"

"Yes," I answered.

"How long would you say you have known Gage?"

"Maybe seven or eight years, we met in high school."

"And you two were close friends right? Some have described you as best friends, is that accurate?"

"Yes."

"So you two spent a lot of time together?"

"Yes," I said, "We spent most of my free time together. We did lots of stuff together."

"What kind of stuff did you do?"

"We played pool, drove around, walked the city, lots of stuff."

"Where did you drive around to?"

"You know, just cruising. We went lots of places. We took a few roads out to see where they went. Just to see where they ended."

"Did anyone ever go with you when you went cruising?"

"No, I only remember Gage and me."

"Who chose where to go? You or Gage?"

"We both did from time to time. Just depended on the night. It was kind of like an escape for us. It didn't matter where we went, just that we could go driving."

"What were you escaping from?"

"Well, maybe escape was the wrong word. We just used it for kind of a getaway from everyday life. Restaurant work isn't exactly glamorous. It can be very taxing."

"Are you and Gage lovers?"

"What? No, we are just friends. Gage is quite straight."

"Mmhmm. You never came on to him? Made a pass at him?"

"Why? Because I'm gay? So obviously I can't keep my dick in my pants, right? Gage is straight, we are friends, that is all."

"You never joked with him about wanting to have sex with him?"

"Sure. We joked about scoring points for running people over with my car and killing customers at O'Charley's too. We joked about a lot of things. But we never killed anyone and we never had sex."

"What if I told you someone had told us you were intimate with him and had, at least at one point, been in love with him?"

"I'd say you have talked to someone who doesn't know me or Gage very well. We didn't have sex, what else can I tell you about that?"

"Ok, ok," he said. He seemed to think he was losing me and decided to change direction. "Did Gage ever have any girlfriends you knew of?"

"Sure, several of them."

"Ok, so he was dating girls then? Does he have a steady girlfriend?"

"Yea, he was dating. He doesn't have a girlfriend right now, but his last relationship just ended about two or three months ago."

"Why did they break up?"

"Why does anyone break up? I dunno really, Gage was a little clingy maybe. He is very overprotective of his girlfriends."

"And they don't like that, do they? What about pornography? Did Gage look at porn?"

"Is there a guy that doesn't ever look at porn?"

"Did you ever see his porn?"

"You mean did I ever see naked children on his computer or in his house? No, I never saw a bunch of naked kids. I'm pretty sure I would have noticed that."

"But you never really went through his collection?"

"Of women? No, I thought you knew I was gay."

"Well we found some gay porn on his computer too. Did you look at any porn for yourself on his laptop?"

"No, never. And I'd find it hard to believe Gage had any gay porn. He wasn't homophobic, but he was very, very straight."

"Well we did find it, no reason for me to lie about it. Who else do you know that might have been close with Gage?"

I gave Detective Hailey a few names of some people I knew that Gage spent a good deal of time with. As I discovered later, some of the people whose names I gave had to go through some terrible interrogations as a result. I had no idea at the time; I thought they were just digging for information. I later found out some videos and pictures they found were of some past girlfriends of his. The cops knew this, I did not.

"So, when was the last time you two went out together?" Detective Hailey asked.

"Well actually, we hadn't been as close the last couple of months. He has kind of drifted into some kind of funk or depression or something. I dunno, but he has been kind of an ass to everyone around him for a while."

"So you guys aren't really getting along right now?"

"Not so much not getting along, just not spending time together like we used to. I kind of felt like I needed a break from Gage lately, ya know?"

"And others felt this way too?" he asked

"Yup, you can ask anyone at O'Charley's and they will tell you he has been an ass lately."

"I may do that. I find that interesting, most people spoke highly of him at the restaurant when we interviewed some people there."

"Yea, well, I guess it is like when someone dies, no one ever says a bunch of bad stuff about the dead guy. No one wants you to think they knew anything about this. They just want to 'be surprised' and move on."

"Do you think anyone there knew he was a pedophile?"

"Ha... no, I can't say that ever came up."

"Well, listen, if you know anything about this or you think you might know someone who does, this would be the time to tell me. This is the time we try to figure stuff out, ya know. If we figure it out from talking to Gage or Joe Blow at O'Charley's, we might get one version. If we figure some of it out from you, we might get a different version."

"Well if everyone tells the truth, you should still get one version. I don't know what you want me to tell you. I didn't know he had child porn on his computer and I didn't know he was into that stuff.

"Ok, Brayden. I believe you. I'm going to give you my card, and if you think of anything at all, please just give me a call. And the manager at O'Charley's has the card too, so if you lose it, they can reach me."

"Ok, no problem. Can you validate my parking or do I have to pay?"

"No, I can get that taken care of. And hey, Brayden, thanks again for coming in. I may call you if I have any more questions, ok?"

"Sure," I said, hoping he wouldn't. This had not been very pleasant. In leaving the police station, I had that dirty feeling you get when you have gone some place you really hate. I felt like everyone was staring at me and all I wanted was to get the hell out of there. It was only 3pm, so I decided to circle downtown for a few minutes before going to work.

When I finally did arrive at O'Charley's, I wasn't even hungry. I had eaten very little all day so I decided to order some food. I sat in the lounge area, which was a popular gathering point for the servers and hosts on breaks. I looked at my burger and took a couple bites. I couldn't eat it at all. I got a to-go box from the back and boxed it up, hoping I could eat later. I decided before my shift began to step outside and call Gage.

"Hello?" he answered.

"Gage, hey it's Brayden."

"What up?"

"I am getting ready to start working your close shift for tonight. I just left the police station. I had to talk to that detective."

"What did he ask you?"

"Pfft. No, it's ok, I'm fine, really. He asked me if I knew you were a pervert."

"Brayden..."

"No, I'm sorry dude. This is just so crazy. They are trying to put you away dude, do you know that?"

"Duh, of course I know that. Nothing I can do now but wait, no sense in stressing."

"Really? Wow, I just can't be that calm and it's not even me really in this situation. Whatever dude, I have to get in here."

"Ok man. It's going to be ok; I'm not going to go to jail."

"Yea, sure. I'll talk to you later."

Every conversation with Gage got weirder and weirder. I wish I could describe how I perceived these conversations, but I really couldn't even process it. I knew this was a huge deal, but somehow it all felt like a big bad dream and eventually I was going to wake up. I can't say I understand how Gage was so calm. He was just trucking along like all was the same. He was secretive about his appearance and where he was for the first day or so, but then it was like he didn't care. Could this really be happening to him, to me?

02/28/2006. I opened this morning. The droning of day to day life was killing me and I was only on my sixth day out. It was steady but not too busy at lunch and the rush seemed to abruptly end around 1pm. It seemed almost like the calm before a horrible storm, but unlike predicting a tornado, I was completely blown away with what was about to happen.

A few minutes after one, Detective Hailey came into O'Charley's. I had just sat down to eat my lunch and, in fact, I hadn't even taken my first bite. He told the other host that he needed to see me. She came up to the lounge and told me the detective was asking for me at the front door. I told Naomi to watch my food while I went down to speak with him.

"I'm on my break right now, just sat down to eat, can this wait?"

"Brayden, I'm going to need you to come with me downtown."

"Right now?" I asked sarcastically.

"Yes, now. I have men serving a search warrant on your home as we speak."

"What?! Are you fucking kidding me?"

"We need to go, Brayden."

"I am in the middle of my shift, I need to talk to my boss," I snapped.

"Hurry up," he said firmly.

"Gordy!" I yelled, "Hey, Gordy, that detective is here and says I have to go with him. He says he is searching my house. Is it a problem if I go?"

"Not yet, I guess you should go if he says you have to."

I was furious at this situation. Gordy was a friend of mine as well as my boss. I didn't screw around with my job. I showed up on time and I didn't leave during my shift to screw up the schedule. I was mad at Detective Hailey. Whatever he thought he had could be nothing more than a screw up. Had he not harassed me enough already? I called my mom for a brief warning of the search.

"Hello?"

"Mom... that detective that arrested Gage just showed up at O'Charley's and he says they are searching our house right now. I need you to come home."

"I thought you weren't involved in this? Why are they searching, what are they looking for?" she asked.

"I don't know, Mom. Look, someone just needs to be there for

Sammy." Sammy was our cat and he was a bit too friendly for strangers most of the time.

"I'll do what I can."

"This is bullshit," I said angrily as I walked out in front of Hailey. "I don't know what you are doing, but it is bullshit!"

We got in his car and I demanded to go home for fear the cat would get out and I really didn't want to go downtown with him at all. He told me I wasn't allowed to go to the house. He agreed to pull up and wait for my mom to get home, but he told me she would not be allowed to go in either. After about twenty minutes of waiting, Mom pulled in. As she got out of her car and walked up to the door, Detective Hailey pulled away.

The ride downtown was silent. I was so angry, I was afraid to say anything thinking he would arrest me for screaming hysterically at him. He pulled in to the same garage I had parked in before, but he pulled to the roof. We entered the building through a special door marked "Law Enforcement Only" and inside was a small area with an elevator. The elevator took us to the same floor I had been before. To this point, nothing was said between us. I was directed to the small room with the funny shaped desk and the two chairs, one clearly more comfortable than the other. I took my place in the uncomfortable interrogation chair. Detective Hailey went to fetch the same folder and he returned with it.

"Ok, Mr. Cooper. Before we start, I need to advise you of your rights. You have to right to remain silent. Anything you say can and will be used against you in a court of law. You have the right to an attorney during any questioning, including today's questioning and, if you cannot afford one, we can provide one for you. Do you understand these rights as I have told them to you?"

"Am I under arrest?" I asked.

"Not right now you aren't. Do you understand your rights?"

"Yes, of course. I *don't* understand who the hell you think you are though. Whatever version you were talking about getting before must have gotten all fucked up."

"Well that's the thing, Brayden; we got our version from

Gage. And he did have some interesting things to say." I didn't say anything and he continued, "You know, he says you are into this child porn stuff too. In fact, to hear him tell it, you introduced him to it a few years ago."

"That's ridiculous," I said. "And it is completely not true."

"Well Gage says we will find our proof on your computer. What do you think we will find on your computer?"

"Hard telling, likely to find a bunch of stuff. I can tell you what you won't find, though. You won't find any child porn. I'm not some kind of freak. And I don't believe Gage would say that."

"Oh he said it. He gave us a written statement. That's how we got the search warrant and took your computers from your home. If you know something or you want to tell us something, this is the last chance you have. Once I empty that laptop, I don't need to hear what you say and I don't need to cut you a deal. I mean, if you ask me, it looks like you were the instigator in all this. Of course, you aren't telling me your side, all I get is Gage's side."

"I don't have a side! And good, since you have my computer, good you will be able to make a complete fool of yourself when you don't find anything. You are wasting your time. Gage didn't make any statement and I'm not a pedophile. You are just wrong."

"Ok, hang on a minute."

Detective Hailey left the room for a few minutes and returned with a thin folder. He sat down and he pulled out a piece of paper. He put it on the desk, turned it so I could read it, and slid it across to me. I picked up the paper and I immediately recognized the handwriting. It was indeed Gage's writing and his signature at the bottom. I read it carefully and, sure enough, it fully described in detail a page full of lies. He *had* written a statement, just as Detective Hailey had said.

"So, can you explain that?" Detective Hailey asked me, sarcastically.

"No," I said. "It is a lie. Every bit of it is a lie. And you won't find what you are looking for."

"Let me see if I understand this. You are such good friends, right? I mean you said you were best friends. And he just says this right out. It's like this is the first thing out of his mouth. "My best friend Brayden has child porn too" is the first thing he says? How did he come up with that story so quick, if it was a lie?"

"I don't know. But it is a lie." I really didn't know. I could hardly digest the fact that he had written such a statement. I had been the *ONE* to support him, to try and be there for him when he needed someone the most. How could this even be real?

My sadness quickly rose to anger. Within minutes of realizing he had in fact written this statement of lies, a statement as hurtful as this, I was flaming mad.

"You know," Hailey said, "if you don't tell me what's going on here, I can't help you at all. I am going to have the evidence off that computer in days, maybe hours after it comes in here. What am I going to find on it?"

"Nothing, I swear. I didn't do what he says. He is a liar."

"You two *were* lovers, weren't you? I understand why you might have lied before. And I am going to forget about that. But now, maybe that's why he told this lie. You were lovers and you had a bit of a falling out a while back, maybe he is mad at you?"

"NO!" I screamed. "We were not lovers, we did not fuck. We were friends, I thought, but nothing more. Not now, not ever before."

"C'mon Brayden. Gage told us. He said you were in a relationship. He said you were angry with him when he changed his mind about it. Is that a lie too?"

"Hell yes it's a lie. God, ask anybody that knew us. They would all tell you this is crazy."

"Then tell me what you think. Why would Gage tell these lies? What would motivate him to do this?"

"What are you thick headed or just stupid? I don't have a freaking clue why he would say that. He is obviously a liar!"

"I know the truth, Brayden. I know how it is. You can talk to me, man. Look, I'll tell you... 70% of the pedophiles I catch are gay. I get it; it is tough out there as a gay man. And you are older than Gage, you could convince him to do things your way. He looked up to you didn't he?"

"So I'm a freak because I'm gay? No, you have this all wrong. Gage wasn't so easily influenced to do anything by anybody. This is not who I am and that is not who Gage is."

"You are a manipulator, Brayden. I can see that. You manipulated this situation to make Gage your puppet. How long did it take to get him looking at this sick stuff?"

I started screaming at him, "You are a sick bastard! I never have looked at this stuff. Not with Gage or on my own and I never talked to Gage about it in any way!! This is such bullshit!"

"Well it doesn't make much sense that it is a lie. What reason does Gage have to lie?"

"Uh, I don't know, he is facing a lot of time in prison for being a pedophile."

"So fear of prison is a reason to lie? Ok, so that being said, you could face the same time if you are involved. Maybe you are lying to cover it up. You know, I have to be honest you. You are a convicted felon; you meet the criteria and the profile for a pedophile far better than Gage. Frankly, I believe him and I don't believe you. This is really your last chance, I'm not going to sit here all day and play this stupid game."

"Fuck you, this is your game. And it is not fun for me either. I didn't start this shit, I'm not involved in it and I don't want to talk to you anymore."

"Ok," he said, "We can be done here. Just remember, that is your decision."

Much like the car ride over and the walk in, the walk out and the car ride back to O'Charley's was silent. I was fuming mad, even more so than the ride over, and now I was worried I might murder a detective, or Gage Tate. By the time we arrived at O'Charley's it was around 4pm. I went inside and was greeted by Naomi and Leala.

"Hey you. I have your money for you. When you didn't get to eat your food, someone else paid for it so I can give your money back," said Naomi.

"Thanks," I said quietly.

"Are you ok?" asked Leala.

"No," I said. "You won't believe it. You absolutely won't believe it."

"What happened?" they asked.

"Gage wrote a statement on me. He said I was involved with this shit too. I am so pissed!"

"Oh my God," said Leala. "What are you going to do?"

"I'd like to kill him," I said softly.

No one said anything. I think they didn't entirely disagree.

After a few minutes of silence I said, "I'm going to call him and tell him I need to talk to him."

Leala and Naomi looked at each other with a look of discontentment. Before much could be said, I walked outside to make the call. Someone behind me asked someone else if they should stop me. But no one did stop me.

"Hello?" Gage answered.

"Hey dude, what are you doing?"

"Not much, how about you?"

"Nothing, just got off work, you wanna do something? I want to talk to you about something."

"Yea sure, have you eaten?"

I hadn't eaten all day. I was interrupted at lunch and haven't eaten since. "No," I said, "I haven't eaten."

"Ok, well I'm at my dad's house so if you want we can meet at Fazoli's on Nicholasville Road."

"That's fine," I said.

I was biting my lip so hard I actually left a mark. That was the hardest thing I had done, maybe ever. I wanted to confront him with this in person though. I needed to see the reaction on his face when I asked him. And, at this point, I still wanted to do something very bad to him. I was told later by Leala that the look in my eyes wasn't so pleasant. She was worried that I might do something really crazy. And not that I think she blamed me for feeling like that, but she was still able to keep somewhat of a level head. She knew going to confront him and doing something stupid, like killing him dead, for example, was not going to be the right move.

No one that I told about my day was happy with Gage. They all completely understood why I was upset and agreed I should be. On the same note, no one seemed to think this meeting was a wise thing to do. However, my mind had been made up. Meeting Gage, confronting him, was the only way I could foresee me handling this. I wasn't sure what was going to happen. Leala actually asked me before I went if I was going to do something stupid. The thought, I think, had crossed her mind to find a way to intervene in this meeting.

I played out several scenarios in my head. Most of them ended in some sort of violence. I knew I couldn't go out there and just kill him, but for the first time in my life, thoughts like that didn't sound so unreasonable. Honestly I think I didn't want to admit my true intentions to myself, let alone anyone else. I can't say I was scared of what I might do, just prepared to do whatever I had to do. It was like preparing for a fight at school with a bully that has been harassing you. If you want to pick a fight with the bully, you would likely catch him off guard and attack. That's what I felt like I was doing. I misled Gage about our meeting. I had plans to carry out something quite down and dirty. He's the one who had burned the rule book.

On the drive out to Fazoli's I ran a red light. I wasn't paying attention. Too many distractions running through my head prevented me from hardly remembering how to drive. Luckily I did not cause a wreck and no cops were there to pull me over. I can't say that would have gone well. "Yes officer, I was in a hurry.

I have to go kill my lying rat of a former friend." I don't think he would have understood.

As I pulled in to Fazoli's, I remember thinking it was busier than I thought it should be for a Tuesday night. Before I could get out of my car, Gage pulled in beside me. I greeted him and we proceeded inside. I ordered a drink and went to sit down at a back corner table. To my surprise, Gage ordered a full meal. The last thing I could think about was eating. As I waited for him to get to the table, I looked around and suddenly figured out why it was so busy in there.

As he sat down at the table I said, "Hey dude, have you looked around? We picked one *hell* of a night to eat here. It is kid's night!"

"Hmm, so it is," he said casually. The last thing I wanted to do in the whole world was to have dinner with a former friend who turned out to be a lying pedophile during kid's night at Fazoli's. Yes, this was pretty fucked up right here. I wanted to run out of there as fast as I could.

"So what's been going on?" I asked Gage.

"Not much, same old stuff I guess. I have been talking to Nicole again a little bit. She is supporting me."

"Have you been talking more to the cops?" I asked.

"Yea, you know, with my lawyer."

"What do you talk about with them?"

"I am really not supposed to talk about it."

"Yea... have they asked you about me at all?"

"Why would they ask about you?" he asked, doing his best confused lie face.

"I dunno, just wondering, have they?"

"Not really, I mean they know who you are and all, that's about it I guess."

I was trying to hint around about it and mostly small talk my way out of here. I didn't want to discuss it in Fazoli's during kid's night. And most uncharacteristic of Gage, he ate unbelievably slowly. When he finally finished, I was ready to go.

"Ok, let's get out of here, take a walk or something. I am not comfortable here."

"Ha ha, I'm not going to just snatch up some little girl dude."

"That is so totally not funny at all," I said directly. I shuttered at his words. Had he done that before? 'Snatched up some little girl?' I was sick at my stomach all over again.

We did take a walk up into the residential neighborhood behind that Fazoli's. A few blocks into the subdivision, I decided it was time to confront him. It was a good spot because there weren't many street lights, no traffic and no one was around us. Seclusion seemed important at the time, just in case.

"So, why'd you do it Gage?"

"Do what?"

"Write a statement saying I'm involved. Tell the cops I had child porn on my computer. Tell the cops we were fucking. Why did you do any of that, Gage?"

"I didn't write any statement..."

"Don't you fucking lie to me Gage!" I interrupted. "I saw the report. I know it was your handwriting and your signature."

"I didn't..."

I interrupted him again along with grabbing his shirt at the collar and moving in close, "You did. I saw it! Why are you trying to lie to me? It doesn't matter what you say, I know you did it!"

After a pause, Gage said, "You don't understand."

"No, you are absolutely right about that. I don't understand at all. Could you explain it to me?"

He didn't say anything and his head fell to make eye contact with the broken sidewalk below.

I got right in his face and said, "You son of a bitch, I should kill you."

Gage quickly reached towards his belt and pulled a knife. I took one step back. He flipped open the blade, like I have seen him do a thousand times.

"Get back, Brayden," he said.

I think this is the first time in my life that I could honestly relate to the term "snapped." I literally had no control over myself. I punched Gage in the face twice, the first to the nose and second to the jaw. As he stumbled backward, I grabbed the knife from his hand and shoved him to the ground. He fell on his back and looked like he may want to get back up. I crouched down on him, with my knee in his chest and the knife he wielded held to his throat.

I looked into his eyes and screamed, "I could kill you right now mother fucker!"

As I watched the trickle of blood come out of his nose and I saw his face swelling practically before my eyes, I was truly intrigued by one thing. As I looked into his eyes, he didn't look scared. He looked dead, like I had already killed him. He was completely empty, a shell of what used to be a person. It reminded me of something you would see on a science fiction show when you look the alien in the eyes.

I felt the tears coming down my face before I even realized I was crying. It took everything in me not to slit his throat right on the sidewalk. I slapped him one time across the face and stood up. I threw the knife a hundred feet or so away and it stuck in the ground, blade down.

I told him, "You move before I'm gone and I swear I will kill you tonight."

And I don't think he did move. I turned to walk away and never looked back. I was so angry at him I couldn't see straight. I got in my car and drove back across town. I was most upset at him lying about it to my face. I already had caught him; the point where you lie and deny had long passed by this point. And how cocky must he be to agree to go to dinner with me, knowing he had written a statement on me the day before? He must have known I would find out. I thought that perhaps he didn't take me for a face to face confrontation type of guy. But what I wanted to do could not be done over the phone and I didn't even do half what I wanted to.

Back across town, I met Leala at O'Neil's to have a drink. Needless to say, she was relieved I didn't kill him. This day could not have gone much worse. I was really starting to feel drained. I had no best friend to lean on and seemingly nowhere to turn. Thankfully, Leala and Naomi were there for me to lean on or I may have gone completely nuts. To this day, they might argue I had already gone completely nuts. Tomorrow, however, was another day. And tomorrow would be even worse.

03/01/2006. I awoke, not to my alarm, but to the ringing phone. Detective Hailey was starting early, it was only 8am. I had to work a "thru shift" which meant 11:30 until whenever we slowed down enough for me to leave at dinner. With such a long day ahead, the last person I wanted to start the day dealing with was Donald Hailey.

"Yea?" I said with a grumbled voice.

"Brayden, this is Detective Hailey," he said, as if there would be someone else calling me at 8 in the morning. "I was wondering if you could come down and talk to me this morning."

"Nah, you know, I don't think so. I have a long day ahead."

"Well I really need you to. Maybe I could come out and talk to you at work?"

"Are you just trying to get me fired?"

"I am trying to solve a case and go home like I do every day. Either way, I need to talk to you today."

"Fine, but I don't have long. I have to work this morning."

"Sure, see you when you get here."

I rolled out of bed and drug myself to the shower. It was way too early to be awake. I grabbed a Pop Tart out of the box in the cupboard, a Mountain Dew out of the fridge and out the door I went. I was actually leaving earlier than Mom today, which was unusual. I usually wasn't even awake before she left for work.

As I drove downtown, I remember thinking about the night

before. Had Gage told him what happened? Was I going to get arrested for assault? I certainly didn't trust Gage, so I knew very well that anything was possible. I pulled in to the garage and went to my usual spot at the front desk to ask for Detective Hailey.

He arrived to retrieve me a bit faster than usual. Same routine as before, up the elevator, long hallways, interrogation chair, small room, he got his folder. He came back in the room and sat across from me.

"Don't play games with me, Brayden," he began.

"Is that one of those one sided contracts or are you going to stop messing with me too?"

He pulled out five photos from his folder and spread them out over the table. He slid them closer for me to see. The first photo was of a girl, maybe 8 years old, performing oral sex on an older man, maybe 60 years old. Another showed a young boy, 6 – 8 years old, pinned down and another 60 something man forcing his penis inside him.

"This is disgusting; I don't want to see this shit!" I said.

"Really?" Detective Hailey said sarcastically. "You haven't seen these before? These very pictures here, you don't recognize them?"

"No!" I screamed, "I told you this is nasty!"

"Mmhmm. Well, you see Brayden, the thing is, I can't believe you. Do you know where I got those pictures?" I shook my head no. "From your computer, the laptop you said I wouldn't find anything on."

"I don't believe you," I said.

"I don't really care if you believe me. I thought you were smarter than this, Brayden. I mean they were right out in plain sight for anyone to see. Buried just a couple of folders deep, it isn't like we had to use special software to recover them. They were right there with hundreds more. How do you explain that?"

"I don't know. If you really got them off my computer, Gage

must have put them there. He had my computer and plenty of access to it."

"No, Brayden. Don't lie to me! Gage is *very* straight, right? Wait, wait, those were *your* words, Brayden! Now, explain why a 'very straight' Gage would have a very gay photo of a boy sucking some guy's dick! You liked this didn't you? The control over that boy... that turns you on, doesn't it?"

I shoved the photos in the floor and stood up with plans to leave. Detective Hailey put his hand on my shoulder shoved me back down in the small chair.

"No, you aren't leaving until you tell me the truth, Brayden!" he screamed.

"I have! I have told you the truth. I don't know where this stuff came from."

"Ok, so let's say I believe you, and I don't by the way, but let's just say I do. Gage said you gave him child porn. He says you have it on your computer and we find some of the same images on both computers. How do you explain that?"

"Gage had my computer several times. When I was serving the time at the jail during my case, he kept my laptop then. He said he needed it for school."

"So back in June of 2005, you were doing a few days off and on then, right?"

"Yes," I said.

"June 18, 2005, you were in jail then? And again a few days later, correct?"

"I don't remember the exact dates."

"But you went in and out over some weekends and some other days on work release, right?"

"Right."

"So I'd like to show you this report. Look here at the dates. See where some stuff was added on June 18? Well look here at some more stuff added on June 24. Now, when you were out of jail in between these times and other times like these, did you get your computer back?"

"Yes, he just took it before I went in and I took it back when I came home."

"So would you agree that this shows child pornography was added to your computer on June 18, 2005?"

"That's what your paper says."

"Right and considering this paper is correct, you would agree that was a fact, right?"

"I guess so," I said.

"Great. And you would say a day or two after this your received the computer back, right?"

"Right."

"So, the computer had child porn on it while you had it back?"

"I didn't know that if it did."

"But you just said you got it back, and the records clearly show that it was added and then you received the computer back, right?"

"That might be the chain of events, but I didn't know."

"But you agree that if all this is right, you possessed the child pornography?"

"I might have," I said hesitantly, "But if I did, I didn't know I did at the time. Not until right now."

"And you then gave the computer back to Gage the next day or a few days later, right?"

"Yes, when I went back to jail."

"Ok, good. So follow with me now. You give your computer to Gage and then he gives it back to you and the computer has child pornography on it. And then the computer, that has child pornography on it, you gave it back to Gage. Right?"

"Well, again, I didn't know about the porn, but sounds right if your dates are right."

"So you can see this, right? You admit you gave the child pornography to Gage."

"No, I didn't say that..."

Detective Hailey interrupted, "You did say that. You said you gave a computer to Gage that we can clearly see contained child porn."

"But I didn't know that *then*. Just because I know it now doesn't mean I am responsible for what I didn't know then."

"Don't split hairs, Brayden. You just told me you gave the child porn to Gage. Don't split hairs."

"Split hairs? This is not splitting hairs; it is completely changing what I said and making it what you want. I didn't say that at all!"

"Well that's what I heard, Brayden. You can call it what you want but if it walks, talks and sounds like a pedophile, it is one."

"This is bullshit, man. You know I did not say that."

"Ok, so you want to make me a believer? Then take a polygraph test. Come in here tomorrow and take the test."

"Fine, I am telling the truth, that is no problem."

"Great! I need some time to set it up and I know you have to go to work. So, why don't we do this; Go to work today and when you get off work tomorrow, just come on down here and we can take the test, ok?"

"Ok, I can do that."

And so it was settled. A lie detector would surely prove that I was telling the truth. I actually wish I had thought of that. It seems it could have obviously saved everyone a ton of time. I was furious about this whole situation. I didn't understand how we had even gotten to this point. All of a sudden, I feel like a big suspect in the case and felt horrible. I couldn't imagine how anyone could think of me like this.

It took the entire ride to work for me to calm down even slightly. I didn't know what would happen next, but surely the lie detector could be nothing but a good thing for my case. Turns out, the idea of a lie detector test helping prove your innocence relies not only on your honesty, but the honesty of the police around you. Their dishonesty, I had not counted on.

Chapter 6

My Arrest.

03/02/2006. As the day ended at work, I said goodbye to several people. Many of them knew I was heading to the police station to take a lie detector test. As I drove downtown, I remember this feeling of calmness come over me. Maybe this would be the ending of all this and I could finally move on with life. That was the train of thought scooting through my naïve mind. After I parked in the garage, I called my cousin, whose call I had missed earlier in the day. I told him I was on my way in to take a lie detector test and I didn't know when I would talk to him again. When I said that, I meant it may be a few hours. It would be longer than that.

As I entered the lobby, the cop at the desk told me to have a seat. She recognized me by now and she knew who I was here to see. After a longer wait, almost a half hour, Detective Hailey came through the door and escorted me upstairs. After we got off the elevator, this time we took a left instead of a right. I was happy to not have to face that tiny uncomfortable chair again. We entered a room that was a bit larger. It was not as bright and the chair was much larger. A man sat on the other side of the table working on a machine I could only guess was the polygraph machine.

"Mr. Cooper, my name is Detective Jeffries. I will be giving you the lie detector today. Go ahead and have a seat and I will explain the instructions."

"Ok," I said.

"Ok, so I just want to go over some myths about the polygraph machine to better help you feel comfortable. A lot of people say that you can fail if you are nervous. This is not true. Most people are nervous and that won't affect your results. The machine produces 99.9% accuracy, but you should know, the results are not admissible in a court of law and cannot be used against you at trial if you get to that point.

I am going to ask you a series of questions. We will start with a group of control questions, such as 'what is your name' or 'what is your birthday' before we get to pertinent questions. This is to help read the machine's signals for when you tell the truth. I will then ask you to look at a square of a certain color and instruct you to lie about the color so we can see the machine's response when you lie. After that, we will begin with real questions. You must remain as still as you can throughout the test because I can only get accurate readings when you sit still. Do you understand all of this?"

"Yes, I think so," I said.

He seemed to be in a hurry and he got me hooked up to the machine. A body wrap went around my chest, small connectors went on ever finger and thumb, and a blood pressure type wrap went around one bicep, although it was not tight like a blood pressure strap. He attached three small, round, suction cup like things to my forehead and put arm restraints on me so I was attached to the chair. After feeling like I was about to be executed in an electric chair, we began.

"Ok, Mr. Cooper. We are ready to get started. Please stay looking forward at the wall in front of you. Is your name Brayden Cooper?"

"Yes."

"Is your birthday September 4, 1982?"

"Yes."

"Did you look anything up online or in a book about how to beat a lie detector test?"

"No."

"Have you ever had any special training to be covertly deceptive?"

"No."

"Look at the projection image on the wall in front of you. Is the color of that square red?"

"Yes."

"Ok. Now I will ask you various questions about the square and I want you to lie. Is the square purple?"

"Yes."

"Is it a circle?"

"Yes."

"Is the square red?"

"No." I felt so stupid at this point. The square was red, can we move on? That is all I could think.

"Ok I am going to start asking the target questions. Are you ready to do that?"

"Yes."

"Do you know Gage Tate?"

"Yes."

"Did you know Gage Tate possessed child pornography?"

"No."

"Did you think Gage Tate may have been a pedophile?"

"No."

"Do you or have you ever watched child pornography with Gage Tate?"

"No."

"Did you know the child pornography was on your computer?"

"No."

"Are you gay?"

"Yes."

"Have you had sex with any men?"

"Yes."

"Did you have sex with Gage Tate?"

"No."

"Were you ever in a romantic relationship with Gage Tate?"

"No."

"Have you lied to me during this test?"

"No."

"Have you lied to Detective Hailey during his investigation?"
"No."

"Have you seen Gage Tate since he made bond?"

"Yes."

"Ok, Mr. Cooper. We are finished. Let me unhook you and you can step outside and wait for the results."

"Well I passed right?" I asked.

"I'll know in a few minutes, just wait outside for me."

So I did wait outside. It took them almost an hour to get the results. I went to the restroom down the hall and spent most of the time pacing the hallway impatiently. Finally, they returned and Detective Hailey invited back to our usual small interrogation room to have a seat. He came in and closed the door as usual.

"So, Brayden, we have a problem here. You didn't pass the polygraph."

"What? I was telling the truth, there must be a mistake. I swear I wasn't lying!"

"I hear that kind of often," he said smugly. "Here's the thing Brayden, nothing you say adds up. And it seems too many things point in a bad direction for you. A few things you said in there were true. But unfortunately for you, they weren't things that are going help you. You care to explain why you met up with Gage after he made bond?"

"We were best friends. I was trying to be supportive!"

"Yea, maybe. Or you were begging him not to tell us about your involvement. Maybe you offered to bribe him? I don't know, but I don't think you were being a supportive friend."

I was in complete shock. I didn't even know how we got to this point. I had been as honest as I knew how to be. I never lied to them and the worst thing I had done was punch Gage in the nose. I remembered how honest the fire department was during the arson investigation. I knew at this point that the police had not been as honest with me as they had. I was so lost.

Detective Hailey continued, "Let me lay it out for you, Brayden. You fit the profile for a pedophile. You are gay and older than Gage. Gage told us we would find child porn on your computer and we did. He said you gave him some child porn and you did. After Gage got out, you went right to him, probably to try and intimidate him. You failed the polygraph; I don't know how else I can approach this Brayden."

"I don't know; this is fucked up. I didn't do anything wrong."

"Well, Brayden, at this time I am placing you under arrest. You are being charged with distributing child pornography, tampering with evidence, and possession of child pornography. You have the right to remain silent. Anything you say can and will be used against you in a court of law. You have the right to an attorney and if you cannot afford one, one can be provided for you. Do you understand?"

"No. I understand my rights, but no I don't understand why I'm being arrested."

"I have explained it to you, I can't be more clear." "You are wrong, you are just wrong."

"I am going to take you to a holding cell. A uniformed officer will be here in a few minutes to handcuff you and take you to the jail. If you want, you can use your cell phone until they get here. By the way, I know you punched Gage. He has a broken nose, ya know?"

"You are charging me with assault too?"

"Not right now. I don't arrest people for assault." I didn't know what to think of that.

The holding cell was next door and was simply a room that was all concrete and had a single bench in it. As soon as I got in there, I called my mom.

"Hello?" she answered.

"Mom. I am getting arrested. This is so crazy; they are locking me up because they think I have something to do with this."

"I thought you weren't involved in all this," she said. "Why are they arresting you? What did you do?"

"Nothing, I promise. They said I failed the lie detector, but I told the truth, I don't know what's going."

"Well there is nothing I can do about it. Are you at the jail?"

"Not yet, I'm still at the police station, but they are getting ready to take me to the jail."

Needless to say, this was not the easiest of phone calls. I had no explanation. Not for my mom, not for the cops, not for anyone. This was screwed up from every angle and there was no explaining it. To hear the description from Detective Hailey, I had to remind myself I was innocent. The evidence looked damning and I didn't even know how it got to that point.

The policewoman showed up and handcuffed me. My pockets were completely emptied and put into plastic bags and labeled. She escorted me to her police car and we headed for the jail. All and all, she was about the nicest one I had to deal with. She asked me if I was comfortable and tried to make things as smooth as possible. I may not have been so easy on a person I was taking in with the same charges. The ride was quiet. I was upset and I wanted to just scream and cry so bad, but by this point, I was almost completely numb. My tears were gone; they had all dried up and no more could come out. I was trying to look forward. Wait until my attorney sees this, I will be ok then. Or so I thought.

Chapter 7

JAIL IS A DIFFERENT WORLD.

Inside the "sally port" we pulled up and stopped by a door. I was told to stay in the car, as if I could actually get out on my own. The officer went inside and spoke with a guard inside the door. She returned and got me out of the back seat of the police cruiser. She took me to the door and pressed a silver button to buzz those inside. Immediately inside the door we were entering, there was another door that was closing. After it closed, our door opened and we stepped inside. I was instructed to sit on the bench just inside. The police officer spoke to a guard and was handed some paper work. She turned over her gun and signed the paper. It was now time to enter the second door.

As the door opened, I could see to the right of me a huge desk that was in an oval shape around the entire room. Above the desk, a huge label read "Intake" and a guard was there to greet us. The guard who I first spoke with seemed friendly.

"Hey man, how are you?"

"Well guess I'm not great since this is jail," I said.

"Yea, I get that man. Are you feeling ok? Sick or injured?"

"No, I'm fine."

"Ok, step up to the counter and the officer will remove the handcuffs."

As she removed the cuffs, the guard asked the policewoman, "Does he have anything on him?"

"No, he's clean."

The guard still proceeded to pat me down. I guess maybe it would have been more intense of a pat down had she not said I was clean. After he was finished, he handed me back my personal belongings, including my cell phone. He told me to have a seat in the chairs anywhere but the first row and to not talk to the women. I did as I was told and turned on my cell phone. My signal was very weak, too weak in fact to make phone calls. Texts would go through during spurts of signal so I continued to talk to a few friends, giving them a heads up about my arrest.

After a few minutes, a female guard yelled, "Brayden Cooper!"

I stood up and approached her. She quickly spouted, "Stand at the line, not over the line, just at the line. Stand straight up and look at the camera. If you make a stupid face, I'll take you right to the hole, understand?"

"Yes," I said. For the record, I did not make a stupid face.

"Do you know what you have been charged with, Mr. Cooper? Did the officer explain those charges?"

"Yes, ma'am."

"Good. Are you feeling sick at all?"

"No."

"Any medications I need to know about, drug abuse, suicidal thoughts, homicidal thoughts, depression, or anything else you want to tell me?"

Did wanting to kill a particular detective or a certain former best friend count? "No," I said.

"Good. There is no preset bail for your charges. Have a seat and the pretrial counselor will call you when it is your turn. He will see if a judge is available to set your bond. Do you have any questions?"

"I didn't get to eat anything all day, just wondering if..."

She interrupted with, "Sorry, we serve breakfast at 6am, you can eat then. Other than that, you've missed the meals for today."

"Ok," I said.

"Hey," she said quickly, "Don't act like that, not here. You hear me? Listen to me; you don't act like that here. Never get that silly little sad face or look disappointed. Don't you do that or they will eat you alive. You listening to me boy?"

"Yes, ma'am."

"Yes is fine, don't be so nice. I'm not saying to be crazy with the guards, but don't be too friendly either. I'm not scraping you off the floor, understand?"

"Yea, I get it."

"Go sit down."

Scrape me off the floor? What a bitch. I know her intentions were well, but at the time, that's the last thing I wanted or needed to hear. Turns out though, it wasn't bad advice. I went over, as I was told, and sat in the chairs once again. They were small bucket like plastic blue chairs. Not particularly comfortable, but not as uncomfortable as my interrogation chair.

It smelled bad in the intake area. Or perhaps more accurately, most of the *people* stank in the intake area. It was cold in there and everything was made from concrete except the plastic chairs. Several people were wondering around and getting in trouble for it. Mostly they were drunk or high, or maybe just completely belligerent. Either way, it didn't seem like the thing to do to make these guards mad.

After waiting about an hour, an older man called my name to conduct my pretrial interview. I followed him back to the opposite end of the big oval desk where there were concrete walls that contained little cubby-like holes with a desk in between. He sat on the side with the computer; I sat on the side next to the drunken hooker who moments earlier puked all over herself. I was, in that moment, a bit envious of the guy at the computer.

"I've spoken to the judge on call tonight and they have set your bond at $12,500. They won't 3rd party your bond or consider reduction prior to arraignment. Can you make this bond?"

"Um... no, we don't have money like that. What is 3rd party?"

"That means the judge will sometimes reduce the bond down to only 10% or maybe just 1% for low income families. Your charges disqualify you for that. You will be arraigned tomorrow morning at 8:30am on the camera. That means you won't go to court, they will do a video arraignment in front of a camera. You can ask the judge then about obtaining an attorney and perhaps bond reduction. Do you have any questions?"

"I don't think so. Is there anything else I need to know?"

"Not right now. Everyone gets a phone call from this free phone to make bail arrangements. I know you said you can't make bail, but if you wanted to call someone and just let them know what's going on, that's ok."

"Ok, thank you."

I did make my one phone call. I called my mom back to give her an update on what was going on. I told her about my bond and about my arraignment. She was noticeably upset with me, largely because I had not kept her informed of the events as they happened this week. She didn't know everything that had happened and she didn't know what to think of my arrest. She was hurt and a bit mad, understandably. We talked for a while, so long in fact that the pretrial guy got in trouble because we were on the phone so long.

After I hung up, I felt as bad as I had yet. I felt completely alone in a totally screwed up situation. Everyone I trusted had either betrayed me or was mad at me. I felt my life caving in on my head and I was in this by myself. 'Hopefully tomorrow I can talk to my lawyer,' I thought. At least then I would have someone on my side.

I sat back down in the plastic chairs and waited for almost eight more hours before I got called on to go to a cell. It was after midnight and I was tired and hungry. I knew I wouldn't be able to eat that night, but at least I could lie down for a while.

A guard escorted me back into the property room where he had me empty my pockets again. I had to make a list of everything I was putting into property and count the cash I had on me. After everything was filled out and logged into property, they said it was time to "dress me out." This means I get to lose my clothes and I get a whole new wardrobe. From now on, I get the fancy green jumpsuit with big white letters on the back that read F.C.D.C.

After stripping me down completely naked, they patted me down again and took mirrors all over in case I was hiding anything in my body anywhere. I had to turn several times and squat and cough for the guard. After a thorough inspection of my body, I dressed in my jumpsuit, and they took me back out to the intake area to a machine. This machine would fingerprint me and record any tattoos I have. I didn't have any tattoos but they sure did get my fingerprints.

The next step was what I had been waiting for. They gave me a "bed roll" which included a blanket, two sheets and a pillow case. I was also given a bag with three pair of white boxers, three pair of socks, one roll of toilet paper, a small stick of toothpaste and the smallest toothbrush I had ever seen. I was then led through several doors and into a unit called 'C' which was used primarily for classification. I was assigned a cell where I would get to be by myself. They let me in and finally I got to sit down. I made my bed and used my very personal toilet, which was so impersonal that you can look straight across the aisle and watch the guy in that cell take a dump. Oh and a toilet seat? Yea, forget that. The toilets were steel and the only source of drinking water was on the back of the toilet. My toilet was broken too, so every time I wanted a drink and pushed the water fountain button, the toilet flushed. The last thing that you want when you leaning over to get a drink is have a toilet flushing and splashing sewer water on you while you get a drink. It was disgusting, to say the least.

About 3 o'clock in the morning, I finally got to lie down and try to rest. As you can imagine, I didn't sleep to well. There were lights on that shined in my eyes and guards came around every thirty minutes to just look at you. Needless to say, 6am came awfully early. 'But at least I can eat something finally' I thought. To my disappointment, I got a hardboiled egg and one powdered doughnut. Not a big one, but one of those mini doughnuts that you normally get in packs of six. I also got a small thing of orange juice that was mostly room temperature now, a cup of coffee, which I totally didn't want, and a mini carton of milk, also warm. This was not enough for a five year old to have for breakfast. I was so mad that I had even awoken for this, and I was still quite hungry.

I decided to stay up because I knew I would be arraigned early that morning. Sure enough, around a quarter of eight, I was called to come down and get in line for arraignment. I was about eight people back in line, which wasn't bad considering there were about sixty or so guys there. But the selection of order was done alphabetically, which kept me near the front.

Once the arraignments started, I was quickly nervous. You could hear everything that went on in there including the charges read and everything the inmate said to the judge. Everyone was about to find out just exactly what I was in here for and I couldn't imagine a more unpleasant way to do it. Immediately after arraignment, you moved to a different line for classification. So, not only was everyone going to find out my charges, I was going to have to stand right there with them afterwards. I was so nervous, I started to shake. I knew what happened to guys like me. People with charges like this were killed in jail, everyone knew that.

The guard instructed, "Mr. Cooper, it is your turn. Step up in front of the camera and stand with your toes on the line. Look at the judge on camera number one."

"Brayden Cooper. Birthday, September 4th of 1982. Is that correct sir?" asked the judge.

"Yes sir," I said.

"Charges are, distributing matter portraying the sexual performance by a minor, one count. Possession of matter portraying the sexual performance by a minor, four counts. Tampering with physical evidence, one count. Do you understand the charges as they have been read to you?"

"Yes sir," I said.

"Do you have or can you afford an attorney?"

"No, your honor."

"The court shall appoint you legal counsel. Your bond is set at $12,500. Do you have any questions?"

"Is there any way to get that bond reduced sir? My family doesn't have money like that."

"Motion for bond reduction is denied. Anything else, Mr. Cooper?"

"No sir," I said.

"Next case," the judge snapped.

As I walked over to the line for classification, I could hear the guard telling some of the guys to shut up. A couple of guys were making comments like "pervert" and "we should fucking get him." The couple of guys in line right in front me for classification just stared at me the whole time, but no one said anything. We stood along a brick wall and I kept my back to it the whole time so if I was attacked I could at least see it coming. Fortunately, I wasn't attacked.

As I entered the room where classification took place one of the inmates yelled something at me. I couldn't understand what he said, but the guard removed him quickly.

"Close the door," the classification guy instructed. "You don't have any violent offenses on your record or in your current charges. You have no drug abuse problems or suicidal thoughts. Is everything I just said accurate?"

"Yes, I think so," I said.

"Good, your classification will be GP. You can go back to your cell now. They will ship you to GP either tonight or tomorrow night."

"What is GP?"

"Jesus," the officer said, "What is this your first fucking time? General population, now go on back."

I figured out that I might be facing this more often than I had known. I didn't know any of this lingo and this basically was my first time going through all this. I remember thinking that if the guards found me annoying or too much trouble that I could wind up in a bad situation if things went sour down the road. They won't protect me if they hate me. And I wasn't flattered with the GP selection either. I didn't want to go into the general population. That seemed like the worst idea I could think of.

About two hours later, it was time for lunch and we got to come out of our cells to eat lunch with the other five or six people in the same housing unit. This was about five minutes before the noon news came on. We all sat at the same table and watched as the news started.

The news announced, "Another arrest in a child pornography ring here in Lexington. We have those new developments in our LEX 18 Big Story at Noon."

"Hey man, that's your picture!" yelled one of the other inmates.

"Yea man," I said, "But this is total bullshit. I got set up."

"23 year old Brayden Cooper has been arrested in connection with a child pornography ring here in Lexington. Investigators say Cooper admitted to giving his codefendant, Gage Tate, child pornography. That is the LEX 18 Big Story at Noon."

Another newscaster began, "That's right, Dia. Brayden Cooper was arrested last night after police say, he admitted to giving Gage Tate child pornography. Tate, who is 20, was arrested on February 22nd on charges that he sent images and videos depicting sexual acts by a minor to an undercover FBI agent. Investigators in that case say some images were of toddler age children as young as two years old."

I was so pissed. First of all, I NEVER told Detective Hailey that I gave Gage any child porn. He twisted my words and has spun it to look like a confession.

"What a crock of shit!" I said.

"Hey man, that's fucked up. They said you confessed dude," an inmate said to me.

"Man, I didn't confess to anything. That is a lie."

"Right, well the news seems to think so. I think you better just get back in your little cell and stay there."

"I'm telling you dude, I didn't do this," I said.

"Yea, well, I don't believe you," the inmate said.

I knew this was going to be a rough road. After I finished my lunch, I returned to my cell and asked the guard to close my door, even though we had another hour we could stay out. I told the guard to deliver my meals through the door and leave my door closed if they could. They agreed and I knew I was safe for now.

As the day continued, so did the news stories. I was on the news again at 12:30, 5, 5:30, 6, and 11. It was basically the same every time, wrong every time. As the day ended, I remember thinking, 'hmm, no lawyer today.'

That night, I didn't get moved. I stayed in classification for one more day. Much like the first day, I stayed in my small cell. I ate in there and did everything in there. It was boring and a bit grueling, but it was safer there. Maybe, I thought, they would leave me there since I had been all over the news. It seemed to me like it would save everyone a lot of trouble if I could just stay out of the path of the crazy people.

But that thought was gone the next night. After another day of being on the news, around came midnight and they told me I would be transferring. Barely an hour after the 11 o'clock news went off, I was on my way to a cell. I thought perhaps people wouldn't recognize me or they hadn't seen it. Turns out, everyone in jail watches every newscast and I seem to have a face that is easily recognizable.

I went to a unit called "KK." As I was escorted into the unit, I noticed it looked very different than C unit. This unit was wide open on the floor and around the sides had 8 pods. Inside those 8 pods were ten guys. I was assigned a bed in KK-7, which was upstairs on the right side. I was not looking forward to entering my cell. As soon as I came into the unit, I could hear guys screaming and banging on the glass. Everyone in the place recognized me. And what do you know? No one was particularly welcoming.

As the guard told me where I was going, he opened up the pod door.

"There's only one bunk up there, they can show you which one."

"I'm sure I can find it," I said, remembering what the guard in intake had told me.

As I walked up the stairs, I saw people looking through the Plexiglas and laughing at me. It was like I was walking right into a firestorm and there was absolutely nothing I could do about it. The door clanged really loud as it began to open. I walked in and most of the guys in the pod were sitting on their bunks looking at me. I looked around for an empty bed.

After a minute or two, a guy in the back said, "Here man, shit. Put your stuff down on the bed, make that shit and go to sleep."

"Thanks," I said.

"Don't talk, make your bed and go to sleep," he said.

So I did just that. I made my bed as quickly and quietly as I could and climbed the step ladder to the top. The whole time making my bed and climbing into it, several of the guys stared at me. They stood by their beds and watched me closely, as if I was going to do a trick or put on a show for them. I didn't say anything, just laid down.

Six o'clock in the morning came awfully early, again. I got up and climbed down my ladder to greet the morning breakfast. In this unit, instead of breakfast being brought to you, they "popped" your door (which meant they opened it) and you walked out to the food card to get your meals. Afterwards, you return to your cell to eat. It seemed much livelier in this unit for breakfast time. In 'C' unit, many people either slept through breakfast or if they did get up, they were quiet and soon went back to bed. In 'KK' unit, there was some noise. People seemed energized to get out of their cells, if only for a few seconds.

As I returned to my pod with breakfast, I sat at the first seat I came to. The tables were all metal with attached round stools to sit on. It was crowded at the table with four guys there.

"That's my seat boy," said one of the inmates, just a few seconds after I sat down.

"Oh ok, sorry. Where should I sit?"

"Do I look like your momma bitch? I don't give a fuck where you sit long as you ain't in my seat."

I wasn't sure how to handle the situation, but I was sure about two things. "Bubba" there didn't need any more caffeine and I wasn't going to sit there again. I decided to stand in the back of the pod and eat my breakfast there.

Another inmate approached me and said, "You that guy on the news? That perv who likes the kids?"

"I don't like kids, man," I said.

"But that was you on the news, huh? You got some kiddy porn charges don't you?"

"That's what they say, but it isn't true. I didn't do it."

"I bet. We are all innocent, right? You better hope you didn't. You might not wake up tomorrow if you did."

I didn't say anything. I expected this to be an issue. Unfortunately, I didn't know quite how to handle it yet. Most of the guys went back to bed after they ate their breakfast. I got back in my bunk too, but I couldn't sleep. The morning crept by and eventually lunch time came. We went through the same process to get our lunch. Again, I ate standing up. And again the news came on. Of course, Gage and I were the top story again on the news.

"They talkin' bout you a lot for someone who didn't do nothing. They said you confessed you lying fucker. Why shouldn't we just kill you right here in the cell?"

"The news is wrong," I said. "I didn't confess to anything."

Three more guys stood up, now four of them moving towards me. Of the ten people in this pod, I was the only white guy facing nine black guys who tended to stick together in prison. I didn't think race was as big of an issue still as it is. In prison, racial lines are much more concise than in the real world. And if you are a white guy in a room with nine black guys, and you happen to piss off four of them, you are in trouble. Race aside; no one would have dared take my side at this point with my charges.

"Look guys, I know it sounds crazy. But those pigs lied about me. Now I'm here and I can't do anything about that today. I'm stuck here."

"Ha! I can fix that real quick. My niggas here can fuck you up. You'll be gone right now. We could just kill you and send you off to hell now where all the pervs belong."

Thinking I could play some mind games, I said, "Yea, I totally agree. I don't like sick perverts who prey on children. That's sick and it is not me dude."

"Hey boy, I suggest you keep your mouth shut." Two of the remaining guys stood and they formed a circle around me. "You ready to die white boy?" one of the guys asked me.

"You guys are real tough in a group. Be a man, take me one on one," I suggested.

"You don't deserve that respect whore. You deserve to die!"

Just about the time he said that, the guard had looked up into our cell and noticed an issue. He saw the circle forming around me and he popped our door open. He yelled on the speaker to break it up. As the noise came from the door, the guy straight in front me looked back at the door. Still with my lunch tray in hand, I decided it was now or never. I put my hand on the bottom of the lunch tray and used it to do a 'pie face' style stiff arm and I ran passed the guy. I went out the door and down the steps. I heard the door close behind me as I left and all the guys were stuck in the cell.

"What the hell is going on up there?" the guard asked.

"Those guys were going to kill me. I can't go back in there."

"Ok," the guard said, "Stand right here." He made a phone call to a supervisor and within a few minutes he came in to see me. The supervisor was a captain, a heavyset guy in his 50's.

"C'mon," he said. "Come with me."

We left the unit and I followed him down a hallway that curved in a circle around what appeared to be the entire jail. We stopped at his office, which read "On Duty Captain" on the door's name plate.

"Have a seat," he said. "What happened up there?"

"Those guys said they were going to kill me," I said.

"Why did they want to kill you?"

"They saw me on the news, didn't like my charges."

"Mmhmm," he said, "I see why they didn't want to make friends. How are you going to handle this?"

"I was hoping you could help me handle this. I can't go back in there."

"So are you asking for protective custody?"

"Yea, I guess so. Do you have other suggestions?"

"Look, if you are telling me you are in fear for your life, I can take you out of that unit and put you in PC tonight. Tomorrow, the dayshift captain will have to review your file. And I'm telling you, having a high profile case isn't a reason to put someone in PC."

"If it makes a difference, I didn't do this. I'm not guilty."

"It doesn't make a difference. I don't care. I'm going to put you in PC tonight and the dayshift captain will talk to you tomorrow."

"Ok, thanks," I said.

He led me back to unit KK to retrieve my things. On our way, he radioed someone asking them to meet us in unit KK. When we went in, I stood by the guard tower and the captain talked to the guard. After a few seconds, two more guards entered the unit. Together, the two guards, the captain and I went up to the cell I was in. The captain stood beside me as the two guards opened the door and went inside. They told everyone to get on their bunks and to not say a word. As they complied, the captain and I entered the cell.

He told me to gather up everything and place it in a plastic bag that he handed me. After I was finished, he took me out of the cell.

We went back out the doors and down the hallway to unit G. I was led into a single cell similar to what I had in the classification unit. I felt like I could finally relax for a while. I wanted to do nothing but go to sleep. And sleep I did until the guard awoke me to eat my dinner.

I spent that entire day and all night trying to catch up on sleep I had missed over the last week and a half. It still wasn't easy to sleep all considering where I was, but it was nice to feel safe for the first time since being arrested.

The next morning, the dayshift captain came down to see me, just as I was told.

"Mr. Cooper, can we talk for a few minutes?" he asked.

"Sure," I said.

He came in and sat on my bed next to me and said, "Tell me what's going on."

"I am locked up on child pornography charges. They are trumped up; I didn't do any of this at all. But I was on the news and all those guys in that cell were ready to kill me because they recognized me from the news."

"Are you still scared for your life?"

"Well if you are thinking about sending me back to that cell then hell yes."

"We will send you to another cell, like that one, but in a different unit. You think that would be ok?"

"I don't know. Everyone knows about this. You think it will matter what unit I go in?"

"Well being on the news isn't a real reason to be in PC. I can't keep you here forever."

"If you send me back to a cell and that happens again, I will defend myself, like I did. If I have to hurt somebody, I will. Just know that."

After a short pause, he asked me, "Are you a religious guy, Mr. Cooper?"

"I'm Christian, if that's what you're asking."

"What would you think about getting into a Christian program here at the jail called Master Life?"

"I would like that. What do I have to do?"

"Let me look into it for you. I will try to get you moved into it tonight or tomorrow, ok?"

I agreed. At this point, praying seemed like a great option for me. As tired as I had been, that small cell and being completely isolated was starting to make me antsy. Staying alive, however, would have calmed me down considerably if my only option was to return to that cell.

The next night, I was transferred to GG-1, which was better known as the Master Life program. It was a unit much like KK, only GG was considered a "program unit" which meant most of the pods there were programs. In one pod, they taught Hispanics English; in another they had a G.E.D. class. And in GG-1, they had the Master Life program. Master Life is a non-denomination Christian program designed to give inmates a chance to build a closer relationship with God. It was a great program but I was still a bit nervous about joining.

As I entered the cell, much like in KK, everyone recognized me. There were a mix of people in this pod and most of them seemed to have a calmer mood. There were a couple of posters on the wall that were Christian themed, which was unusual because posters were not allowed on the walls. This pod was also cleaner than I was used to. Clearly, these guys were a step up from the thugs in KK.

As I entered the room, I was greeted, "Hey man, I'm Chris." We shook hands and he said, "Your bed is over there, you can put your stuff there. When you make your bed, I can give you a rundown of the rules here, ok?"

"Sure, sounds good," I said.

Another inmate looked over from across the room and said,

"Aren't you the guy from the news that was looking at that porn?"

"Yea," I said, "I was the guy on the news. But I didn't do that stuff man. I was set up by my co-defendant."

"Mmhmm, ok," he said. I wasn't sure what to think about that at this point.

I finished making my bed and Chris came back over to me. "Let's take a walk while we still have recreation time."

"Ok," I said.

"So, let me ask you something. Be honest, that's all I ask. I want to tell you that I am a friend. I won't judge you at all and I won't tell anyone what you tell me. But did you do what they say on the news?"

"No," I said, "I wasn't involved at all. I swear, my co-defendant made it all up, I just can't prove that yet."

"Cool man. I know this must be hard. Do you know who I am?" Clearly, I didn't.

"No," I said.

"Do you watch the news on the street?"

"Yes, when I can."

"Do you remember the story about the guy labeled the "UK stalker" who was flashing women on campus?"

"Yea, I do remember that."

"Yea, well that's me. Guilty here, I know it is crazy. That's why I said I wouldn't judge. I mean being into kids is crazy. I know flashing isn't a respectable thing to do, but I wouldn't flash kids or nothing. But I know what you must be thinking being all over news. I was too when I was arrested. I wasn't the most popular guy, but I wasn't as unpopular as you probably are right now."

"Yea, they tried to kill me in my last unit. I think that more than qualifies for unpopular."

"Ha ha, yea I guess so. You might not meet a lot of friends here, but I don't think anyone is going to try to kill you in the church pod."

"That's a step up," I said.

"That guy who asked about you being on the news... His name is Bear. He is kind of the 'unofficial leader' of our group. He knows a lot about the Bible and he's a great guy. He kind of has a pet peeve for guys who use our pod as a safe haven for sex offenders. I know you came from PC, that's just what it looks like ya know?"

"Yea I get that. I'm not going to lie; it kind of was like that. But I really am Christian and I really do want to be involved in the program and do what I need to do here. There's nothing wrong with building a closer relationship with God, even if it is in jail."

"Well you could say there couldn't be a better time. He can guide you through Hell, quite literally."

"So true. So what do I need to know about the pod?"

"Well we get lights on at 8AM and you have to get up and make your bed. You aren't allowed to lie back down until after 3PM. We say grace before every meal, no cussing, no fighting, and no yelling. If you don't follow the rules, they can kick you out of the pod. And that means back to GP for you."

"Yea that's cool though. I can do that."

And I knew I could do that. The Master Life program was an actual learning course that is available to learn more about the teachings in the Bible and how to build a closer relationship to God. I considered this a safe place, at least, and a place where I could learn something valuable about something I should have always spent more time studying.

As I began to relax a bit from thought of being killed, I began to worry about my case. I replayed every conversation with Gage and Detective Hailey in my head repeatedly. I thought about everything Gage and I had ever talked about or done together just to see if I could find something strange. How could I have really missed this? How could I honestly be caught up in the middle of this? I should have prevented this, stopped this, somehow. My family didn't know what to think and I had no explanation for them. The Commonwealth's Attorney isn't going to understand. The cops didn't believe me, changed my story to fit their version of the crime and now here I sit. My lawyer, I hoped, would surely be my knight in shining armor, a true advocate.

Chapter 8

Lawyers, Judges, And Charges, Oh My!

"Cooper! Get out here! You have an attorney visit!" yelled the guard on the loud speaker in our cell.

"Ok, where do I go?"

"Upstairs; see that door up there?" he asked as he pointed above our head to a door.

"Yes," I said.

"Go up there and wait outside the door, I'll be up there to unlock it in a minute."

I went up the stairs and to the door. Inside the door I could see a concrete bench to sit on with a counter and window. On the other side of the window, I could see a man with mustache, a little heavyset, writing in a notebook. The guard let me in the room and told me to push the button on the wall when I was finished.

"Brayden Cooper?" the man asked without looking up.

"Yes," I said.

"My name is Robert Frumkin. I'm your attorney as appointed by Judge Cantrell. Have a seat."

"Ok, nice to meet you," I said.

"Why didn't you ask for a lawyer when the cops were questioning you? Says here they practically got a confession out of you."

"What!? I didn't confess to anything and never even suggested that. I didn't ask for a lawyer because I didn't do anything wrong and I didn't think I was a suspect. I didn't think I needed one."

"Hmm, well looks like you did, huh? Says here 'suspect admitted to giving Mr. Tate a computer that contained child pornography.' Is that what you did?"

"No! Absolutely not. And if you get the video of my interview, you'll see that is not at all what I said. That's what the detective said 'he heard.' I told him that during a brief incarceration, I lent Gage my computer. He said a bunch of stuff about when some of these things were put on my computer and said that if I was still lending Gage my computer after *he* put the stuff on there then I was distributing. But like I repeatedly told Detective Hailey, I had no idea the stuff was on there!"

He shrugged his shoulders and said, "That's what his report says."

"Well he's lying, how can we prove that?"

"Prove that a decorated detective is lying? Ha ha, that's funny. Listen, you are a convicted felon, you fit the profile for a pedophile, they have all that in the report. Says here you failed a lie detector test. And then this is what Hailey says that you said. He wouldn't have written it up like that if he couldn't play it back and prove it at trial."

"Well get that tape and listen to it yourself. Then you tell me what the hell I said to him! And as far as the lie detector, I dunno what happened. I told the truth!"

"Look kid, you don't have a case here. All I can do is ask Hailey for the tape, but they don't have to give it to us unless we go to trial."

"*Unless*? I didn't do anything wrong! I need to know you are going to fight for me!"

"I will do what I can, Mr. Cooper. But I have to tell you, there is no case here. I will talk to Hailey and the Commonwealth's Attorney handling your case and I'll get back to you. You can expect to see me in a couple of weeks."

"Please get the interview tapes; you will see I am telling the truth."

I was so angry I was shaking from one end to the other. *This guy* was supposed be my lawyer!? Really? I knew I was just another number to him. Another stupid case that he has to handle, just a burden. Again I wondered just how the hell I got in this situation. I was completely helpless and I knew it.

For the next two weeks, I talked to my mom more in depth about the case details that had previously not been told to her. She was equally upset with my attorney. She tried to call him several times to talk to him about the case. He never once returned her call. We were looking at every chance to help my case and we weren't getting anywhere. Every phone call, which by the way costs $1.80 for ten minutes, was centered around this case. Every visit we spent our entire twenty minutes talking about the case. I suppose, considering where I was, it makes sense. But I still wanted to think about something else occasionally.

When Robert Frumkin returned, I felt like I was ready. I was going to tell him how it was. He sat in the same little room and I was escorted there to be let in by the guard once more.

"Mr. Cooper, have a seat. I have looked into some stuff. First of all, tell your mother I am not going to return her phone calls. You are my client, not your mom and I don't want to talk to her."

"She's trying to help my case; she knows some stuff that might be..."

"I don't care what she knows, I won't call her," he interrupted. "Here is what I found out. The DA, Ray Larson, is not a big fan of yours. They are willing to offer you a reasonable deal if you plea on rocket docket. That means you need to plead guilty before you are indicted or the deal goes off the table. I talked to Hailey and he says you clearly admit that you gave Gage the child porn and if he has to show the video to the court at trial he will."

"He's a liar! He is bluffing and you are falling for it! That is NOT what is on that tape! I'm telling you, just get it."

"He is not going to turn it over until the last minute and..."

I interrupted, "That should be your first freaking clue man. If he didn't have anything to hide about the tape, why wouldn't he just show you now so you know he has a slam dunk? He won't show you because what he says is on that tape is not on there!"

"How old is your mom, Mr. Cooper?" he asked.

"She is 56, why?"

"You two are close?"

"Yes."

"And you have a grandmother too, right?"

"Yes, why?"

"If you hope to get home to see either of them before they die, you had better listen to what I'm saying. If you don't take this deal and you are talking about going to trial, then they are going to push for 35 or 40 years. You think your grandmother or even your mom will be alive in 35 years? She'd be 91, unlikely. If you won't do this for you, do it for them. Let me see what kind of deal I can get and we can go from there."

"You don't understand. Why do I have to take a deal when I didn't do anything wrong? This is crazy!"

"Look kid, I don't believe it and if you can't convince your own lawyer with the evidence in your case, then you aren't going to convince a jury. They will rip you apart. Don't risk 40 years, let me try to get you a deal. I might be able to get it under 10."

"You are a piece of government shit just like Donald Hailey. Can I fire you?"

"Not without good reason, which you don't have. I will be back when I have a deal. Think about what I said."

He left the room and I was once again stunned. Not only did I feel completely helpless, I really understood the severity of my situation for the first time. Everyone really thinks I did this and I can't prove otherwise. How could anyone who knew me even think this for a second? But that was the problem. None of these detectives and lawyers and judges knew me. They saw me as another number, another conviction. A statistic, at best, is all I could even be considered. I would never hurt a child and this was so agonizing to have it dumped in my lap to deal with. And how to deal with it was something I had failed to figure out.

Over the next month, I began to become close to Bear. He was kind to me and was a good listener. He was one of a few who believed me and knew how screwed up our justice system truly is. He directed me to several passages in the Bible that helped keep my sanity. And really, I think prayer and the word of God was the only thing that kept me sane through most of this ordeal.

Leala and Naomi also came to visit me several times during this time. They started coming to see me soon after I was arrested and continued until I left the jail. I think they were both a bit horrified at the situation and didn't know exactly what to think. And if you want to know what they really thought, you should ask them. But I have my own opinions about their views.

When you get incarcerated, it is common to hear inmates say 'this is where you find out who your real people are' and that simply means you learn who your true friends are. Leala and Naomi were true friends at a time I desperately needed a true friend. I can't help but believe that Leala being present when I found out why Gage was arrested helped form her view of the situation. I don't know what I looked like or how I acted exactly, but I've been told I impacted a few people during the week before I was arrested. You can fake many things, but there are some things you can't fake. The best way I can describe myself during that week was pure shock. I was a shell going through the motions of daily life. That, I believe, you cannot fake. After knowing me for a while, Leala and Naomi viewed a side of me that I must say was my lowest. I was not at all myself.

These type of emotions are impossible to hide and equally as hard to fake. Many things didn't make sense when you looked at whether or not I was guilty. I could have ditched my laptop, in fact I had six days from the day Gage was arrested before the search warrant to discard it in the river. The thing is I had no idea I needed to. I had friends in different states. I could have run and stayed hidden for a good while. I could have immediately refused to cooperate with police and ask for an attorney. While it turns out I should have, I didn't think I needed to. This is the beginning of things I could have to done to get away with this crime, had I known I committed it. But I didn't commit this crime and I didn't know Gage had set me up.

From outside, all of these things seemed bizarre looking at my case, but my reaction to Gage during that week seemed proof enough of my innocence to those who knew me. My opinion of my reaction was one of shock and loyalty, at first, turning later to anger and confusion. Most that paid any attention at the time would likely agree with that. In my opinion, Leala and Naomi paid attention to those details. And this, I believe, contributed to their continuing loyalty to me. I have never had better friends in my life. Certainly better than the one I called my best friend.

After about a month of stressing out, my attorney came back to talk.

"Ok, Mr. Cooper. I have a deal for you. And you need to take this deal. I got you 5 years, that's it. I know you aren't a fan of taking a deal, but listen, they are coming after you with PFO and 40+ years if we go to trial." PFO stands for persistent felony offender and is a time enhancement charge that can be added to any felony a convicted felon is facing.

"Did you see the tape?"

"I'm not going to see it if we don't go to trial. And Mr. Cooper, we don't need to go to trial. I'm telling you that would be a mistake. You will lose at trial. That jury will see those videos and pictures that were found, they have your profile and your confession that Hailey says he has. Just take this deal."

I was so deflated by this point, I didn't know if I had a chance doing anything else. I had talked to my mom, who understood the situation. She offered her full support whatever I decided to do. But that was just it; I didn't feel like I had a choice. Frankly, I didn't have a choice. The police conducting the investigation, supposedly looking for truth, reworded what I said to be what they needed, the Commonwealth's Attorney hated me and wanted me in prison, and my own lawyer didn't want to fight for me. I had no money to hire a private attorney. I couldn't fire this attorney, though I had tried. I was truly stuck in the most horrible and impossible position ever.

"What happens if I say yes?" I asked.

"Well I take your informal commitment back to the prosecutor. This doesn't commit you to anything until you change your plea in court. You should know the media will be all over this. Keep your family away if you care about them. They can't help you here anyway. They are willing to lower the distribution charge to criminal attempt to distribute. The only felony you will get is tampering with evidence. This is actually very good for you."

"Good? For an innocent man, this is horrible."

"You have to understand, they will convict you at trial. Here is the layout. You will have one felony in the tampering charge. You will have five misdemeanors, the criminal attempt to distribute and four possession charges. The tampering charge would be 1 year enhanced to 5 by the PFO. The five misdemeanors will all be 12 months of jail time; all run concurrent with the five. Gage got his deal, he's facing at least 11 years in prison and he's going to take it."

"He's guilty! And so you're saying that if it wasn't for my other charges, I could walk right here. They are holding a grudge. They are screaming 40 years and then come down to one year, enhanced only by the PFO, which is directly related to my prior? This is such bullshit."

"It doesn't have to be fair. But that's how it is. Can you do this?"

"Well, you are my lawyer and you don't seem to give me any other options."

"You can always go to trial. You have that right. But I don't think we can win at trial."

I reluctantly agreed to sign that paper. Ironically, I was

committing a felony by lying about my guilt on an official court document and swearing it to be the truth. But I guess they will let the perjury go for this conviction.

Breaking the news to my family was the hardest. I was really backed into a corner. I had been lied to and my words twisted so much, and now to take a plea, I didn't think anyone could ever believe I wasn't involved. I had said many times, why would a guy plead guilty to a crime he didn't commit? Well, now I know why. I was one of those guys I used to make fun of just months before.

As my court day arrived to plead guilty, I was having second thoughts. The guards at the jail got me up and told me to be ready early to go to court. I got in my green jumpsuit and lined up with the rest of the guys going to court. They shackled me at the ankles and hands. They then wrapped a chain around my waist and cuffed my hands to my waist. It made moving nearly impossible. To make it worse, they took a long chain and chained a group of twenty prisoners together in what was commonly known as the chain gang.

They loaded us on a bus and drove us to the court house. My lawyer met me in a window and confirmed that I was ready to enter my guilty plea. I told him that I was nervous and still didn't like the idea. Once again, he insisted it was the only way and I was making the right decision. He reminded me this was the only way I could be with my family once again. When it was my turn, a bailiff came to retrieve me. As they escorted me into the courtroom, there were cameras everywhere. I had asked my attorney to try and get them banned but he said it was hopeless. To him, I think, everything was hopeless.

"Your honor," my attorney began, "My client wishes to change his plea from not guilty to guilty."

Judge Cantrell said, "Ok and I understand there is an arrangement with the Commonwealth's Attorney's office, correct?"

"Yes, your honor." They passed the paperwork to the judge.

"Mr. Cooper," Judge Cantrell said, "Are you prepared to enter a guilty plea to the charges you discussed with your attorney?"

After a short pause I said, "Yes."

"On count one, tampering with physical evidence, Mr. Cooper, how do you plead to this charge?"

"Guilty."

"On count two, criminal attempt to distribute matter portraying the sexual performance of a minor, Mr. Cooper, how do you plead to this charge?"

"Guilty."

"On counts three through six, possession of matter portraying the sexual performance of a minor, Mr. Cooper, how do you plead to these charges?"

"Guilty."

"Having talked with your attorney, are you prepared to recount what you did in commission of these felonies?"

I turned to my attorney and he spoke to the judge, "Your honor, as a condition to the plea agreement, Mr. Cooper is not required to give a description of the crimes."

"Is this correct?" Judge Cantrell asked the prosecutor.

"Yes, your honor," he said.

"Brayden Cooper," the judge began, "I hereby find you guilty of the charges as you have pled to them today. I will set sentencing for two weeks from today. You are dismissed."

You are dismissed. That is what the man said to me on the worst day of my life. My life had been dismissed with those very words. With the five years I had on the shelf from my previous conviction, these five years would stack on top to make ten years. I was going away for a long time and I knew it.

After leaving the court room, I didn't say a word to anyone. I had to wait several hours to be returned to the jail and all I wanted to do was crawl in bed and curl up. As I arrived back in my unit, I knew right away that my plea was on the noon news. When I entered my pod, Bear asked me how it went. Of course, I wasn't too chatty. It went horrible and I didn't want to talk about it. When

I finally got to see the news that evening, LEX 18 called the plea deal a "surprise guilty plea" as if they knew the intimate details of the case. Or perhaps to them it was surprising because they knew something no one else did. I was innocent, but was now legally guilty.

Most of that night, I stayed in my cell, in my bunk. This couldn't get any worse, I thought. But little did I know the next day would bring light to so many things. My life would go on entire one hundred story roller coaster the next day. And I already couldn't sleep tonight...

Chapter 9

The F.B.I.

"Cooper, get out here!" yelled the guard into our cell. I was still groggy at 7:30AM and didn't know what the guard could want. I left my cell and approached the guard tower.

"You have a visit."

"A visit?"

"Yes," he said, "Go up to the door and wait for me to unlock it."

"My attorney is here? I really didn't think he'd want to rub in yesterday, and so early, damn."

"I don't think your attorney is here, I think they said cops." About that time, he got a phone call at the tower and after a few seconds of saying 'ok' to the other person he said, "Well you aren't going to that room actually. Wait a couple minutes, the Sergeant will be here to escort you."

"Escort me where? Am I in trouble for something?"

"I don't know. Not in trouble with the jail, maybe the cops have something else for you."

As the Sergeant walked in, he motioned for me to come with him. We left Unit GG and went back out to the big round hallway. He took me to a room I hadn't seen before with a sign that read 'Interrogation' on the door. He unlocked the door to let me in and then left. In front of me was a middle aged guy, around 35 and clean shaven. He was good looking and clean cut, stood with confidence. He was definitely a cop.

"Brayden Cooper?"

"Yes."

"Mr. Cooper, I'm Special Agent Zach Greene with the F.B.I." he said as he sported an unfolded wallet-like badge with a picture ID and shiny badge. It was just like something out of every movie with a fed. "Have a seat, we need to talk."

"I want a lawyer," I said quickly and before I sat down.

"I want you to sit down. You don't need a lawyer, you need to sit down."

I sat. He seemed like a small guy who was confident but I got the feeling he could kick some serious ass if he needed to. He had with him two folders that both read "Sealed" in bold black letters on the front. He opened the first one and looked up at me.

"You didn't do what the state charges you are facing indicate, did you?"

"No sir," I said. "But try telling that to the cops, the prosecutor, or my lawyer."

"I don't need to, I know you weren't involved. And I need your help with an investigation."

After a pause I said, "I don't understand."

"I'm not at liberty to discuss details with you at this time. I have in my possession a gag order, already signed by a federal judge and the F.B.I. Before I can talk to you, I need you to sign this order. I can prove your innocence, but you'll never know what I know if you don't sign this paper. Do you think you could do that?"

"What does that mean if I sign the gag order?"

"That means everything we talk about, my existence to you, everything stays in this room. Everything stays between you, the F.B.I. and no one else. You can't tell your buddies in the slammer, you can't tell your mom, mammy, or cat. I don't care who you think you can trust; this gag order seals our deal as confidential. And if you violate it, I can put you in federal prison for 20 years. If you don't sign it, I can't use you to help me. You don't help me, I can't help you. You tell me to get lost; I'm walking out that door and not coming back. I didn't come here to waste my time."

"So if I sign this, you can get me out of here?"

"I'm not at liberty to discuss that. You have to sign it or I can't talk to you any further."

"Can I consult with my attorney?"

"You don't have an attorney, not one you want to consult with."

"True, but I don't know if this is the right thing to do."

"Tell you what; I'll give you one chance to talk to an attorney. I will provide you with a federal legal aid counsel. I will be back tomorrow at the same time with an attorney to discuss this further. Then, you need to sign the gag order or I won't be back. Deal?"

"I'll talk to the attorney, go from there."

As he left and I was escorted back to my cell; I didn't know what to think. He said I was innocent and he knew that but in order for him to help me, I had to sign a paper. At first look, I was skeptical of him because I had learned to be skeptical of any cop. But in thinking about it, things began to not seem so unreasonable. He had folders that said sealed. He said he couldn't share that info with me unless I agreed to not tell anyone about it. That seemed fair. I wondered what it could hurt. At least someone would know I was innocent for sure. That meant a lot to me.

The next morning, when Agent Greene returned, he had a second man with him. I was led to the same room as before and as soon as I entered, Agent Greene excused himself and told us we had 10 minutes.

"Ok Mr. Cooper. My name is Nathan Reeves. I'm your attorney in this matter. What are your concerns about the gag order? Have you read over it?"

"Yes, I have read it. I don't know my concerns. Is this a common thing? It seems like it's a little crazy and I just don't have a high trust level for the police."

"Listen, Agent Greene says he has information about your case. He claims to have proof you didn't commit the crimes you are charged with here in Kentucky. He can help get your name cleared up. This gag order doesn't commit you to helping him with any investigation. It only helps him explain what he knows and you can decide then if you want to help. Does that make sense?"

"Yes. So basically I just sign the order saying I won't discuss what we talk about here. Kind of like confidentiality with doctor and patient right?"

"Exactly. Only, this can send you to federal prison for 20 years if you violate."

"Ok, I understand. Let's do it."

Agent Greene re-entered the room with his folders and said, "Mr. Cooper, again I am Special Agent Greene with the F.B.I. You have agreed to sign a gag order and I am now presenting you with that order. You will need to sign and date at the bottom of the page on the dotted line."

I signed the order and slid it back across the table. Agent Greene opened the folder on top and slid over to me two 8 ½ X 11 photos to look at.

"Do you recognize the place in those photos?" he asked.

"Yes," I said. "This is my bedroom in my apartment. When were these taken?"

"They are still shots from video that was taken as part of surveillance on Gage Tate. They were taken several days before he was arrested. He is attempting to remove some photos that he is copying onto an external drive and he will add some videos to your computer in a hidden folder. We believe Tate wanted you to be in possession of very specific pictures and videos. The date we took this video of Tate corresponds exactly to the dates that Detective Hailey says you had some files that were moved around on your computer. It is the same files, in fact, that brought your tampering with evidence charge."

"This is great then, right? Can you get me out of here? You know I'm innocent."

"It's not that simple, Mr. Cooper. We..."

I interrupted, "Yes, actually. It seems to me to be quite simple. I didn't do it. You know I didn't do it. You have proof I didn't do it. You tell the prosecutor that I didn't do it and I get to go the hell home. Now that I have spelled it out, it should be easy."

"Watch your tone, Mr. Cooper. You need to let me explain. You don't understand the magnitude of this case. This case is not about some pictures and videos. This case is going federal. We have child trafficking and homicide cases tied to this investigation. This is a big deal."

"But I didn't do any of that and I don't know anything about it."

"That may be true," Agent Greene said, "And that's what we are banking on. None of the major players in this child trafficking ring have been taken down yet. We don't know enough about most of them to take them down. Gage Tate was a key player in the mix. They know he got busted. They need to think it has gotten partially pinned on you and that all we have is some pictures of some random young girls. Otherwise, they get spooked and disappear without us ever being able to track them. You are an intricate part of that equation. You stay here, you work with us and help us out, they don't run, we get some big busts here. Then these children can be rescued and families can be put to rest."

"So I can't go home?" I asked.

"I know this is a bunch to take in. But no, right now you can't go home. But I do have a proposal for you. I have an agreement here from the F.B.I. saying if you cooperate with our investigation, then when we are finished we will take care of your record. Think you could do that?"

"First of all, I don't think I know anything that can help you. Secondly, why couldn't I help you from home?"

"We'll decide whether what you know will help us. And you

can't go home or everyone knows there is another investigation. You are safer here and our investigation is safer like this."

"So I get sacrificed because you need to bust some guys? What about me, my family, what about us?"

"You have to understand how the priorities are decided. You aren't facing much time and may not even be convicted..."

I interrupted, "I have already been convicted. I took a plea two days ago because my attorney said I didn't have a chance in hell at trial."

"Anyway you can retract that? It will be easier to help if you haven't already pled out."

"I don't know; what could I do?"

Mr. Reeves interjected, "Ask your attorney to talk to the judge and see if you can take back your plea. Tell him you changed your mind and you were pressured into it. That will stall some things a bit."

"Ok, I can try that."

"Now we have an agreement here," Agent Greene continued. "This would state that you would cooperate from beginning to end in our investigation and prosecution of Gage Tate and that, upon completion of the case, we will notify you of your record being cleared up. I'm not going to lie to you, this could take a while. This is a true time investment. And you would have to go and do as the state says in the meantime. If you can make parole, great, if not, I'm afraid you'd have to stay. Don't think I am trivializing this Mr. Cooper. I know what I'm asking you to do and I know how big of a deal it is."

"Do you? Let me talk to my lawyer in private."

"Sure," he said. Agent Greene left the room.

"What is the real deal here? Do I get to keep a copy of this agreement? How can I enforce it?"

"Listen, the F.B.I. doesn't often make promises but when they do, they usually come through. But as your attorney, I must advise you, there is no recourse if they don't. You can't take a copy of this, it is under seal. You can't sue them if they breech. You really have no way to enforce it and as part of the gag order, you can't even acknowledge the existence of the agreement to anyone. That being said, I don't think they will screw you."

"You don't *think*? I need more than think. If you were in this situation, knowing what you know, would you sign it?"

"Yes. You have nothing to lose. If you don't sign it, you do your time. If you do sign it, maybe things can get wrapped up and you can get out early. At least your charges could go away sometime instead of having them forever."

"How long could this really take?" I asked.

"Hard to say. Likely years though, these things don't move quickly."

"Years! What do I do in the meantime?"

"Be a model prisoner and try to get out of prison on parole. It is a bad situation, but you don't have many options."

"That seems to be a theme among my attorneys lately. I never have any freaking options. Ok, I'll do it. Send him back in."

After I signed the agreement and listened to the thirty minute speech about how I would be buried under the jail if I breeched, I was told Agent Greene would be back the next day to begin interrogation.

I called my mother that night and told her the F.B.I. had come to see me. I told her they knew I was innocent but they weren't going to let me go home unless I helped with their investigation. Yes, I immediately violated my gag order. But this was too much for me to handle on my own. I had to talk to someone who had my best interests in mind. I knew I had to keep her updated. This was becoming by far the hardest thing I had ever done. She wasn't in favor of signing the gag order. Agreeing to be quiet about anything wasn't something she thought was a good idea. But what was done was done, and I didn't get the mom consult until after it was all said and done. I think we both decided that trusting anyone was risky.

The next day, Agent Greene returned, as promised. He was alone this time.

"Mr. Cooper, Agent Greene, F.B.I." he said has he showed me his badge, again.

"I know who you are by now; you don't have to tell me every time."

"Yes I do. Protocol. I know that's not something you are familiar with since you violated your gag order on the first day. I'm going to let this one go, but don't think you can get on these phones and we aren't listening. I said you don't tell your mother. You don't tell a single sole, is that fucking clear!"

"Yes," I said.

"Good. I hope it really is this time. I'm going get to some questions, ok?"

I guess it was ok, I didn't really know what to expect. I didn't know anything about what Gage had done and I felt like I didn't really know anything about Gage at all. But I had signed this agreement and I wanted nothing more than to be free, so I was committed to trying.

"First of all, do you prefer to go by Brayden?" asked Agent Greene.

"Yes sir," I said.

"Ok, Brayden. I'm going to ask you a bunch of questions that might not seem to you to be related to anything. Some of the questions you may have been asked by the local police. I don't care what you told them, ok? I don't care if what you tell us is different from what you've told them. All I ask is that what you tell us be the truth, 100%, ok?"

"Ok," I said.

"Good. Do you have any questions before we get started?"

"No, I don't guess so."

"You are gay, correct?"

"Yes."

"Did you or do you find Gage Tate attractive?"

"I *did*. Not so much now, I guess for obvious reasons."

"Were you two ever involved sexually?"

"No, never."

"Did you two ever talk about it?"

"Having a sexual relationship? No, not seriously. We joked, or more I joked and he rolled his eyes. It really was just joking. He liked to kinda tease me sometimes like 'you know you want my body' but it was seriously just all joking."

After a pause, Agent Greene asked, "Did you want there to more than joking?"

"Not really. It was just joking."

"Ok, let's switch gears a bit. What do you know about Mike?"

"Mike who?" I asked.

"Tate's stepfather. His name is Mike, do you know him?"

"Yes I know him. I don't know much about him. He doesn't work because of some back injury that he gets a check for. He smokes pot and is an ass hole. Other than that, I dunno much about him."

"So, you say he is an ass hole, so Tate and he didn't get along?"

"No, not at all. Gage hated him."

"I guess his relationship with his mom must have been shady too then?"

"Well, it was weird. I dunno what he really thought about it. He hated that she smoked pot but they didn't seem to fight much. He was close to his real dad though. Mike was an ass, but being close to his real dad probably helped drive a wedge between Mike and Gage."

"How often did he see his dad?"

"I don't know. Used to be every other weekend. For a while

it was every weekend. I think basically he saw him whenever he wanted."

"What do you know about the trip Tate was getting ready to take?"

"Oh yea, his vacation. He was visiting family in North Carolina. He tries to go once a year, usually with his parents. I don't really know what relation they are though."

"And he hadn't mentioned going anywhere else?"

"Not to me."

"When was he going to North Carolina? Was that going to be on his vacation from O'Charley's?"

"Yea I think so."

"What if I told you Tate wasn't planning a trip to North Carolina?"

"I dunno; that's what he told me."

"Has Tate ever mentioned taking a trip out of the country?"

"Not to me."

"Well he was planning a trip out of the country. Does Tate speak any other languages? Specifically, does he speak Czech?"

With a chuckle I said, "No, Gage doesn't know any other language that I know of. Why would he learn Czech?"

"Because he had plane tickets to the Czech Republic that would land him there during the week he was planned to be on vacation."

"Why would he want to go there and why would he tell me he was going to North Carolina?"

Agent Greene nodded and said, "Yea, he had good reason for that. The Czech Republic is one of the few places around the world with no legal age of consent and legalized prostitution. The combination means Tate could go there and have sex with minors all he wanted and it wasn't illegal. It's a child trafficking safe-haven"

"Do you think that's why he was going there?"

"No, I don't think that's why. I know that's why. He has received mail from the Czech Republic that contains maps of hostels in the area where minors solicit sex."

"Man," I said, "He was really deep into this shit wasn't he?"

"Yes he was. You knew Tate's girlfriends, right?"

"Yes," I said. He proceeded to list a few names that I remembered as clear girlfriends of his. "Yea I know all of them."

"And do you notice something about all of them, like some similarities?"

"Like what?"

"Oh come on Brayden. They all had a small figure, baby face, nice skin. You didn't notice that about every girl he was interested in?"

"Yea, well, they were young, thin girls. I knew that. That was Gage's type of girl."

"You never thought it was bizarre?"

"Well, I don't really understand. Why would that be bizarre?"

"They all looked like 12 year olds in the face. Did you not notice that?"

"I didn't think about it like that. So he liked young women with a petite body style. A lot of guys like women like that. None of them were really younger than him. They were all about the same age, a couple even older than him. So if you think I should have thought it was weird that he liked young looking petite girls his own age as opposed to old fat bitches, yea I guess I didn't think it was a bad thing."

"I just look at this case and there so many warning signs, Brayden. He paid cash for his new car too. Did you think that was weird? You sure can't say most guys do that."

"Well I knew he *told* me that. I didn't really believe him."

"You didn't believe your best friend? Did you have a reason to think he was lying?"

"It wasn't *that*," I said with irritation in my voice, "It's just that lots of guys our age say stuff. I dunno, I thought maybe if he paid cash his dad helped him or something. I didn't think he did all himself. He doesn't make that much money, but then again, he had no bills either. I thought it was weird but I figured worst case scenario he was dealing some pot or something. I knew his brother was involved in the drug trade, I just figured he might have been doing that."

"Well it wasn't drugs was it? He didn't need his new laptop to deal drugs."

"He said he needed that for school," I said.

"Right. And his bad attitude, did he need that for school too?"

"Hey man, what the fuck is your problem?" I screamed.

"I don't have a problem. I'm just trying to figure out how you missed all the warning signs. You weren't involved, so you say, so how do you explain all the signs you missed?"

"You KNOW I am not involved. You showed me the proof yourself!"

"I know you didn't do what the state says. That doesn't mean you didn't know what Tate was doing. You have to explain the things that don't make sense here. Just help me understand how this came to be what it is."

"I don't know how it happened. But you are crazy if you think *that* goofy list is supposed to tell me something like this. A bad attitude, extra cash, young women with a petite figure and not getting along with his stepdad doesn't scream pedophile. Or at least not to me it doesn't. And if it does, you better arrest every teenage boy around here. So I'm sorry if I was supposed to take that and run with it, but if you were expecting me to have caught that, you are crazier than he is."

"Ok, Brayden. I think that's enough for today. Don't be so combative with me. I'm trying to help you."

"Yea that doesn't sound like help to me."

"I will be back tomorrow and we can talk some more."

As Agent Greene left, I got this feeling of doubt. I felt like I should have never agreed to this. I had this self-righteous feeling like 'how dare he treat me like that knowing what he knows?' Once again, my stomach was tied up in knots and I knew I wouldn't sleep a wink. Tomorrow's meeting better be more like an interview, less like an interrogation, I thought, or else.

Agent Greene's attitude about this was surprising to me. Perhaps the things that Gage Tate did and said were warning signs of something bigger, like being a child predator. I questioned myself constantly and wondered how I could possibly have missed it. But I didn't know how anyone could take those particular signs and determine someone is a pedophile. In fact, I'm not the only one who missed this. If the signs were so obvious and I was so dumb as to miss it, at least everyone around me was dumb enough to miss it also. The satisfaction of that realization was minimal. I still felt largely responsible for not doing more. I was, after all, his best friend.

After a very poor night's sleep and bad headache later, I was again summoned to the interrogation room. He came later this time and he had again brought someone with him. He was not my attorney and he was an older man. He had a large case and some equipment with him. As I entered the room, I smelled food immediately. I looked on the table and back of Hardees® was on the table.

"For you," Agent Greene said. "I know the food here is awful. Consider this a peace offering of sorts. I need you in good humor today, ok?"

"So because I'm fat, I'm for sale for a cheeseburger?"

"Well I'd be glad to eat it for you."

"Thanks. What are we doing today?"

"Well first, you are eating. Then we need you to take a polygraph."

"Great, that was fun last time," I said sarcastically. "Apparently I fail those things even when I tell the truth. Are you going to turn on me too?"

"I'm sorry, forgive me if I wasn't paying attention, but I must have missed something."

"Oh, I just assumed you read all the police reports and whatnot from Detective Hailey."

"I did, I read them all. What are you talking about?"

"The polygraph," I began, "I failed it. That's why they arrested me because I failed their polygraph."

"No. You didn't fail it. I have the report from the detective who administered the polygraph. We obtained the actual test results, the output from the machine. You clearly passed the test. The only deception occurred during control questions, right where it should have."

"What the hell? Are you serious? They lied to me?"

"Looks that way. Listen, we are not going to lie to you. I will give you the results right here as soon as we are done."

"Ok," I said.

After I finished my cheeseburger and fries, the polygraph examiner began attaching me to the machine. It was similar to the machine I was tested on before, but this one seemed to have a few more gadgets. This one had a shoulder pad piece that sat lightly on my shoulders. It wasn't so uncomfortable as it was just humiliating. To me, lie detectors are used to prove you aren't lying and such means the person asking you questions doesn't really believe what you are saying. It made for a setting of awkwardness.

"Ok, Brayden. I am going to ask you a few control questions like your name and birthday. Then I will ask you at the end your birthday again. The first time I ask you, I want you to list your real birthday. The second time, I want you to tell me a different date.

You need to give a different month, day and year from your real birthday. Do you understand?"

"Yes," I said.

"Ok, remember, try to sit still and only answer yes or no to target questions. Here we go. Please state your name."

"Brayden Cooper."

"Birthday?"

"September 4, 1982."

"Sex?"

"No thanks."

"Ha, funny. And a lie. You know I mean gender. What is your gender?"

"Male."

"Ok, again, what is your birthday?"

"April 1, 1974."

"Good job. Now we will get to target questions. Are you ready?"

"Yes."

"Are you attracted to men?"

"Yes."

"Are you attracted to boys under the age of 16?"

"No."

"Did you know Gage Tate was a pedophile?"

"No."

"If you had known, would you have reported it to the police?"

After a pause, I said, "I don't know."

"Have you ever been suspicious of Gage Tate's involvement with younger women?"

"No."

"Are you mad at Gage Tate?"

"Yes."

"The police found child pornography on your laptop. Did you download those files?"

"No."

"Talking about the same files, did you obtain them from Gage Tate?"

"No."

"Did you find those files prior to the police seizing the laptop?"

"No."

"When often means once a week or more, did you often let Gage Tate use your computer?"

"Yes."

"Did Gage Tate have your password to enter Windows on your computer?"

"Yes."

"Did you have the password to Gage Tate's computer?"

"No."

"Did you know where Gage Tate got his 'extra cash' that he had?"

"No."

"Have you told anyone anything about the things we have talked about in our interviews with you thus far?"

"Yes."

"Other than your mother, have you told anyone else about these conversations or given any details about this case to anyone?"

"No."

"Have you tried to beat this lie detector using special training?"

"No."

"Have you been completely honest with me?"

"Yes."

"Ok, Brayden. We are finished."

"Good, how did I do?"

Agent Greene interjected, "Decent as near as I can tell. Let the printer spit it out and we will see for sure."

As the printer spit out the page, the polygraph examiner was reviewing data on his screen. When the paper came out, Agent Greene quickly skimmed over it. He pointed to something on the screen and showed the polygraph examiner something on the paper.

He looked up at me with a grin and said, "You only showed deception on one question. That was the birthday question. You passed with flying colors. Just like the other one. We just like our machine better. It is more accurate. You won't have to do this again. Thanks for your cooperation."

"No problem," I said.

"We will be back next week to begin the more intensive information search, ok?"

"Ok. Thanks for the burger."

As they left, I actually felt better again. I knew a few things at this point. First, Detective Hailey is a liar and manipulator and shouldn't be a detective. Second, the F.B.I. truly believed in me and seemed to be more interested than ever in talking to me. I felt for the first time like I might be able to sleep that night. Rejuvenation can mean a lot to someone in my position and I was more rejuvenated than ever.

Chapter 10

As one chapter ends, another begins, even in life.

I called my attorney to fill him in on some of the updates and the new evidence I learned about. That lie detector result was in itself a lie. Detective Hailey was the only liar there and I need to withdraw that guilty plea. My lawyer would have the answers for me now; he couldn't deny I was telling the truth. When I called him, I told him I had new evidence in the case. He needed to come see right away, I assured him. He wasn't greatly fond of the idea. He didn't believe me and I had already entered a plea. He was basically done with my case and wanted to be done with it.

After some coaxing, I convinced him to come to the jail. When I entered our usual room, he was tapping his pen on the pad of paper in front of him. He was clearly in a hurry and not too interested in what I had to say.

Before I could say anything, he said, "Well, what is your evidence you have?"

"The lie detector test they said I failed, I didn't fail it. I passed it, 100%. And I passed another one now. Detective Hailey lied about that just like he lied about what I said."

"What are you talking about? How would you know he lied about the test results?"

"You listen to me carefully man. I told you from the beginning that I wasn't lying. I told you then that I knew Hailey was lying about the results. But the day after I pled guilty, I got a visit from the F.B.I. who is also investigating Gage Tate under seal. They asked me to cooperate with their investigation and they had proof I was innocent. They had the results of the first lie detector test and they showed it to me. I passed that test. Then, just to be sure, they retested me on their machine with their examiner. I passed that one too.

Now, *you* had me rush into this plea deal and I have pled guilty to something I didn't do. I told you from day one, I didn't do it. The F.B.I. made me sign a gag order. I can't talk about the stuff they showed me. This means I can't take it to court and use it to argue why I should be able to withdraw my plea. So, since *you* didn't believe me, and since *you* wanted me to plead out because I had no chance, then *you* can figure out how the hell I'm going to fix this!"

"Well first things first," he began, "I need to talk to the F.B.I. When are they coming back?"

"I don't know, they said next week."

"Ok, I can find out. If everything you say is true, I'm still not sure how we can take back your guilty plea if we can't prove any of it. We can't just tell the judge to trust us when we tell him the lead detective is a liar."

"That's not my problem. You created this mess, you have to fix it. This is my life! You're talking about me going to prison here. You need to figure this out!"

"I'll come back in the morning," he said. "I'll have more info for you then. Just hang tight."

So I hung tight. Waiting was something, by now, I had gotten good at. It seemed waiting was all there was to do in this place. I was surrounded by people who made my IQ drop steadily and besides that, there was really nothing to do. While 'waiting' for a number of things, I found myself developing a closer relationship with God. The Master Life program was a chance to learn some things about the Bible that I had never learned before. And I had time to read and study. I learned to treasure these studies. It was my best and only escape from reality.

When my lawyer came back to see me, I was interested in what his plans were. I was also ready to kill him a little. I just knew there had to be a way to make all this right. When bad guys do bad things, a loophole seems too frequent to bail them out. Now, I need the screwed up system to work for me!

"So here's the thing," Robert Frumkin began, "We don't have a lot of options. I talked to Agent Greene. We can't bring this up in court. If we do, you may get out of this case for a far more serious one with the feds. So, there is only one way to play this. At the sentencing date, you have to ask to speak directly to Judge Cantrell. You need to tell him that I misrepresented myself in the offering of the plea into consideration. You need to tell him that you are not guilty and don't want to plead guilty. You need to tell him that, while I was supposed to be your advocate, I pressured you into taking a deal offered by the Commonwealth's Attorney. Hopefully, he will let you rescind your deal and we can go from there."

"What if he doesn't?"

"Then we will ask for a continuance and see what we can figure out. I have an idea about a way to get that. Some of the files they say were tampered with may have been before your previous charge. That's important at sentencing because if this crime was technically committed prior to your first felony, then you are still a candidate for probation. I will ask for that."

"So what if he does let me withdraw, then what happens?"

"Well then I go back to Donald Hailey and string him up by his balls in front of the prosecutor so I can try to get this case thrown out."

"I am hoping for that option. I will see you at court then?"

"Yes, I won't be back before then. Be ready to be forward with the judge. We can't have you pulling punches."

"I'm not known for having problems being vocal," I said.

For the first time, I truly felt a bit of hope. I only prayed that my attorney hadn't waited too long to get on my bandwagon. I was going crazy in here and desperately wanted to go home. But it finally made a little more sense how I wound up where I was. Gage is crazy, Hailey is a liar, I was careless... Yes, it was starting to come together.

Early the next week, as promised, Agent Greene returned. In lieu of a cheeseburger, he was armed with a large box filled with folders, a laptop computer and what looked like endless stacks of forms. The cheeseburger, I thought, was better than all that.

"Today we have an unpleasant task to begin. How do you feel?"

Not liking the sound of that, I said, "I'm ok. What are we doing?"

"I need to make identifications if we can. I'm going to show you some pictures and some videos. I need you to pay close attention and tell me if you recognize anyone. Some of them are children, some are adults. Some of it isn't easy to look at, but I need to know if anyone looks familiar. Even if you don't know a name, anything you could tell us may be helpful. Do you think you can do that?"

"Sure, I guess. You just want me to look at some pictures and tell you if I know the people in them, right?"

"Right," he said. He proceeded to take a folder that was stuffed full out of his box. He positioned the folder in front of him and began pulling out the pictures one by one and sliding them over to me so I could view them.

"This one," he said, "is someone we know. Her name and identity are known to us, but we still don't know who is responsible for her death. We are hoping you recognize her because we have information that suggests she was being held by Tate for up to three days."

The pictures, four of them, were spread out in front me. The first was a nice picture of this girl, 11, taken on picture day at her school. She was adorable, cute face and lovely smile. She was dressed nice and looked very well taken care of. The next picture was a still photo from a video that was taken. In this photo, she looked very much different. It was a shot of her head, from the shoulders up. You could tell she wasn't wearing a shirt and the look in her eye was pure fear. Her hair was messed up, like you would expect just after she woke up in the morning. I did not like the way this was going.

As I looked at the last pictures, they were of her body, as investigators found it. Her face was barely recognizable it had been beaten so badly. She was covered by a tarp to shield her naked body from view. Every visible part of her body was bruised and swollen. She had been literally beaten to death.

"She was raped repeatedly," Agent Greene said. "She was beaten from head to toe and her fingers were cut off, all before they killed her. They tortured and brutalized this poor child and then put her body in a duffle bag and tossed her off a bridge. We had to use dental records to identify the body. Is there anything you can tell us about her?"

I was speechless. I could not muster words for the thoughts that swirled through my head. I thought this reminded me of Law and Order®, not real life. People didn't really do these things to other people, to children.

"I don't know her," I said.

"You have never seen her before?"

"No," I said. "I almost wish I had. Could I have stopped this? When did this happen?"

"Her body was found about eight months ago. If Tate had her in his house for three days as we suspect, you may have seen something. You knew him then, that's all. Let's move on."

I was on the first pictures and I didn't know if I could move on. I hoped the other pictures weren't as bad as these. I didn't recognize anything in the photos that I was asked to look at. No personal effects looked familiar and she wasn't someone I had seen before. Is this why Gage had been coming to work late all the time? My head was spinning with insanity.

"Now I'm going to give you a stack of photos, each of a different child. Some of them we know, most of them we don't. We want you to see if you can identify who any of them are or if you can verify that Tate was in personal contact with any of them."

As he slid the folder over to me, I began to thumb through the photos. Most were girls in the age range of 9 – 12, but scattered in and throughout were a few boys in that age range too. Some pictures were taken by a predator and later recovered on Gage's computer. Some photos were taken by investigators at a crime scene after the child was discovered.

One picture was especially disturbing to me. It showed Gage engaged in anal sex with a young girl on his bed. He had his hand in her hair and had pulled her head back. He was penetrating her from behind. His head was looking down and back towards the camera and he had a smirk on his face. He was enjoying this and that poor girl had a look of unconscionable fear and pain. They were both completely naked and she was bound by a leather collar attached to her neck at one end and the bed frame at the other.

She had bruises on her back and a trickle of blood on the tip of her hairline where it appeared Gage had pulled her hair out at the roots. On Gage's left hand, which hung to his side, you could see a scratch on his knuckle where he had done something to her that was so violent it cut his knuckle.

Gage seemed so calm. I thought of this like a movie with a really bad guy character, someone who is just complete evil. Then, the casting director casts someone who is traditionally a good guy to be that really bad guy. It just doesn't fit; you can't imagine *that* guy playing a bad guy in the movie. And I couldn't imagine *Gage* playing this role. The more I saw, however, the more I began to believe it. And the more I began to realize this was so much more than just a 'role' for Gage. This was a lifestyle, a hobby of his. How this sort of thing could be fun was beyond me.

After a week more of these meetings, looking at disgusting pictures and videos, I was becoming numb to the experience. I remember Leala and Naomi visiting me in the jail and feeling like I was so disconnected. I very much wanted to talk about nothing but what was going on outside the walls of the jail. And, naturally, they wanted to get the latest on the case. I saw my family on the weekends and Leala and Naomi came during the week. Every visit each week was the same visit. A rehash of the same events I had lived through the week. Sometimes it was truly hell enough to live it, but to rehash it was sometimes worse. Thankfully that gag order prevented me from giving specifics.

I used that to my benefit more often than not. A part of me was ready to explode and I just needed to tell someone something about what was going on and couldn't really talk about it. Another part of me wanted to curl up in the corner in the fetal position and cry. I did learn one important avenue was God. I could tell him anything, ask for advice and disclose my true feelings without fear of it getting back to feds or fear of ridicule. I still felt great guilt and very used in this situation. To this day, I still feel that way.

As humans, we give out unconditional love and trust selectively. Maybe family, a spouse or a close friend, but not just anyone gets that sort of loyalty. People take time to make that decision and opening those doors takes courage. That is simply natural human development. But when that trust is broken and those doors are slammed shut by the other person, it remains nearly impossible to reopen them. God, blessed are we, never slams that door. He may be the only one that is guaranteed to never betray you. For that guarantee, I stand completely loyal to Him.

When the day came for my sentencing hearing, I was a wreck. It was my chance to stand up to the judge and declare my innocence. It was time to start over with my case and hopefully go home soon. While those thoughts were exciting, nervousness overwhelmed the excitement.

"Are you ready?" Robert Frumkin asked.

"I think so," I said, unsure of anything at this point.

I was escorted into the courtroom where I felt most alone. I had told my mother and the rest of my family to stay home for fear the news media would swarm them. My attorney had not been my best ally until now, which may very well be too late. No one was in there to support me except me.

"Mr. Cooper," Judge Cantrell began, "You understand what we are here for, to sentence you?"

"Yes, your honor," I said, "But I have something to ask, if I may?"

"Go on," he said.

"I am not guilty of this crime. I was pressured into taking this deal by my attorney who misrepresented this deal to me. I did not fully understand all of my options at the time of the plea. I was told it had to be done quickly and I made a hasty decision to plead out when I was not guilty. I would like to withdraw my plea and go to trial, sir."

"Have you discussed this with your attorney?"

"Yes and he agrees we had some miscommunication."

"When you entered your plea, Mr. Cooper, I asked you if you understood what you were doing. I asked you if you felt pressured. I asked you if your attorney had explained your other options. You said you were of sound mind and completely understood your options and you told me you were guilty. Am I to understand that you were *confused* the last time in court?"

"I wasn't confused, your honor. I was misinformed."

"Is there new evidence in this case that I am unaware of?"

"No your honor," answered my attorney.

"Mr. Cooper, were you or are you now on any medications or under the influence of any drugs that may affect your judgment?"

"No, your honor," I said.

"Then your motion to withdraw your plea is denied. I hereby find your guilty of the crimes you are charged. Any more motions before I proceed with sentencing?"

My motion was denied. The system, I knew at this point, was completely screwed up. I was empty inside and had lost my faith in humankind altogether. How could he sleep tonight knowing that he had sentenced a man to prison time who claims he is innocent? Sure, he may not know for sure that I'm not guilty, but that's why the justice system is in place to have a jury trial. With that one statement, 'motion to withdraw your plea is denied,' I had no recourse action. My attorney asked for a continuance to check into the crime dates associated with this crime as we had talked about so he could explore options for probation. I did not have my hopes up.

My family and friends were naturally upset. My mom, I thought, might murder my attorney. Thankfully, she didn't. I was on probation for a previous felony and had five years pending in that case. If I was convicted in this case, as I just had been, I would have to tack on those five years to my sentence in this case. My plea deal was for five years in this case as well. Ten years in prison was my sure fate. Shortly after this hearing, I got the very disturbing news that Gage had received probation on his 11 year sentence. I was at the lowest of low points, heading to prison for a crime that was committed by a man who got probation. I felt true hate for the first time in my life. Hate for my situation. Hate for the system. And hate for Gage Tate.

My jail life had not started great but finally had calmed down. Prison, I thought, would not be as easy. People in prison had longer sentences, less patience and less to lose. That deadly cocktail leads to no fear and the murdering of guys like me. As hopeless as it sounded, the feds seemed to be my best bet to this point. Perhaps before I had to be drug off to prison, they could help get me home.

Chapter 11

The F.B.I. and Gage Tate, Evil.

"I'm going to go to prison!" I yelled as I entered the room where Agent Greene and I always met.

"That often happens after a conviction of a crime," he said smugly.

"Don't you take me for granted! What can you do about this?"

"Nothing, I told you at the beginning we can't do anything. The faster we move the better. Until we are done, you are here or wherever they send you."

"Well I can stop it whenever I want. So let me be clear with you for a change, my family is suffering. I'm suffering. I am not your puppet. I am a person who has been treated incredibly unfairly. My mother could go to the press and have a front page story in the Herald Leader by tomorrow morning and your case would be blown up. So don't take me for granted! I am helping you, so you need to help me!"

"If you tell anyone to do that, your mom, or anyone and we see a story like that on the front page, you will regret it. You won't ever see your mom again. I can see to it that you both go away, and apart, forever."

"Unless you are bluffing," I said sarcastically.

Agent Greene took his gun out of his holster and laid it on the table in front of him. He stood from his chair and leaned over the gun to come face to face with me. He was close enough I could feel the warmth of his breath when he spoke.

He said, "Do what you think you need to do, *if* you think I'm bluffing."

"Are you threatening me?"

"Yes, you will definitely go far, far away from your family and everything else you know if you fuck me over."

"So why did you set the gun on the table? You going to kill me if I say something?"

With a shrug he said, "Don't say something."

"You are threatening me."

"I can't say I see it that way. And after all you have been through to this point; you should know it isn't what really happened that matters. It only matters what the cop says happened. And *I* didn't see it that way."

"You are just as bad as the local police."

"Except I have much more power. And when I'm done, I can take care of you. Hailey doesn't care about screwing you. I'm not screwing you. The Feds aren't screwing you. We have a deal, remember?"

"Awfully one-sided deal to this point," I said.

"Yes it has been. You have endured a lot. I get that. All you have is a cheeseburger and that's just a freebee. But in the end, working with me is better than fighting with me. Please trust me when I say that."

"I don't trust you. But I don't have any choice but to make this work."

"Another true way to look at it. Listen, we are close to arresting Gage. We are wrapping up a few loose ends. I need to ask you some questions. You think you can do that today?"

"I guess," I said with a shrug.

"Where did Gage hang out the most?"

"Uh... well he liked the Rack Club; it's a pool hall near where we live. I don't know really about hang out places. Gage and I did a lot more driving around than hanging around at any place. He couldn't get into most bars because he's underage. So we didn't have many places to go. He liked the Rack Club because they would serve him alcohol underage."

"What about common places to get gas or eat or whatever you did do in between driving?"

"Well there are only a few 24 hour places that we ever went. We liked Perkins the best. There was a server there, a lady, she was getting older and needed a friend. She was nice and we enjoyed chatting with her. And we tipped her good so maybe that's why she's so nice too."

Agent Greene quickly shuffled some papers and said, "Perkins, is that on Richmond Road by a Home Depot?"

"Yup, sure is," I said.

"How often did you go there?"

"I dunno, often. Mostly late at night after we had been out and needed some food. It was usually our last stop before heading home."

He pulled out a photo and slid it to me. "Do you recognize this man?"

"No," I said. "He doesn't look familiar at all."

"Do you recognize the setting? Can you tell me where he's at?"

"Yes, he is at Perkins. I recognize the game machine where you try to get the stuffed animal out here and look, their doorway is very distinctive."

"We have believed for a while that Tate was meeting contacts here. You think that's possible?"

"I dunno; he never met anyone there when I was there."

"Well still, this is a big help. We haven't found a bit of evidence that Tate was ever at this Perkins. What was that waitress's name that you two like?"

"Her name is Anna."

"You think she will remember you two?"

"Oh yea, for sure. We were good tippers."

"I'll be back tomorrow. I'm going to go talk to this girl tonight. This could be a break, kid. Get some rest and I'll be back tomorrow."

Get some rest. Yea, I didn't rest any. Resting was a rare thing in jail. You could sleep for a few hours, but to really rest is an unreasonable expectation. That meeting was truly a rollercoaster for me. I went in so angry and left feeling like I had maybe really helped their case. If I was valuable to them, they'd want to help me faster for sure. Or at least I had hoped that. As good as I felt though, I couldn't help but wonder if he played me there.

That night, I didn't sleep well. I was scared to go to prison and with the images Agent Greene had showed me racing through my head every time I closed my eyes, sleeping seemed hopeless. I stayed up late that night and read the book of Job in the Bible. This was the first time I felt a connection to a story in the Bible. Not that I had endured anything compared to Job, but my faith in God was more important than ever at this point. That story was inspirational enough to keep my faith strong. If Job could keep his faith facing all the horrendousness he faced, then surely I too could do this.

The next day when I entered our room, Agent Greene had a smile on his face.

"I got him," he said.

"Gage?" I asked.

"Yes. I arrested him this morning on Federal charges. He is in the jail right now. I just brought him in myself just before I came here to meet with you. He is being charged with voyeurism, promoting the sale of material depicting a sexual performance by a minor, and trafficking in minors under the age of 16. He is going to be given a $100,000 full cash bond."

"That's great! What happens now?"

"Well we think he may post bond. Or his associates may post his bond. If they do, we are hoping to get a lead on some of his connections. We'd like to know where the money came from and who his connections to the ring are, that's the most important. If he doesn't post bond, he isn't going home for a long time."

"Is it going to be all over the news again? And am I going to be on there again?"

"No. No media is going to know about this. He was arrested under seal, which means the warrant was not public record. But we aren't finished here. I need to get all those guys in the ring. And Tate's charges are expected to grow. We wanted to see if he can post bond first. Then we can arrest him later and retract the bond or increase it. The entire bond from his case will go to the crimes against children fund and spread among his victims so the more the merrier."

"That sounds good. So I guess you have some paperwork to do today?"

"No, unfortunately, I have something else we need to go over today."

"What is it?" I asked as his face grew more serious.

Agent Greene spoke softly and said, "I want you to watch a video, Brayden. It is not going to be easy to watch, but I really need you to pay close attention to detail. This video has a camera man that we are trying to identify, but we only have a very tiny, very short look at him. Also, anything else that you might recognize would be helpful. And Brayden, this girl is missing. We are trying to find her and we can't get a lead. This is the only lead we've had in two years. I'm not going to sugar coat this, it is ugly. It will be tough, but do you think you can handle it?"

I didn't immediately respond. I had seen many things to this point that I thought were horrible. I saw things that no person should ever have to see. But this was the first time Agent Greene had made such a big deal about how bad something was. For people that see this everyday as part of their jobs to think it is especially bad, I didn't know if I could do this. I was shaking and my stomach hurt from anxiety.

"Her name is Lindsey. She was 12 at the time of this video. She'll be 14 this year. Her parents need this. Please, just try. For her, for her parents, please." Her name is not really Lindsey, but if there were ever a name to change to protect the innocent, it is here.

"My family," I began, "also has lost someone. They have lost me. And they too are grieving. I might not be 12, but this is not easy on them either. I know you guys do this every day, but I don't. And I don't know how you do it. How much more of this must I do with no real quality *anything* from me? I don't know anything except I want to go home." I began to cry. I was in so much pain on the inside; I couldn't imagine what it felt like to not hurt. No one could call this their worst nightmare because no one could think up such ungodly treachery as this.

"Brayden, you have provided us with quality information already. I may not be able to go into detail about it, but believe me; if you weren't helping I wouldn't keep coming back. That waitress at Perkins, I talked to her and she gave us enough information to make a case on Tate. That's how I arrested him today. That info came from you! Now I can't tell Lindsey's family that you are sad so I can't talk to you about our best lead. And that's not what you want."

"No, I don't. I wish nothing ever happened to the poor girl... I wish nothing happened to me." I was on the edge of losing control. I could not stop crying.

"I know you do, Brayden," he said. After a pause he continued, "I'm not trying to downplay how hard this is. I understand how you feel." He did *not* understand how *I* felt.

"Let's just get it over with, please," I said, fighting the tears.

As the play button was pressed in, you could see the camera jerking around. Someone was trying to get it in the correct position. After the camera settled, you could hear some movement, but no one spoke. As I looked at the setting, I knew immediately that this was Gage's room. His sofa bed in his room was unfolded.

"The sheets," I said, "They are black, I've never seen those before, but this is definitely Gage's room." This, I'm sure, they knew already.

The sofa bed had standalone bed posts that didn't go with it. They were tightly wedged in between the night table and the bed on the right and the wall and the bed on the left side. The camera was focused on the center of the bed where a girl, Lindsey, was tied to the bed posts. The top of her right hand was wrapped around the bed post on the left side that faced me and what appeared to be another sheet was tightly binding the palm of her hand to the post. The sheet fit in her palm, while the back of her hand was tightly pressed against the post.

The pole at the top of the bed post had a large, thin, blue towel tied to it. The other end bound her left hand. She was wearing a pair of blue denim shorts and a Sponge Bob® t-shirt. Her shoes had already been removed but she was still wearing white socks with little hearts on them. Her feet were not bound or tied up, but she didn't squirm or move much during the beginning of the video.

After a few seconds, the camera man zoomed the lens in to get a close up of her face. She had a ball gag that had been shoved in her mouth. It was clearly too big for her mouth and looked uncomfortable. Although she wasn't making any sound, as the camera got in close, you could see the tears streaming down her face. She was scared to death of these evil men. I could feel her fear in the pit of my stomach. I put my hand in the air briefly and turned to the trash can beside me. I vomited in the can and began crying. The video paused and the jail guard opened the door to our room.

"Is he ok? Does he need to go to medical?" asked the guard.

"Get out of here," Agent Greene snapped.

When I was finished vomiting, Agent Greene picked up the can and set it outside the room. He grabbed the can from his side of the room and set it next to me on the table.

"Just in case," he said.

As I began to calm down, he once again pressed play on the remote. I heard a voice on the tape ask "are you ready" and I knew it was Gage. I was horrified at how cavalier my once best friend had just asked the camera man if he was ready for him to rape a precious child. His tone suggested he was ready to run to the grocery, not do something so unbelievably evil.

As he went over to the bedside and sat down next to Lindsey, he grabbed a tissue off the nightstand. He wiped tears from her face.

"I'm not going to hurt you, ok?" he said to her. But he was going to hurt her and she knew it. Gage proceeded to kiss her on the forehead, in what appeared to be a consoling manner. You could almost believe he cared for her if you didn't know what was about to happen. He stood up and took off his shirt and his pants, leaving him in his boxers. He unbuttoned her blue jean shorts and removed them. He opened the drawer in the nightstand and pulled out a pair of scissors. He cut her shirt off of her, right up the middle in the front. He then cut down her sleeves and pulled the rags from under her.

After he finished removing all of her clothes, he removed his boxers. He raped and sodomized this innocent child. She cried and fought for a while, and then she gave up. It was like she knew not only could she not get away, but she wasn't going to leave that house alive. She fell limp to the point that Gage checked her twice to see if she was unconscious. He slapped her in the face to see if she cried; this was his cruel method.

At one point in the middle, the camera turned slightly to get a different view and you could catch a glimpse of the camera man's face. The FBI had been able to get poor quality still shots printed out in picture form to look at. I did not recognize this man, to the disappointment of the feds.

After Gage was finished brutalizing this child, he got dressed. About the time he buttoned his pants, Gage's stepfather knocked on the door and called for him. Gage told him to wait a second and he put his hand on top of the camera and pushed it down onto the chair beside the camera man. He told the camera man to hide in the corner, which was cut out so it would be impossible to see anyone there from the door. He grabbed a bed spread and he threw it over Lindsey. He opened the door, which you could clearly see from where the camera was now sitting. When the door opened, you could see his stepfather standing in the kitchen and he looked up, right at Gage.

The way the house is laid out, his stepfather had a clear line of sight into the bedroom as well as anyone in the bedroom had a clear line of sight to the kitchen. After a few seconds, Gage returned to his room and closed the door. The camera man came back to his post and picked up the camera. It was pointed back at Lindsey. What blew me away was that you could see her arms up on the posts outside the bedspread. Had Gage's stepfather looked in that room, he could have seen this too. This raised many questions with the FBI about whether his stepfather knew what was going on in the house.

After a few seconds, I asked Agent Greene, "Why is the camera still recording?"

"You'll see. We aren't sure why they recorded this part, but that's something we are highly interested in."

Gage finally removed the bedspread from Lindsey and refolded it. Again, Gage asked the camera guy if he is ready. My first thought was that Gage was going to start over again. But the video was about to turn even more bizarre. The camera man set down the camera on something where the camera could still see Lindsey. The camera man approached Lindsey, being careful to keep his face out of the camera. Though his face was not shown, this was more of the camera man than we had seen to this point. He seemed as tall as Gage, but appeared older and had a medium sized potbelly. He wore jeans and a very long black t-shirt.

Gage left the view of the camera and may have left the room. You could hear a noise in the background that could have been the door opening and closing, but whether he left could be debated. The camera man began to untie Lindsey and then stopped to get something from his pocket. He pulled out a small box and removed something small. The video freeze made it look like a clear breath strip. He instructed Lindsey to open her mouth and stick out her tongue. When she did, he placed it on her tongue and closed her mouth for her. He finished untying her and when her left arm was untied, she fell limp. She appeared to be unconscious.

He sat her up and folded her legs under her as if she were sitting on her knees. He folded her arms in and bent her body over so she was almost in a ball. He set a large duffle bag on the bed next to her and opened it. He picked her up just as he had positioned her and set her in the duffle bag. He zipped it up and set it on the floor.

He then got a plastic bag and gathered up all her clothes, the linen used to tie her up and the sheets and placed them in the bag. He carried both the duffle bag and the plastic bag over to the camera and stopped the recording. It was as if this was planned exactly how it went. Everyone knew their role and followed a script. The FBI said it was calculated and well thought out. I said it was sickening and horrible.

"What are your thoughts, Brayden?" asked Agent Greene.

"Really?" I asked. He nodded. "Wow, well he's sick. They are both sick, whoever the other guy is. It was in Gage's room, I had never seen the sheets before. I don't know; nothing else really stuck out to me."

"You have never seen Lindsey before?"

"No, never."

"Ok. What do you think about the possibility that Gage may have known this girl?"

"I don't know... do you think he did know her?"

"We don't know. Her family is from Nashville, so it seems unlikely. Has Gage ever been to Nashville?"

"I don't know, he never mentioned it."

"Well we think this was a murder. We don't think they had any intention to do anything else but murdering Lindsey. Too many things seem so careless for such a well scripted plan. They didn't cover their faces, they almost got caught by the stepdad, they spoke to her and all this was filmed at Gage's house. This girl would have a great chance of identifying them if she got away. So, I don't think she got away and I don't think they ever planned for her to get away. Have you ever seen that duffle bag before?"

"No," I said, "I don't think it belonged to Gage."

"Whatever they stuck in her mouth appeared to knock her out. The curious thing is, they filmed that part. We think they were required to show this video to the 'boss man' for proof they acted correctly. What we do know is there was a digital copy of this made, because we never found the tape itself, we found it on Gage's computer. This is the video that Gage's attorney continues to say is proof that he was "forced into this and had no choice," but we don't buy it."

"I don't either," I said softly. "He looked so calm, so... comfortable. How can someone be so cruel?"

"You don't think Gage and his stepfather had a good relationship, right?"

"No, they didn't much get along."

"You think that could be a front?"

"I don't know. I guess anything is possible, but if it was, they were both awfully convincing."

"Did anything about the camera man's body look familiar to you?"

"No."

"Anything else you can think of that might help here?"

"The look Gage had on his face. When he used to push hair out of the eyes of a girlfriend he had, I remember the same look. He wasn't scared is all I'm saying. I've seen him scared and this wasn't it. This was crazy."

"Interesting you should say that. Our experts said the same thing. Anything else?"

And, as usual, I was continually answering no to most of their questions. I had no idea what to think about anything and I certainly didn't know any of these people except for Gage. My stomach ached and I vomited several times a week. I couldn't eat properly without getting sick and I couldn't sleep at all. I had nightmares about the things I saw in this little room. I knew it was literally killing me from the inside. I didn't know how to endure the images I continued to replay in my head over and over again. I couldn't even process it all at the time. Some of it I blacked out almost immediately, only to begin to remember the gory details months later. This was so difficult; I had this strong desire to give up, to just quit. But in the back of my mind, I could always settle with the idea that perhaps I could make a difference to just one child. All of those children, every one of them had it so much worse than I did.

The next morning, Gage posted bond in the form of $100,000 cash. I was astonished. I knew he couldn't have that kind of money. I was told that Agent Greene had interviewed the guy who bonded Gage out. Apparently he was no one that was connected to anything. He was a random guy who was paid $10,000 to walk into the courthouse, pay his bond and leave. In the federal system, bond is rare and when bond is granted, whoever posts the bond must offer a personal guarantee that the fugitive will return. That detail noted; it is illegal to bond out a complete stranger. The state of Kentucky doesn't operate like that. You can bond out anyone you want and anytime you want. This random guy just got paid to get arrested, likely the reason he was paid.

Again I was sitting in a jail cell while Gage Tate roamed the streets. Life seemed so incredibly unfair to me at this point. When Agent Greene returned to me, he offered up some information that I had yet to hear.

"How did he post that kind of bond or who posted it for him?" I asked.

"The boss posted the bond. You need to realize, we are dealing with some dangerous and powerful people. Do you know what the number one business in the United States is?"

"No," I said, "But I would guess maybe food of some sort since we need that to live."

"Drugs," he said. "Drugs are the number one source of revenue in the U.S. And I'm not referring to OTC's or any prescription drugs. I'm talking narcotics that are being used illegally, cocaine, meth, that sort of drugs. You know what the number two business in the U.S. is?"

"No," I said again. This time I didn't offer a suggestion.

"Child trafficking. The sale of children for the purpose of sex and imprisonment in this country is second. It is a multi-billion dollar industry here. We generate more revenue from the child trafficking business than countries where it is legal. You see, here it is much more a luxury for pedophiles. In other countries, it is no harder to get than a pack of cigarettes."

"That is unbelievable."

"Gage has earned over $2 million thus far making videos and aiding in the trafficking process. He is a small player by comparison to the industry. But around here, he's a big player. And no, he didn't post his own bond because we seized his money and all assets. But the boss paid for his bond by using the decoy."

"It seems crazy that we were so close I didn't have a clue."

"He needed a good cover. And he was good at saving face in that cover. I know this can't be easy on you. I get that. But look at me, if only for a second. I have over 30 cases open in front of me that Tate was involved in. All 30 cases are classified in two categories; homicide or missing persons. None of them have been solved and we are closer than ever. The oldest victim is 16, the youngest is 5.

We are currently digging through this case trying to determine the extent of Tate's role. See, all of these cases that I have discovered we have either a video or picture of the victim in Tate's room at his home or he is in a picture with them at an unknown location. We believe he may have murdered some of these children or at very least handed them off to a hit man. If he didn't kill these children, he knew they were being killed. We just need anything that can help us solve this case."

"I wish I could be of more help, I just..."

Agent Greene interrupted, "You are being helpful. The

association with Perkins was enough to get a warrant with the other evidence we had. We have arrested two people from that alone. Please don't think you aren't helping. We just need you to hold it together."

"I'm sorry if this sounds selfish, but when will all this be over?"

"I wish I could tell you. But I can't. Listen, I have to talk to you about something. I don't want you to worry about it, but we have received a couple of death threats towards you at the F.B.I. office here in Lexington. We are sure Tate is involved, but he didn't make the calls himself."

"What kind of threats? My mom lives alone. I swear to God if they try something, I will kill them."

"The threats were directed at you. We have people watching your family. You don't need to worry about that. They probably aren't legit; I just want to make sure you know the whole story here."

"So what is the plan to get Gage off the street?"

"I'm not at liberty to discuss that. Just trust I will."

"That doesn't sound like the whole story."

"Some things I can't tell you. He has an arraignment tomorrow morning. I will be there. I'll let you know how it goes." And I wait, again.

Chapter 12

Case Closed and the Phone Call.

"Unfortunately, the dates don't match up right. There was nothing I could do about trying to get you qualified for probation. I'm sorry this went down like this," my attorney said.

"Me too. He's going to send me to prison for sure?"

"Yes. I think he will."

As I waited to be called into the courtroom, I remember feeling alone again. No one was here because I told them to stay home. I sat in corner of the holding cell and I began to cry. I was about to be sentenced to five years in prison for a crime I didn't commit. Judge Cantrell looked at me like I was a monster, as did everyone in the gallery. The news painted me out to be Gage Tate's sidekick, an equal accomplice, a dirty, perverted freak. I reverted to my empty feeling of confusion. I second guessed everything I had done to this point. Surely, I thought, I must have done something wrong or something to deserve this.

I wasn't always the best person. I didn't always tell the truth and sometimes manipulated people to get what I want. I was selfish and rude, labeled ruthless and an ass hole by some. I didn't pray often and certainly didn't give my relationship with God the time or attention it so much needed. In a way, this must be karma. I had heard about karma and that it was a bitch. What goes around comes around. But I remember thinking I would rather it had come back to me in small bits as I had dished it out instead of one big kick in the nuts. I had this overwhelming feeling that while God condemned those who lied and abused power to get me in this situation, He didn't feel that sorry for me. From that minute forward, I promised to be a better example for God and for everyone.

"Cooper, your turn," the guard said.

I walked slowly into the courtroom, heavily shackled. As I looked around, the courtroom was full as usual. My attorney stood at the podium closest to me. We made eye contact and his head fell. He knew this was his dropped ball. It was also my inexperience in the system. I should have never pled guilty to a crime I didn't commit. If I had only taken a day longer to think about it, perhaps I wouldn't be here right now. Nevertheless, I am here.

"Is there any reason I should not continue with sentencing counselors?" asked Judge Cantrell.

"No, your honor," my attorney answered.

"Mr. Cooper, I have found you guilty of one felony count and five misdemeanor counts. I understand you have a deal with prosecutors in this case. With a persistent felony offender enhancement, they have recommended a five year prison term and you have accepted this offer. Is that correct?"

After a short pause and a glare at my attorney, I said, "Yes."

"Mr. Cooper, this case disturbs me. You are a young guy and yet so twisted. The crimes which I have convicted you of in this courtroom are reprehensible. To think that someone could find a child sexually attractive is not only disturbing, it is worth much more time than five years. I am disappointed in the prosecution here for offering such a low sentence. Do you have anything to say before I sentence you?"

With careful thought, I said, "Nothing I've said to this point, nor anything I should say in the future has made a difference. I have nothing to say to you."

"Your mother must be proud," he snapped sarcastically. And he was right about that at least. "I only wish a stiffer penalty would be handed down today. I refuse to probate this crime. This is not only too serious in nature, but too you were on felony probation. Mr. Cooper, I hereby sentence you to a term of five years' incarceration at a facility to be determined by the Kentucky Department of Corrections. This term shall be run consecutively with any other time that you should be given to serve. I certainly hope you can get some help, Mr. Cooper. Good luck."

Good luck? I was not a fan of this man. While he didn't know the whole story, something told me he wouldn't have been patient enough to listen if he was told. I remember thinking that afternoon that I had originally been threatened with a forty year prison sentence. The case against me could have never given me forty years. They didn't have the evidence against me and what they did have was based on lies and fabrication. Only in a case like this, where charges could bring forty years, do you get a deal for one year enhanced to five by a PFO. Judge Cantrell liked being on TV, and he enjoyed showing off his sarcasm.

And as broken as this system is, so openly broken and in my face, I was still amazed I had agreed to work in it to help investigators. This hearing was also only part one of two that I had to face a judge and quietly bow to accept prison time. My probation judge would still get to add her time onto the time I just received. I was destined for two five year sentences run together for one ten year sentence.

These numbers seemed so big to me. Prison was this word in which the meaning had been almost sensitized inside me. I didn't really know what it meant to go to prison. After all, I had never been before. Some of the friendly jail inmates had told me of murders, shankings and beat downs for guys with charges like mine. I was told I'd be killed within a year, which wasn't a pleasant thought since it so appeared to me I was facing ten years. I can't imagine being diagnosed with an incurable disease and having doctors tell you that you have a year to live. The fear that must overwhelm you, however, must be similar to that of being told

I have a year to live in prison, facing a ten year sentence. Like a terminal patient, I was frantically considering ways to live beyond that year and into the remainder of my sentence until I could get out. And, much like a terminally ill patient, I didn't know what to expect which made planning my defense quite difficult.

In two weeks, I would have to go before Judge Angela Gailey to be sentenced on my probation violation. Shortly after that I knew I would be transferred to a prison. Agent Greene returned, as he was supposed to, three days after my sentencing.

"So I heard that you got five years," Agent Greene said softly.

"Yea, well I knew that. I took that stupid deal."

"I also heard you kind of gave it to the judge. Nothing you say matters so you have nothing to say to him, huh?"

"What was I supposed to say?"

"No, that was fine. I didn't mean it was bad. Just want you to know that what you say to me matters. The bureau cares what you say too. I know it wouldn't have mattered with that judge but it was still funny to hear you give it to him."

"You were there?"

"Yes, in the back."

"Hmm, well like I said, what I have said through this whole thing hasn't mattered. And I really don't want to hear how you or the bureau cares about me. You care what I have to say only because it may pertain to your case. You don't care about me or my family or I wouldn't be here."

"I do care. I just don't have a lot of options. I do what I'm told here. I didn't choose this."

"I'm sure you didn't come here just to give me pep talk. Can we get this over with so I can go lay back down?"

After what they knew about the night I met Gage in the park after he made bond, the FBI thought I may be able to get a confession out of Gage. After all, he had admitted some involvement to me already. From jail, there wasn't much chance I would get to see Gage in person, nor if I could would he agree to talk to me. A phone call, however, may be just the answer. All phone calls made from the in house jail phones are recorded. You can put money on your commissary account and make calls to any number you wanted. If you didn't have money on your account, calls could only be made collect and to a land line telephone. I did not have money on my account because I owed the jail for booking fees that had not been paid.

"I just want you to see what you could find out, see what he would say to you," said Agent Greene.

"What makes you think he would talk to me? Don't you think he will be suspicious?"

"Probably. Tell him you had to talk to him. You had to hear from him what was going on. Tell him you are worried about him."

Angrily I said, "I'm not worried about him! He could drop dead and not hurt my feelings. I don't know if I can be convincing. I am not comfortable with this."

"You're not comfortable? Right, and well I can see that. I can see why you wouldn't be comfortable. But what you must understand is this situation is not comfortable for anyone. Not for you, not for the FBI, not for Gage... Certainly not for the children who have been hurt. The children who have been brutalized, raped and murdered. Would you want to tell their parents how we couldn't convict the man who did this to their baby because you were uncomfortable? I don't want to have to do that."

"This is so hard," I said. I had to pause, fighting back the tears. "Why do I have to be in this position? Why does it *have* to be this way?"

"The world is not fair, Brayden. You have to be strong here. This is not about what you are getting out of it. This is just a phone call. Those poor children, they would have given anything to have to make a phone call. But we both know what they had to endure. This is nothing." He was so matter of fact about it. To me, this was very much something.

"Just shut up, please," I said, "I'll do it, ok? Just tell me what I need to say."

"I can't tell you exactly what to say. You know Gage better than we do. We have an account and we will give you the numbers to use the phone. All you have to do is get Gage to tell you he was involved. Even if you say something like 'why did you do this?' and he can say he's sorry for dragging you in it. That would be something. More details, better for court, that's the rule."

When you make phone calls collect from the jail, the recording tells you where the call originated from, who it is from and that the call will be recorded. When you make a call from your account, the person you are calling doesn't get such a message. It is not clear where you are calling from or that the call is recorded. But it is. Every call is recorded. And that's why, no matter what was said or what I could remember about the call, it would be fine because there is a recording.

I struggled for days trying to decide what I could say and how I would do it. I waited long enough, in fact, that Agent Greene came back and asked if it was done yet. They were in a hurry. They wanted it done now. I didn't ever want to do it. What do you say to your once best friend who framed you and turned out to be a lunatic?

After building up the courage, I entered the numbers and dialed Gage's cell phone number. My hand was shaking so hard, I could barely keep the phone up to my ear. I remember the phone rang precisely two times.

"Hello?" he answered.

"Gage?"

After a pause, I repeated, "Gage? Are you there?"

"Why are you calling me?" he said.

"I had to, Gage. This is so hard. So many things I don't understand."

"I shouldn't be talking to you, Brayden," he said.

"You're right, but I only have ten minutes, please don't hang up."

"What... what do you want?"

"How are you?"

"Fucking bullshit, Brayden! What do you want!?"

"Yeah, ok. Yeah I want to know why, Gage? I want to know how you could do the things they say you did? Did you kill those poor kids?"

"The police are liars, Brayden. Have you not learned that?"

"You are a liar too, Gage. I have to know if you did those things. You told me in the park that you were involved, just not like they say. I mean, it seems to me it is way worse."

"If what they say about me is true, aren't you scared to talk to me? Aren't you scared of what might happen?"

"Do I have a reason to be, Gage?"

"I can't talk to you about this, but I will tell you one thing. I'm not going to prison for this. I have many friends. Call it the mile high club for people like me. I have money and I have power. I think it is best if you don't call back."

"So it is true. You drug me into some kind of sick game. Why, Gage, why would you do that?"

"I had to do whatever it took. You were like an innocent bystander I guess. At least you have your life."

"You son of a bitch. I can't believe you are even saying that!"

"Well there is a lot you wouldn't believe about me, ha ha! These things would happen anyway. Sad, yes. But I might as well make some money. You don't have to get it, Brayden."

"You are a heartless bastard. I don't know how you can live with yourself, how you can sleep at night." I was holding the phone so tight I could hear the plastic giving way.

"Well here, it is quiet. Eat a good meal, relax, and fall right to sleep, Brayden. What did you expect out of this call?"

"Nothing, Gage. I expected nothing and got so much more. You remember being at the jail, right? Using those shitty pay phones on the wall? You know the ones that record every conversation?

Oh yea, this one too. You will burn in hell for what you've done, Gage! But before you do, I will do everything I can to help make sure you rot in prison."

"Fuck you, Brayden, you have nothing. Goodbye."

He hung up the phone, but he was wrong. I did have something. He all but admitted his direct involvement in everything. He might as well have given a full confession. This was one of only a very few times I felt as though I may have made a real difference. While the thanklessness of the position I was in wasn't the easiest to deal with, worthlessness was much worse. If I could at least do some good, then I could feel like I was helping some child somewhere out there. Otherwise I was just another thankless federal informant.

Agent Greene wasn't as excited as I was. Apparently it wasn't as good as a full confession, but he was happy. I got enough that we could certainly use it in court.

"It may hurt that you taunted him at the end. You know, his attorney will argue entrapment." I wondered if I could do anything without facing criticism.

"So, it doesn't change what he said. Who can ignore that?"

"Brayden, if it is ruled out during a suppression hearing, no jury will ever see it. It will never make it to evidence."

"Did I do something wrong? I don't know how to do this stuff; I did what you told me. I'm not some trained agent, I'm just a guy in a really shit ass situation."

"You did ok, no sense in worrying about it now," he said.

But I did worry about it. I worried about everything regarding this case. I didn't know what was going on most of the time. I always felt I was disadvantaged and I was screwing up everything I did. I sort of felt like I was the kicker trying to play quarterback in the Super Bowl after injuries left me the only option. I truly felt like I was playing a game I barely understood, and I wasn't very good at it. I so incredibly wanted to awaken from this nightmare.

Chapter 13

The Interruption and Gage's 3rd arrest.

Those two weeks seemed to pass so quickly. I think time was moving faster during this period because I didn't want to go to prison. I wasn't a fan of the jail, but I felt reasonably safe there. On the bus ride over, some of the guys were taunting me because they recognized me from newscast two weeks prior. There wasn't much that could be done on the so called 'chain gang' because everyone was chained together and access was limited. But just to be safe, I was placed in the special cage in the back of the bus for inmates in protective custody.

When you are taken into the holding area, the space is split up into two sides and there are two visiting windows on each side. Those windows are where you are supposed to see your attorney. Inmates look in the windows to see if they can see their attorney through the window and jump in to get final details squared away before they get in front of the judge. As always, I was looking for Robert Frumkin.

"Brayden Cooper?!" an inmate yelled out.

"Yea?"

"Your lawyer is here looking for you."

It wasn't Robert Frumkin. It was Kimberly Huffman, the attorney I had in the first case two years ago. I can't tell you how pleased this made me. Kimberly Huffman was the best attorney I could have asked for.

As I approached the window, she smiled and said, "Hi, Brayden. How are you holding up?"

"I've been better," I said.

"What is going on here, Brayden? This just so doesn't sound like you."

"It's not me! I didn't do this, I swear. I was pressured into taking a plea deal. My attorney was Robert Frumkin and he was horrible. Is there anything I can do? He totally pressured me into my plea and I didn't do it."

"After the sentencing, there isn't much to be done about that. But I will fight for you in here. I just knew something had to be wrong. This just doesn't fit you."

With a tear in my eye, I said, "Thank you. You don't know how much that means to me. No one has believed in me from the start."

"We'll do our best in there. I'll go talk to Robert before we go in too. I'll see you in a few."

I was thrilled. Someone not only believed in me but was willing to fight for me. And not only that, but she was a great attorney. If anyone had any fight in them it was her. As it was my turn to enter, I saw her standing at the podium much like my first attorney would, but she was confident. She smiled at me and then turned her serious face on.

"Mr. Cooper," Judge Gailey began, "This is not what I expected to see. You don't strike me as the type to be involved in this. What do you have to say?"

"Your honor," Kimberly began, "My client was forced into a plea deal in this case. He is inexperienced in this system and doesn't believe he got a fair shake. We would ask for leniency from you here, your honor."

"Mr. Cooper," Judge Gailey began, "What happened in this case that makes you feel that you were pressured into taking a deal?"

"My attorney didn't explain everything properly to me. He didn't try to find a way to fight this at trial, he just said a deal was the only way."

"And why were you so against taking a deal?"

"It wasn't the right thing for me to do. I tried to withdraw it, but the judge wouldn't let me."

"Why did you want to withdraw your plea?"

"I wanted to go to trial, your honor," I said with some confusion in my voice.

"If you are trying to say something, Mr. Cooper, I suggest you say it."

I leaned in to Kimberly's ear and said, "There is a gag order, I can't say I'm not guilty." I saw her concerned look.

"Mr. Cooper, what are you trying to tell me!?" Judge Gailey snapped.

"I didn't do it, ma'am! I'm not guilty," I said.

"Your honor!" a familiar voice yelled from the back of the courtroom.

"Sir, you had best have a warrant to be barging in my courtroom!"

"I am Special Agent Zach Greene, F.B.I., your honor. I do have a warrant. May I speak with you in chambers please?"

He approached the bench and handed over a piece of paper to the judge. She agreed to meet in chambers and we were told to hold for five minutes. Kimberly grabbed my arm and pulled me down to the bench directly behind us.

"Is there something you want to tell me? This would be the time."

"I don't know what he's doing. I wasn't allowed to say

anything. There is a gag order in the federal case. But he knows I'm innocent."

"You don't know what he's telling her?"

"Not for sure, just what I told you."

"Ok," she said, "Don't worry, we will sort this out."

As Judge Gailey reentered the courtroom, she slammed the door behind her and quickly took a seat. She seemed flustered and upset. That didn't seem to be a good thing coming from a judge who was about to determine my fate. I was pretty sure I wanted her in a good mood.

She said, "Mr. Cooper, you have been convicted of a felony while on felony probation. The law ties my hands a bit. There is no sense in leaving you on probation being that you will be in prison. I am hereby ordering your probation to be revoked and I am sentencing you to the five years in prison, as per your probation conditions. That, Mr. Cooper, I cannot change. But what I can do, and what I will do, is I will run that five years *concurrent* with your current sentence."

"Objection!" screamed the prosecutor. "Your honor, you can't run that time concurrent. Judge Cantrell ordered his time to be run consecutively to other time the defendant may be sentenced to."

"I don't care what Judge Cantrell ordered. He doesn't run my courtroom, nor does he dictate how I sentence anyone," she said sarcastically.

"The statute says this is prohibited, your honor," said the prosecutor.

"I don't interpret it that way. I read it as Judge Cantrell could not have ordered *his* time to be run concurrent with my time. And I understand it to read that his time must run consecutive to any *future* time he may receive. My time came first and I can do this."

"Your honor..."

Judge Gailey interrupted and said, "I suggest you sit down,

counselor. If you don't like my ruling, you can appeal. In the meantime, shut up."

"We will appeal, your honor," said the prosecutor.

"Not another word. Mr. Cooper, this is all I could do for you. Have a good day and don't come back to my courtroom."

"I promise, your honor," I said. "Thank you."

Wow! A victory, or at least what felt like a victory at the time. My sure fated ten year sentence had just been cut in half. I would only be serving a five year sentence. As I left the courtroom, I could hear mumbling and unrest in the gallery. This had been something most unprecedented. In fact, I had researched this possibility quite thoroughly. It turns out, according the statute, the prosecutor is correct. When you are on probation or parole for a felony charge and you are convicted of another felony, and that felony crime occurred during your period of probation or parole, those two sentences cannot be run concurrent. Apparently, and thankfully for me, Judge Gailey didn't care what the statute said.

I was so excited to call my mom and tell her what happened. I was dying to know what Agent Greene had said to Judge Gailey. And that would be the first thing I asked him the next time I saw him. My mom, as expected, was very happy. We had not only prepared for, but completely expected me to get a ten year sentence. The statutes were clear, my attorney had told me so and nothing had gone my way to this point.

As exhilarating as this was, it too was a sad moment for me. I could count on one hand the number of people who stood behind me in support. Out of the dozens of people I called friends, even some of them whom I considered good friends; they had less faith in me than an attorney and judge who saw me on three occasions, less than five minutes at a time, months prior. The exploration of this thought pattern led me inside myself with questions. Had I been so deceitful or hateful to those around me at times that they trusted me this little? Had I truly let lifetime friendships loosen so much that my once best friend wanted nothing but distance between us? Had I maybe just picked a shallow group of friends? Or maybe this was just an impossible situation.

Whatever you call this situation, under a picture of it, a caption would surely read 'painstakingly impossible.' As much as I have spent weeks, almost months, despising what Agent Greene was doing to me, I felt now an odd obligation of thanks.

The next morning, when he returned, I was anxious to meet with him. I wanted to thank him for the day before in court. I did feel like he was making a difference to me for the first time, and I felt more motivated than ever to help him. I know it must seem crazy to need motive to want to help with a case like this. But considering my entire situation, fully in context, I was at a loss for what was right and wrong. I had lost touch with reality and my self-confidence was nonexistent.

As the door to our meeting room opened, I said to Agent Greene, "Hey man, starting to think I might have not given you enough credit."

"Sit down," he snapped. "You weren't supposed to say that yesterday. You have caused me some problems."

"What? Well I am so sorry indeed that I have caused *you* some problems. Why did you help me if I am so much trouble?"

"I wasn't helping you; that was just a positive consequence to me covering my ass. And your ass by the way."

"So am I in trouble?"

"You need to understand that I have more power than you can imagine. My boss has more power than that. I can bury you and your family under a federal prison and none of you will be seen or heard from again. You keep fucking with me; I will prove that to you. I didn't say this was going to be easy but you have to be a man about this. I don't care why you keep your mouth shut, be it your family, your fear of federal prison or me, or you want to help those kids. It is irrelevant to me. Your reasoning just needs to be discovered so you can stop blurting this stuff out. I'm not going to warn you again."

"You can't let me be happy about anything, can you?"

"You want happy? Fine. I arrested Gage Tate this morning, again. I have added rape, sodomy, murder, conspiracy to commit murder, murder for hire, and sexual abuse to his charges. His bond is being raised from $100,000 to $1,000,000. We don't expect him to post bond so quickly this time. We got him, now we have to make this big case that I just created."

I was silent and Agent Greene said, "You ok?"

"I don't think so," I said, as I began to cry.

"This is a good thing, Brayden."

"I know," I said. "I just still can't believe it all. Even with seeing it with my own eyes, I can't believe it. What is the next step?"

"Well these are serious charges. He will be arraigned like always. Then the next major step, the first of which you will be needed in court, will likely be a suppression hearing. Do you know what that is?"

"Like where the attorneys for both sides argue about evidence they want or don't want to be shown to a jury?"

"Yes, just like that. You may not have to testify. It depends on what the evidence in question is. But just in case, you will be transported to the courthouse for it."

"When will that be?"

"I have no idea yet. It could be a couple of months off yet. Just depends on how this all goes and how fast attorneys work."

Another piece of reasonably good news, mixed with a tough lecture was at least good news nonetheless. Gage would finally be in jail instead of out on bond. That made me feel especially good. One of the hardest things about this ordeal was knowing I am locked down in a jail cell rotting away, while Gage is out gallivanting around town and living his life. And as for Agent Greene's lecture, I really heard him this time. I wasn't just scared of going to federal prison. I wasn't just worried about being able to live with myself for screwing up a case like this and having another child get hurt. I wasn't just scared for my family. I was scared because I believed Agent Greene when he said he had more power than I knew. Prison would be lucky, I believed. I was convinced if I crossed him, I would wind up dead.

All those conspiracy theorists out there make wild accusations about the federal government. All the hiding and secrets, the government must be responsible in some way for every bad thing that happens in the world. At this point, I was starting to see why they thought that. And for God's sake, could they be right? Probably not, of course. I am not a conspiracy theorist, not before this and not after, but I can see where someone could be convinced of that. I would argue there are less so called 'conspiracies' in the world and more just stuff we don't know. Most of that 'stuff' that we don't know, I believe the average citizen doesn't want to know.

Given my situation, being locked up for a crime in which the government knew I was innocent, imprisoned and forced to cooperate with an ongoing investigation, all the time being threatened, a government conspiracy didn't seem so unbelievable. A gun had sat on the table in front of me allowing my mind to wonder about the possibility of being killed by the government. They went behind the local police's back to get what they want, when they wanted it. They have unlimited resources to make anything happen they so choose. Yes, given my circumstance, I could certainly see some believable conspiracy theories about the government.

After a bad night's sleep, Agent Greene showed up again in mid-morning. He said he would be back in a few days, but this had been a few hours. As I entered the room, Agent Greene was sitting at the table with his hand in his hair, looking frustrated at some paperwork.

"He did it again," Agent Greene said.

"Can you start from the beginning? That would make it easier on me."

"Tate posted the million dollar bond. Well, someone posted it for him. This time, he knew the person or so he told the federal judge. He is going to his dad's house now and apparently this guy is a good friend of Tate's. His name is Mario Rodriguez. Do you know him?"

"Short guy, black hair, Mexican-American with little or no

accent. We went to high school together. I haven't seen him in years though. You sure it is the same guy?"

"Well you described him pretty well, look at this. Is that him?"

After a pause of disbelief I said, "Yes, that's him."

"Did he go by a nickname in high school?"

"Yea, weird though. Everyone called him Frankie. I know that's nothing like his name, but people just called him that."

"Weird you say? How about this, the secret questions that the bailer must answer and then the bailed must also answer to confirm a connection, Tate was asked about a nickname. Frankie was the answer. He's our guy. How well did you know him?"

"Not well. We were friends in high school but I can't see him being involved in this."

"Well he may not be really involved. He might have just been a connection that Tate has that was willing to post the bond for a cut. Either way, it is enough to meet the loophole requirements and get him out."

"So what does this mean?"

"It means Tate is back out, roaming the streets again. We have a tail on him still. Hopefully he will lead us to someone this time, a mainstream player."

Hope seemed to be common in this investigation. I would be far more comfortable with some 'I knows' and some facts rather than a bunch of hope. Again, I sit in a jail cell, rotting away from the inside out and Gage is out on the street living his life.

My jail life had started rocky, to say the least. And all this contact with the F.B.I. doesn't look so hot as far as popularity either. But I had found a better path inside the jail. Master Life was a great program and I was encouraged to pray often. One night, when I was overly concerned about my survival in prison, I prayed for guidance. I know people sound crazy sometimes when they say 'God spoke to me' but that day, I truly believe he did. It was clear to me for the first time that, while I wasn't the most popular guy, I did have valuable skills.

Throughout my stay in the Master Life program, I began having meetings with inmates about their cases. I was more educated than most of the guys there. Some didn't understand their charges or their options. I was able to give free advice and it kept me safe. Along the same lines, many of the inmates could not read or write. I often found myself helping someone write a letter to a loved one or reading a letter to them from a loved one. It was so sad to hear some of the stories I did. I won't share them, out of respect to those guys, but I can assure you, these guys seemed so unprepared in life. A drug dealer for life was a common theme. To me, even in my circumstance, that was so sad. Where can they go and what can they do after prison?

On August 2, 2006, our door was opened at 6AM and the loud speaker screamed, "COOPER! Pack your shit, you're heading down."

Chapter 14

A Fish In The Fish Tank.

I was shaking with nervousness. It was finally here. I was on my way to prison. The idea of a road trip kind of excited me, but the arrival is what bothered me. I was instructed to pack all of my belongings, minus any food or hygiene products in clear plastic bags. I did as I was told and was escorted out of the unit by a guard. No one else from our unit left with me. When I went out the door, there was a small line of men awaiting the trip already. This process reminded me of going to court, only there were less people.

We were escorted in a line down the hall and into the property room where we very first entered the jail. One by one they called us up to the window and we were given our original clothes back. We were strip searched just like when we first came in only this time we concluded by ditching the jumpsuit and getting our clothes back. We also got back our keys, cell phones, money, wallets and any other personal items that were in property. All of our property was in small vacuum sealed bags and we were told not to open them.

My clothes made me stand out a bit. I was wearing a black button down dress shirt and black pants, the dress code for a host at O'Charley's. It didn't smell the best, after being warn all day hosting in the smells of the restaurant and then shoved in a bag for a few months. The other guys didn't look particularly flattering either and no one really commented on this. Actually most of us were comparing how our clothes were bigger than when we came in. Of course, we had all lost weight eating the pathetic jail diet.

After we had our belongings, we were escorted to holding cells. We were grouped into several groups. My group was a group of all first timers except one. That, I was told, was customary. The 'fish,' as we newcomers to prison are called, all rode up to the big house in the Sherriff's vans instead of the large bus. They felt that safer than mixing us with the violent repeat offenders who might fry us up for dinner. Personally, I agreed. I wasn't a huge fish fan anyway, especially when I'm the fish.

After nearly two hours of waiting, we were finally taken to the vans. Before we got in, we were shackled heavily. Our hands and ankles were cuffed, along with a chain that linked our handcuffs to our ankle cuffs. This was very similar to our transport to court. The difference this time was the black box. I had heard rumors of the black box, but this was the first time I saw it. The black box is just that, a small black box that locks down over your handcuffs so the key hole in the cuffs is not visible to the inmate. This would prevent those amazingly coordinated escapes you see on TV where the inmate cleverly hides a paper clip in his mouth only to later remove it and pick the lock on his cuffs. He then takes the guard's gun and gets away. This would not be so easy here.

After we were all seated in the van, two Sherriff's got in the front seats. There was cage separating us from them, much like the type of cage in a police car. The driver started the van and then turned in his seat so he could see us.

"Listen up, guys," he said. "For those who might not know, we are going to the Roederer Correction Complex, commonly known as the Fish Tank. It is located in LaGrange, KY, a few minutes outside Louisville. I expect there to be no problems. If you had cigarettes in your property, note, you are not allowed to smoke in this van. That being said, I don't care if you smoke. If you try to escape, I have a shotgun up here and we both carry pistols. We will shoot you if you get out and run. Neither of us runs; we are old fat guys who drive a van. So, simply, if you run, we will shoot you. Does everyone understand? Any questions?"

Everyone affirmed their understanding and no one seemed eager to challenge them. As we got out on the road, I could see the sun shining. It was amazing to me to be able to see the simplest things, like sunshine and growing grass. It had only been five months, but still, I already was feeling weird about not seeing the outside in so long.

The van rode smooth and aside from the black box that made moving so incredibly difficult, the trip went smoothly. On our approach to the Fish Tank, the feeling of entrapment truly set in. This place looked like a prison you would see on TV. There were three fences surrounding the facility with razor and barbed wire and one was an electric fence. Guard towers stood tall too with armed guards ready to fire on anyone who attempted to escape. The van pulled between two fences and up inside a gate enclosure. There was barely room for the van and a doorway inside this enclosure.

We were taken off the van and unshackled just inside the doorway. After being unshackled, we were taken into this huge room, which looked like a really long, wide hallway. There were people sitting at desks and offices on the side at the front. Along the wall were showers, wide open in front of everyone. We stopped at the table just inside the door. A guard gave us a box and told us we had to ship all of our belongings back home if we wanted to keep them or we could trash anything we didn't want. Shipping, of course, was at our own expense and would be charged to our inmate account. If we didn't bring money from the jail for the account, we had to get family to send money and get it on the books within 14 days or the box would be trashed.

After boxing up my stuff, I was handed a bag containing the one item I was allowed to keep, my bible. We went down the hallway and were put into a holding cell with a bunch of other guys. We waited there for over six hours before we were called upon. All of us were hungry and annoyed at the long wait. It was pushing 8PM and we had been doing this since that morning at 6AM.

Finally, we were called out, one by one, to get our hair cut. They shaved all of our hair on our head and face. You had to be bald coming in to the Fish Tank. After we were bald, we could begin the process of getting checked in.

The first step in the process was to have our fingerprints taken and our naked bodies examined for tattoos, injuries, birthmarks or any other identifying feature to prepare in the event of an escape. After standing naked in front of many guards, both men and women, for about 45 minutes being interviewed and checked over completely, we were instructed to stand in a line and await the shower. Still naked, we stood in line and watched as those in front of us were sprayed down with a cold, green chemical. When it was my group's turn, we stood under the shower heads and listened to lady guard give instruction.

"Do not touch the shower head. I will tell you when you can turn on the shower. I am going to spray you with this chemical. It cleanses you of bacteria, viruses, lice and anything else that may be growing on your bodies from the jail. Face front and stick your arms above your head."

She sprayed us from head to toe and then said, "Now turn around and keep your arms in the air. Lean your head back so I can get your head soaked real well. Now, bend over so I can get your ass soaked well."

After she finished humiliating us and soaking us in this green, slimy chemical that made me sneeze, she told us to stand there for ten minutes. During the ten minutes, the chemical began tingling, which she said was the way we knew it was working. I got yelled at for sneezing, although I didn't know how to stop. After the ten minutes were up, she told us to turn on the shower heads and rinse off thoroughly. By now, of course, there was no hot water left.

We were given towels to dry off with when were done. We then went to a room just behind the showers to collect our clothes. They were all different colors, mine were green. The pants were like sweat pants only a coarser material and the shirt was the same material with a low v-cut shape to it. We were handed a hygiene pack that contained one bar of soap, a tiny toothbrush and toothpaste, and two rolls of toilet paper. No deodorant was included and I found out later, the only way you can get any is to buy it off commissary.

After we were dressed, we finally were led to our respective dorms. My dorm was called C dorm and everyone there wore green. I was told it was the newer section. It was one huge room that was wide open with about 200 guys in it. I remember thinking that I would never get any sleep in that room with that many guys. There were bunk beds, just like the jail, but here you weren't as close to everyone else as you were at the jail. There were two TVs up high, about thirty feet off the floor that you could watch. Although, good luck hearing it or getting to watch anything you want when you have to compete with 200 other guys. The only two things that everyone seemed to agree on watching were wrestling and football. At least I had football.

That night, it did quiet down much more than I had imagined. When the lights finally went out, I got a couple hours of sleep. The next morning, I got to go to orientation. It was kind of like when you get a new job, they want to show you the ropes and let you know what you can expect over the next few days. Basically they would run a multitude of medical tests on you and you were required to see a psychiatrist. Also, during this time you would get classified.

Classification was quite important because the level you get from the classification director would determine what level prison you would go to. Prisons were classified in three categories: maximum security, medium security and camps. Camps were the lowest security and they had the most freedom. Everyone wanted to go to a camp. Anyone with thirty years or more automatically had to spend at least six months at maximum security, even nonviolent offenders with large sentences. Also, anyone with murder charges or extreme violent charges, and some inmates with escapes on their records, all went to maximum. Medium security was often referred to as 'behind the fence' and was really a melting pot. Violent offenders, sex offenders, escapees who didn't go to maximum and anyone with a twenty year sentence or higher had to start at medium security. Camps had only nonviolent offenders, mostly drug offenders, theft convictions and some other lower class felonies.

Maximum security and most medium security prisons have controlled movement. This means that you can't go anywhere or do anything other than on the prison's specific set schedule. In some cases, that included restroom and shower use and always included recreation time. You are truly at the mercy of the institution in maximum or medium security prisons in Kentucky. Camps gave inmates the freedom to roam around a bit more. There is often no fence around the prison to keep inmates in because the trust level is higher. That being said, most of these prisons are in remote areas and it would be very difficult to make an escape.

My felonies were both the lowest level felonies you can get and all my possession of child pornography charges were misdemeanors. That is important because they don't classify inmates, generally, on what misdemeanor charges they have. With felonies being the most important determining factor, the fact that this was my first time down and I had no history of escape or bail jumping, I should have had no problem getting sent to a camp.

After letting the medical team take what seemed like gallons of blood from me to make sure I don't have AIDS or some other highly contagious and deadly disease, I was finally sent to the shrink. This, I knew was important. If you said the wrong thing, like you feel depressed, or you are extremely unhappy, the shrink could order you be sent to suicide watch. This would also prevent me from going to a camp. I knew I had to be as happy as possible in this meeting that I so much dreaded.

"How do you feel, Mr. Cooper?" asked the psychiatrist.

"I'm good," I said, with a smile.

"I am told your case was quite public on the news. How was that for you?"

"Well it wasn't a field of roses and chocolate," I said. "I didn't enjoy it, but it's over now and no one here knows about it."

"So you are not afraid of anyone here?"

"Well I don't want to bunk with a serial killer, but I'm not afraid of people finding out why I'm here. They don't know so far, anyway."

"Otherwise, you are feeling healthy? No bad thoughts?"

I thought of slapping her, but instead I said, "Nope, I'm good to go."

I was given a clean mental health paper that I had to take to classification when I go there. For this day, I was finished, but the next day would bring classification, hopefully. They didn't seem to have an order of classification. They get to you when they get to you, but one thing is for sure, everyone comes here and no one leaves before they are classified.

As I walked in the door to my dorm, a tall, thin man with many tattoos waved me to come over to him. He said, "Hey man, what are you here for?"

"Arson," I said.

"Really? Hmm... that's weird," he said.

"Ha ha, why is that weird? Don't peg me for an arsonist?" While I wasn't proud of this part of my past, I learned quickly that you fit in far better boasting about your crimes than playing the remorseful type.

"No, you don't. But it ain't just that. A guy next door says you are in here for messing with some kids."

"What?!" I said, trying to sound as shocked as I could. "Well that's a fucking lie!"

"You been classified yet?"

"No," I said.

"Cool. Well we can straighten all this out when you do."

"I don't understand."

"Oh yea, first timer, huh? Ok, well let me spell it out for you, fish. When you go to classification, they will give you your time sheet. That time sheet will have your charges and how much time you got for those charges. When you get back from classification, you can bring your time sheet over here. If you got sex charges on there... well let's just hope, for your sake, you don't."

"I don't. You'll see when I get it, man. I'm not some kind of sicko, unless you count arsonist as sicko."

"Nah, arson is cool. Liking kids will get you killed. See you when you get back."

Before this conversation, I was looking forward to classification so I could get transferred to where I was supposed to go. Very few inmates stayed at the Fish Tank and everyone wanted to get where they were going to stay permanently so they could get settled into a routine that would make their time pass faster. Now, my main concern was what I was going to do when I got that time sheet. I'd have to tell them to lock me up in protective custody.

I spent that night talking to other inmates, looking as slyly as possible at their time sheets to see if their misdemeanors showed up. If only my felonies showed up on the time sheet, I would be ok. The misdemeanor charges were the only charges that look like sex charges. I began to feel sick to my stomach throughout the day. To think that Gage Tate had done all of this and drug me right into it and now, a few months after my life was turned upside down, I felt like I was battling to survive pending what was printed a dumb piece of paper. I was truly reduced to one of *them*. I had to become a criminal to live in their world. I was not given a choice.

I had a plan. If I got classified, and all my charges were on that time sheet, I would ask for protection. If they deny me, I would return to the dorm and attack the guy who asked for my time sheet. It was my only hope. This guy was going to kill me if he found out, so my best bet, if I couldn't get protection, was to hurt this man so I could be locked up in segregation. Stab a guy and they will definitely lock you up. I didn't want to stab this man or to hurt this man at all. In a strange way, I totally agreed with him. The thought of someone doing the things Gage did and I was falsely accused is sickening to think about.

The next morning I was called down to classification. On the way down, I had calmness about me. I was on a mission of sorts. Obtain the time sheet, evaluate the situation, and act accordingly.

This was my plan. Though I didn't know the night before if I could actually stab this man if needed, I had convinced myself that it was the only option if the time sheet was revealing and all I could do is block out my concerns.

When I entered the office area, I was directed down a hallway to the last door on the right. The sign on the outside of the door read 'Classification Director' and the door was open. I stepped in front of the door and there were two people inside, one man and one woman. They motioned for me to come in and have a seat in the chair provided. It was a padded chair, much more comfortable than those interrogation chairs or the chairs in the jail.

"Mr. Cooper, I have your file here. Due to the arson charge and your misdemeanor charges being sex crimes, I'm sending you to level 3." Ok, so to clarify, there are actually five levels of classification. Level one is halfway house eligible, level two is camp eligible, level threes and some level fours go to medium security and some level fours and all level fives go to maximum security. "Here is your time sheet, look it over and let me know if there is a problem."

I was so concerned with looking at the time sheet; I didn't even notice that she said level three. Medium security, not where I wanted to go, but I hadn't even heard that. As I looked it over, I quickly spotted my charges. I took a huge sigh of relief in noticing that *only* my felony charges were listed. No misdemeanors, no sex charges, no nothing but arson and tampering with physical evidence.

"Does everything look ok?" she asked.

"Yes," I sighed. "Everything is great."

After I was dismissed, I started to replay that conversation in my head and getting a closer look at my time sheet. I discovered some serious problems and everything was *not* ok. Level three?? I knew I was going behind the fence somewhere. And my time sheet, now that I got a close look, had me sentenced to ten years, not five. I know the commonwealth's attorney appealed my probation time being run concurrent with my new time, but they had lost that appeal. I was set to serve only five years, which means this is wrong.

Instead of stabbing the man in my dorm, I thought it would be better to friend him and ask for some help. On my arrival to the dorm, he and his two or three friends were waiting for me. Like before, they waved me over.

"So, how'd it go?"

"They are sending me behind the fence. I can't believe it!"

"Let me see it," he said.

As I showed him the time sheet, I said, "See this too, they have me down as ten years. But those sentences were to be concurrent for only five years. Who do I talk to about that?"

"Legal aid here, an inmate. Don't go through the prisons cause everything will get messed up. And if you need it, I know a solver too."

"Yea cool, I need this solved for sure."

Huge laughter busted out, though I wasn't aware I was being funny. He said, "No, no, fish. A solver is like a prison hitter, a hit man. They fight for you, kill for you, whatever you want to pay for. This is the best place for that."

"Uh... I don't think I need someone like that for anything. At least not yet."

"Well you need to do something about that fucking midget wetback mother fucker next door talking that shit about you. I won't trust what he says anymore, but you don't want no problems around here because of some wetback spreading rumors like that."

"Oh yea, true that. I will let you know, trying to get some money here. So what about that legal aid? You know a good one here? And what can I do about my level three status?"

"Damn twenty questions guy. I'm not a legal aid. I can point you to one, but you gotta ask him those questions bro."

And he did point me towards a legal aid. He was much friendlier than he might have been had he known my plot to stab him only hours before. Friendly might sound like a loose term here, but when you offer to help someone kill someone else, that's about as friendly as you get in prison.

The legal aid turned out to be pretty good. Turns out, he hooked me up with all the forms I needed and I got all my time issues worked out within just a few days. I appealed the decision to send me to a medium security prison but as most other appeals, mine was too denied. I found that a group of men to the back of my dorm would get together every night around eight. They stood in a circle and they prayed for each other and their situations. I joined this group to pray for family and myself. I needed extra strength to get through this. I had only arrived at prison and was turning into a criminal with thoughts of stabbings and violence. This was hard to take in after it sank in. I knew it was a good thing I didn't have to do it because I had not let the thought sink in enough to process what I was even considering. I wouldn't have been able to live with myself if I had chosen to do that.

Prayer, I learned, did help. God does answer prayers. He gave me the strength and peace of mind I needed to survive what I was going through. I had learned that I was given credit for sixty days of time prior to this charge that I had served on the arson case. That, with the time I had served on this case already meant I was eligible for parole as soon as January. It was only August, but January didn't seem so far away. If I could just make it until then, I thought, maybe, just maybe, I could get out of here and go home.

After only 11 days, it was my turn to get transferred. I was going behind the fence and I was wondering, where had the F.B.I. been the last 11 days? It was the longest since their first appearance that I had not seen them. Waiting to be put on the bus, I was told I'd be shipped to LAC, which stood for Lee Adjustment Center in Lee County. Inmate.com, as we call the inmate rumor mill, had reported this was a big boxing match here. That, I knew, was not what I wanted to hear...

Chapter 15

Lee Adjustment Center, 'The Promise' And The F.B.I., Again.

As the bus pulled into LAC, I was ready. I was prepared to walk into this great big boxing arena and take out the biggest guy I could see, just like in the movies. Thankfully, that would not be necessary. The warden of LAC actually came on the bus to welcome us to the facility. I remember thinking, 'right, this isn't college and we aren't happy to be here, let's get on with it,' but in looking back, it was a peaceful gesture. Between the guys at the Fish Tank waiting to leave and the guys on the bus, I was a bit worried about this prison's reputation.

Of course I didn't show any concern, because as I had learned early on, inmates, like dogs, smell fear. It really is a fine art, impressionable emotion. If you come in scared, they will give you a reason to be. If you come off as the 'tough guy' then they will challenge you at every corner to see how tough you are. So, inmates had to either think you were completely insane or they had to like you. Insane was going to be harder than liking, I thought. And what could I possibly have in common with *these* people?

After we were unshackled, we were all put into a room where inmate entry bags were handed out. We were sized for clothes, which were considerably different here. Instead of parachute pants or jumpsuits, we were given khaki slacks and button up shirts. Five pair of pants, five short sleeve shirts and five long sleeve shirts was our full allotment. We would be required to wear these every time we left our dorm. Clothes must be pressed and shirts tucked in for a neat look or we could get a write up. The entry bag also included some socks, underwear, towels and washcloths. Our bedding, such as sheets and pillow cases, we were to get at the dorm we were assigned.

Dorm assignments were done here much like in other places, based on classification. This was the first lesson I would learn about being transferred; you are reclassified every place you go. Initially I would be placed in a lockdown dorm with two man cells. Then, within a couple of days, I would be classified again and either left in the two man cells or transferred to an open dorm. As we were led outside to the dorms where we'd have our initial stay, I recall many inmates with a northern accent.

"What's with everyone's northern accent here?" I asked the guard.

"Oh, that's the Verms," he said.

"What is a Verm?" I asked.

"Vermont inmates. Lee Adjustment Center is private, ya know? They take inmates from other states and house them here too sometimes. About 60% of the gen pop here is from Vermont."

I wasn't sure if that was a good thing or not. Or maybe it didn't matter at all. We were given a brief overview of 'breakfast, dinner and supper' hours, as the folks called it here in Lee County. So much for lunch out here and dinner was at noon. From what I had heard, the food was quite an improvement on the Fish Tank. When we arrived at the dorm, I learned I'd be first housed in Unit C, which had now become a pattern for me. I wondered if all places put you in a C unit before anywhere else. That had at least been my experience. I was told to take my stuff to cell 22 and my roommate would give me the rundown of the setup.

As I walked through the unit, it was much different than any place I had been previously. There was a huge open area, maybe 5,000 square feet in the middle of the room. In that area there were tables that would seat four. Several of us that were shipped together scoured the area for clues of lifestyle changes we may face. The front wall, which all the dorms were angled to face, had the showers. There were no walls or barriers to protect the view; it was just eight shower heads on a wall with tile area and a few drains underneath. In fact, there were only three drains in the middle. We found that kind of disgusting, since if you picked one of the middle shower heads, other people's dirty waters would flow down to your feet. I finally found my door, downstairs, it was number 22. I opened it and went inside.

On the bottom bunk was a large man with a big smile who said, "Oh thank God! Please tell me you are my new roommate!" He had a strong northern accent, clearly a Vermont inmate.

"Yup, I guess so," I said.

"The last guy they sent in here came yesterday and that fucking nigger had to go."

"Oh... yea?" I said, hesitantly.

"Yes indeed. I hate those niggers. They just think they can be crazy and disrespectful. The only niggers we got in Vermont are the ones working in the field and hanging from a tree."

"Wow," I said, in shock of what I was hearing.

"My name is Gage Tate, what's your name?" Seriously!!?? Could he have had a worse name?? I was absolutely in disbelief at the utter ridiculous odds of this.

"I'm Brayden Cooper. I used to know a guy named Gage Tate. Not my favorite person."

"Was he a nigger?"

"No, just an ass hole."

"Least he's not a nigger. So what are you in for?"

"Arson," I said.

"Oh my God! Man you are meant for this dorm. I'm in here for

Arson too! I burnt down this fucker's house because he owed me money. They said I got a fire addiction, I told 'em I got a money addiction. And I don't see it as a problem. The mother fucker paid me and he won't stiff me again, will he?"

"I sure wouldn't," I said.

"So what'd you spark up?"

"State office building," I said.

"Oh man, I do like you already. Well look, here's the deal. I go out and come in a lot during the day, but at night, I kick back and watch TV. I know you don't have a TV yet, so as long as you don't mind watching what I watch, you can feel free to join me. If you need to shit, there's the toilet. Just tell me and I'll leave for a rotation. Oh and rotation is one hour. If you leave during movement, you can't get back for at least an hour, so don't forget that. No one comes in our cell but me and you. Don't hang out with the niggers or the fags and we have no problems. Any questions?"

"No," I said. "Can I use those phones to call collect?"

"Yea man, you should be able to. And if you can't, let me know and I'll give you my number. You can use it to dial out. Just don't threaten the president or nothing."

"Ha ha, just want to call my mom, let her know I'm here."

"Commendable... Moms are important."

A racist, arsonist and a momma's boy; wow, what a character AND he had to be named Gage Tate. What are the freaking odds? At least he didn't seem like he wanted kill me and since he hates 'fags' he didn't want to rape me either. He was quirky and a bit crazy, but I didn't feel threatened, which was good. This guy was a real character. He was really cool to me, but he has some issues he'll probably never work through. He treated me good, and that was all I could ask out of anyone at this point. But please note, words cannot describe how insane he really was. When supper time came, he was excited to show me the chow hall and the way to get the most food.

"Ok now," he began, "we go up this side of the wall. They are going to give you a tray with some meat, bread and dessert on it. Then you take the tray over there to the bar. Don't forget to get a cup off the cart. You can get all you can eat salad, potatoes or pasta and veggies. You can get more drink too, so it's really a good deal. The food ain't bad, but when they serve turkey surprise, keep in mind that you won't like the surprise. Sometimes when they have leftover meat or desert from supper, they put it on the dinner line to be eaten. You can eat good here, better than most places around here from what I know."

As we went further into the chow hall, I noticed that all the black guys sat together at one table and the gay guys all sat at one table. Everyone else was straight white guys, or so it appeared. I wasn't about to announce I was gay, for fear I'd have to sit at that table. I needed to make friends, not turn into a target. Overall, 98% of the population was white, which seemed crazy for the black population. It seemed they were so greatly outnumbered by racists that it must be extremely difficult.

As a white guy, I didn't see much in the way of racism on the street. To this point I hadn't seen much true racism in the prison system. It certainly was common for like races to stick together in prison, but the open racism wasn't evident until here. I thought, for anyone who doesn't think racism is still a big issue; they must never have accompanied a black man to Vermont. From the appearance here, everyone from Vermont was racist. Clearly that may be a complete stereotype, and I have never been to Vermont, but I was in Little Vermont, and it was otherwise known as LAC.

The next day, I was well rested and ready for anything. It was my day for classification. When the time came, the guard came to my cell to let me know.

"Mr. Cooper?" he asked.

"Yes, sir," I said.

"How are you holding up, buddy?"

Skeptical of his kindness, I said, "Fine so far."

"Good to hear. How's Tate treating you? He's kinda crazy," he said with a laugh.

"He's cool," I said. "I like him."

"Ha ha, lucky for you a dorm is likely in your future. Classification is ready for you. If you come with me, I'll take you."

I was unbelievably impressed at how nice this guy was. In fact, everyone I had met thus far who worked at LAC was nice. He led me out of the unit and to the room right across from our dorm. He asked me to wait in the hallway while he poked his head in and told them I was ready. After he was done poking, he waved me in the room.

"Mr. Cooper, this is David and he is the classification manager. He will be conducting your classification. I'll be waiting in the hall when you get done."

"Thanks," I said. Extending a handshake, I said, "It's nice to meet you, David."

"You too. Can I call you Brayden?"

"Sure."

"Ok, great. We like first names around here. So, I see the Roederer Farm classified you level three because of the arson charge and some misdemeanors. What do you think about that?"

"With all due respect, they didn't care what I thought. I appealed it because I disagreed and it was denied."

"Well I care what you think. This is your first time down. You don't seem like you need to be a level three. Are you going to try to escape?"

"Lord no," I said. "Maybe escape in thoughts, like watching TV or something, but never for real. I couldn't go home to my family with a story of escape," I said with a smirk.

"That's what I thought. Well listen, I'm going to re-class you as level two and send you to a camp, if that's ok with you?"

"That's great! Thanks."

"Any place in particular you want to go? Like a specific camp?"

"Yes, actually. Not that I've been to any of them, but Blackburn is closest to my home and my family isn't all in good health. Blackburn is in Lexington and would be the best to get to if possible."

"Ok, Brayden, I will see what I can do for you."

"I appreciate that."

"And we are going to get you moved to a dorm in the next day or two. That ok with you?"

"I guess so, sure."

"It's better there, more to do. I'll process all this and let you know in a few days about the transfer, ok?"

"Sounds great, thanks again!"

And it seemed people were getting friendlier and friendlier as I went. I couldn't wait to call my mom and tell her I may very well be coming right back to Lexington to serve time. That would make everything so much easier. I could see all of my family much more often. LAC was a little less than two hours from Lexington, so the drive wasn't so bad. But ten minutes across town would have been so much better. When I got back to my cell, I was anxious to tell my new celly about my classification results.

"Hey, Tate. I got classified. They are going to send me up the hill to an open dorm and he said I was classified too high before and he's going to get me transferred to a camp. Good news, huh?"

"All but the open dorm shit. Those fuckers up there will drive you crazy. All those vine swinging niggers screaming, ugh, it will make you want to kill them. That's why I'm here now, taking my vacation. About once a year they put me back in a dorm and I do ok for a couple months. Then when the niggers drive me crazy, I beat one down and they send me back here. This is my home really, a single cell."

"That's cool. How long have you been here?"

"Almost six years. Long time, huh?"

"Yea it is," I said. I couldn't imagine being there that long.

A few days later, just as David had said, I was moved up to a different dorm. The dorm had a big cage around it, mostly providing a clear boundary between being on the grounds of the dorm and being in an unauthorized area. The building was split into a four-plex, two huge dorms on the bottom and two huge dorms on the top. Downstairs was just the general population and upstairs on the right was too. Upstairs on the left was SAP which stands for Substance Abuse Program and is the most intensive rehab offered to prisoners in Kentucky. I was housed upstairs on the right, next door to SAP.

This was certainly a different type of dorm than I had been in. The right side was divided into two sides. Two hundred inmates slept in each section, making four hundred in the side. The good thing was, no bunk beds, so no one had to climb up top. Each area was now called a 'cube' instead of a cell and instead of a celly, we had cubies. Each cube had two bunks with lots of space in between. I wasn't crowded at all like I was in other places. My new cubie's side was very neat. He was waiting when I arrived.

"Hi. My name is Craig," he said with an extended hand. He was an older guy, around fifty years old. He was in shape, clearly from working out. He was a small guy wearing a gray t-shirt and sweat pants. He had a cross hanging from his neck and, of course, he was white.

"Hey man, I'm Brayden."

"Cool. You'll like it here, I think. Just get all your stuff settled in and if you have any questions, just let me know. I'm on my way to the track, but I'll be back later."

At some point while Craig was away, I remember considering that, though my fondness of sci-fi was miniscule at best, perhaps I had fallen into the twilight zone. Everyone here was so friendly; it felt like a trick waiting to happen. Just when everyone I knew said 'do not trust anyone in prison,' everyone has decided to be really nice. I decided then to take the niceness in stride but to keep my eyes and ears open. After about an hour, Craig returned from the track.

"Hey buddy," he said, "You get all settled in?"

"Yea, I think so."

"Cool man. So, you are a Kentucky inmate, right?"

"Yup."

"I'm from Vermont, if you can't tell by the accent," Craig said with a smile. "So what are you in for?"

"Arson," I said.

"I'll have to hear that story sometime. Well listen, when I'm not here, I have a TV and a CD player here. You're more than welcome to use them. Just be sure to put them back like you found them so I don't get a write up. You going to get a TV?"

"I don't know. My family is pretty screwed right now with me in here, so I don't know yet."

"I understand that. Well if you need anything, just let me know. I may not have it, but you don't know if you don't ask."

"Thanks man. So, what are you in for?" I asked.

Craig put his head down and said, "Murder. I am serving a thirty year sentence for murdering my wife. But before you think I'm crazy, I didn't mean to. I know it sounds stupid. But I was drinking, drunk really, and I black out when I drink. I have had a couple of DWI's in Vermont and it was documented that I black out when I drink. I wasn't supposed to be drinking at all on probation for the DWI. But I'm an alcoholic. I got drunk and I guess we got in a fight. I got mad and I shot her six times. I don't remember that at all, but when I came to, I had the gun and blood all over me. I know I blacked out."

"Man, that's rough," I said, grasping for an appropriate comment.

"Well anyway, now I'm a born again Christian and I won't ever drink again."

"That's good. You seem like a good guy."

"Are you a Christian?"

"Yes," I said.

"Awesome, well they have church services here, if you want

to come with me. I go every Wednesday night and Sunday night. Wednesday is an hour and Sunday is two hours."

"Yea, that'd be great," I said.

"Mr. Cooper?" said a guard behind us.

"Yes?"

"You need to come with me. There are some law enforcement folks here to see you."

"Ok," I said, wondering if he meant the F.B.I. "I'll see you later, Craig."

He led me out of the dorm and to a meeting room inside the building. Inside, Agent Greene was sitting, twirling his pen like usual.

After the guard closed the door, I said, "I was wondering where you were. Been a while."

"Yea, you are kinda hard to track down. I keep missing you when I show up to see you. Listen; straight to business, Gage is going to have a suppression hearing in two weeks. I need you to be there, to testify."

"Ok," I said. "What are the topics?"

"Well we are going to ask to revoke Gage's bond for the threats he was involved in making against you. We can't prove he did it, but he did. Also that phone call you made from the jail, the defense wants that gone. Some other stuff too. Hey, you might not have to say a word, but as a witness, I have to have you there just in case. U.S. Marshals will be here to get you that morning, really early. They will take you to Lexington, do the hearing and then they will bring you back. And I'll make sure you get something to eat."

"Ok. You think this is going to be a good step, this hearing?"

"I hope so, if we win some points it will. I will be back just before the day to make sure you are still here and all that. You holding up ok?"

"As ok as I can, I guess. I like this place better than the jail, that's for sure."

"Good. Try to stay positive. I will talk to you soon."

And he was gone, about as fast as he came in. Perhaps, I thought, this would be the chance to get Gage off the street. I so wanted him to be locked up for a while. I was also looking forward to seeing him in court answering for his charges. As embarrassing and humiliating as the process was for me, I wondered if Gage would even care one way or another. This new Gage Tate that I was learning of didn't seem to have much remorse or concern for anyone but himself. Other than the disappointment in getting caught, I have to wonder if Gage even cared about what he had done and what people thought of him for what he had done.

On my out of the meeting with Agent Greene, David, the classification manager, stopped me in the hallway.

"Hey Brayden. How do you like the new dorm?"

"It seems ok," I said.

"Great, glad to hear it. Listen, I wanted to let you know that I sent your paperwork to Frankfort for processing and got a signed copy faxed back to me this morning. I have you down as level two and I got that transfer to Blackburn approved too."

"Oh wow, that's fantastic! So I will be going to Blackburn for sure then?"

"I promise, buddy. I got it in this morning."

And finally some good news. I was coming home to Lexington and would be much closer to my family! Excited couldn't describe the level of happy I was. I didn't want to stay in prison and wanted nothing more than to go home. But if I have to stay, being closer to home was the best move for me.

Chapter 16

Objection, Your Honor!

It was late August of 2006 by now. My cubie Craig was cool and I got my first visit. My mom was super excited to come see me and my grandmother joined her. Visits here were called contact visits, and that meant we got to hug for the first time in 6 months. That was one thing better about prison. I told them about our local TV stations and how we got Lexington channels at LAC. My grandmother insisted that since my birthday was close, she would buy me a TV for my cube. I was so excited. In prison, this was truly the best gift. TV was largely your only connection to the outside world. And with cable selections, it was really a great pastime.

It was also time for that suppression hearing that would determine several very important talking points. The U.S. Marshals came, just as I was told they would. They handcuffed me, but no ankle cuffs or black boxes. They stopped by Hardee's to buy me breakfast, which was nice. We rode in a black SUV with dark tented windows and the words 'bullet proof' were written backwards on the inside of the windows. The Marshals were somewhat chatty and very amicable.

When we arrived at the courthouse, we drove into a parking garage and up to a garage door. The door opened and we pulled inside. The door closed behind us and we got out. We were in an enclosed area big enough for the SUV and a small walking area around it and that's it. There was a door just in front of us that I was escorted through. A narrow hallway lay on the opposite side of the door and just a few feet from that door was another door across the hall.

This was an important hearing as the judge was to decide about the inclusion of the recorded phone call I had with Gage from the jail. He would also decide about the computer they recovered from Gage's house. Since they took the computer from the house and removed evidence before returning it to the state, they violated Gage's civil rights and obstructed justice in the state case. The FBI was planning to argue that it was a domestic terrorism case, they invoked national security with the Patriot Act and because of that, they didn't do anything wrong. This would, of course, be up to the judge whether that's what *should* have happened.

Interestingly, I was never heavily shackled when being transported to the courthouse from any place I was incarcerated, except when going to my own court appearances in state court. But, at the courthouse, I had to be shackled per protocol. Just outside the second doorway, in that narrow hallway, my ankles were chained together. I was handcuffed and a chain link was wrapped around my waist to keep my hands close to my body. Another chain linked my handcuffs to my ankle cuffs. This made it hard to walk but I guess it made sense to me at the time. When it came to a prisoner in front of a federal judge, they took no chances.

As I entered the court room, Gage was sitting just a few feet from the door. He was dressed nice, clean shaven and he made eye contact with me. I shot him a glare that I'm sure made him a bit uneasy. He turned his head quickly and focused his eyes on the ugly carpet below him. As it turned out, per the pre-designated seating arrangements, I sat directly behind Gage, just a few inches from him. A US Marshal sat on either side of me. Escaping was not only not an option, but seemed like a sort of life ending type of decision. They did not fool around and I had better not either.

As the hearing started, the mood was tense. It seemed as though Gage's attorney and the District Attorney didn't get along. Beyond just being on opposing sides, it seemed they had a personal dislike for one another. A sarcastic undertone could be heard in every conversation they had. I was hoping for a fist fight, but no luck.

"All rise, court is now in session," the U.S. Marshal in front announced.

The judge quickly began, addressing the attorneys.

"Are there any pressing issues counselors, or shall we begin at the top of the list?"

Neither side seemed to have anything pressing, so the judge began with issue number one. In the federal system, and many state systems, the defense must turn over and have approved by a judge, a list of possible defenses or defense strategies in the trial of a case. Gage's attorney was especially interested in two defenses he wanted to be permitted to use.

"I understand the defense has some strategy to introduce that the prosecution objects. We'll start with the defense."

"Your honor," Gage's attorney began, "We would like the court to consider a defense of Not Guilty because of Extreme Emotional Disturbance. Also, we would like to reserve Not Guilty by reason of Extreme Forcible Duress. Your honor, some of the evidence presented by the prosecution will be questioned in this hearing today, but some of the video evidence points clearly to forcible duress. Regardless, we have several experts prepared to testify that Mr. Tate has been and is under extreme emotional disturbance."

"Objection, your honor," announces the prosecutor. "Your honor, the evidence presented does not show or present any forcible action at all, except the defendant forcing himself on a minor during a sexual act. The defendant's experts have not testified to date and our evidence presents no force by nature. The premise of the argument is invalid."

"I agree," said the judge, "Do you have any evidence that the prosecution has brought forth to further your claims?"

"Yes, your honor. In one video, a camera operator is present and presents forcible duress. Forcing Mr. Tate to perform these acts, in itself, presents extreme emotional disturbance."

"I agree, counselor. I think we are more in an area where a jury needs to decide whether they buy the story. They should at least be given the chance to hear it. I will approve both defenses."

"Thank you, your honor. May we approach?"

"Yes," said the judge.

The judge turned on some speakers with some white noise that was broadcasted over the microphone. The purpose of this is to prevent those in the gallery from hearing what is said by the attorneys and the judge. After a few seconds, both attorneys returned to their rightful tables.

"Marshal," the judge said to the U.S. Marshal that sat to my left side.

He looked confused and said, "Yes, your honor?"

"Sir, will you escort your witness to the other side of the gallery, away from behind Mr. Tate?"

He was so confused. He looked immediately at my shackles to make sure I had not somehow shimmied out of them or picked a lock. He looked back at the judge and said, "Your honor?"

"Mr. Tate is uncomfortable with your witness sitting directly behind him."

The Marshal nodded and said, "Ok, your honor."

He got me to stand up and as he walked behind me, he whispered, "What a pussy. What are *you* gonna do?"

I smiled, but chose not to answer. This was the most emotion or sign of a sense of humor I had seen out of anyone associated with the FBI. I refuse to name him out of fear he will be fired for such a sense of humor. Personality is not welcome in the FBI.

"Ok guys," said the judge, "May we continue?"

"Your honor," Gage's attorney began, "We'd like to exclude the phone call with Brayden Cooper. The call was made under circumstances that couldn't be called anything but entrapment. The call is largely irrelevant to this case, as it contains mostly ranting by Mr. Cooper and Mr. Tate didn't wish to carry on the conversation..."

"He did," the prosecutor interrupted, "carry on that conversation, though. Didn't he? I remember a conversation where both parties spoke."

"Ok, ok," the judge interjected, "Let's here the call."

They played the call on the loud speaker in the court. They began with the phone ringing so as not to miss a detail. During the time this recording played, I couldn't help but stare a hole through Gage. I wanted to see any type of reaction or remorse. Even a hint that he may wish he hadn't said something. But no, I wouldn't see any of those things. He put on the most serious poker face I have seen. He stared down as if to be listening most intently. It would seem as if he has never heard what was on this tape, even though it was him listening to himself.

When the tape finished, Gage's attorney spoke, "Your honor, a clear violation of Mr. Tate's rights should have this call thrown out. My client was unaware this call was being recorded from the beginning. No recording notified him that it would be and Mr. Cooper didn't tell him until his ridiculous taunts at the end of the call."

The prosecutor said, "The calls made from the jail are all recorded your honor. Mr. Tate was in the jail before this call. He in fact made phone calls from the jail. He should have knowledge, common knowledge, that the calls going out of this jail are recorded. While it wasn't said directly to him, we found it understood."

"I can hardly think of what must have been going through my client's head after being put in the jail back then," the defense attorney argued. "He was only there a few hours and made *one* phone call. I hardly think that qualifies as common knowledge."

"The phone call is shaky," said the judge. "I believe that Mr. Tate would have been distraught facing such serious charges in the jail. He spent a mere eighteen hours there and did only make one phone call. In addition, Mr. Tate was hardly expecting any call from Mr. Cooper. I can't say for sure common knowledge would apply here. Motion to suppress granted."

Motion to suppress granted. This meant the phone call I stressed over, agonized over, and made against my better judgment was pointless. No one would ever know about it. I turned and looked ahead of me where Agent Greene sat.

"What the hell?" I whispered loudly.

The Marshal told me to shut up. I was mad, really mad. I was hurt too, like I had been betrayed. It was like the prosecutor didn't even try. He all but admitted his involvement in this case and I couldn't even get a prosecutor to fight for it. All this happened to innocent children. All the guilt for even questioning my cooperation constantly weighed heavy on me. Like if I let up for a minute, more children could be hurt or killed. And this prosecutor has the audacity to come in here and fight like a ninety year old woman against a pit bull?

I was having a hard enough time staying in this. Staying away from my family for what they called the "greater good." And if the people who are paid to fight this battle can't care about it, how could I continue to sacrifice anymore?

The next topic at the suppression hearing would be Gage's computer. His laptop had been confiscated by the FBI during the search of his home at the time of his original arrest. They held it for only a short time. But what happened during that short time threatened the entire case.

Agent Greene had taken the computer and combed through the evidence. When they found images and videos that contained children as young as eight or ten performing sexual acts with Gage Tate, they immediately knew this would be a federal case. However, Agent Greene recognized one of the girls in one of the videos. It was a girl he knew was missing and had never been found from closer to his home base in Florida. He ordered all material that contained evidence of Gage Tate's direct involvement in producing his personal pictures and videos to be wiped clean off the drive and backed up to a drive in possession of the FBI. The computer was then ordered to be given back to Detective Hailey with the Lexington Police Department. The state of Kentucky could then only prosecute him for possession and distribution of child pornography.

This deception could cost the feds their case now. Evidence has a certain chain it must follow and certain procedures must be exact to have the evidence admissible in court. Needless to say, Agent Greene's method was completely outside those procedures.

"These videos and pictures," Gage's attorney began, "They came off the computer, the laptop, the one that the FBI confiscated at Mr. Tate's home the day he was arrested on state charges. The state of Kentucky never charged Mr. Tate with having sexual relations with a minor, only distributing the work of others. The reason is, Agent Greene of the FBI removed this evidence before handing it over to Kentucky detectives. This taints any evidence that may or may not have been removed. We ask it to all be thrown out. The computer, the hard drive, the pictures, the videos... all of it should go."

"Your honor," the prosecutor began, "We had to act quickly in this case. Many things didn't happen according to normal protocol. However, I assure you that a warrant was signed by a federal judge authorizing this action under the Patriot Act. We considered this a matter of national security. People's lives, children's lives were at risk."

"What threat could Gage Tate have to national security, sir?" asked Gage's attorney.

"Gage Tate has been labeled a domestic terrorist, which defined by federal law, is anyone who commits violent crimes against a group of people whom are otherwise defenseless. I personally consider children a group of people and rather defenseless. And if you don't consider raping and murdering them violent, I don't know what is."

"Objection, your honor! My client has been charged with no murder, nor has that issue come up."

"Sustained."

"Your honor," Gage's attorney began, "Since 9/11, the FBI has used the Patriot Act to do many things that are unjust. This is one of those things. If a crime was committed based on what was taken off that hard drive, it should have been first viewed by detectives in the state of Kentucky. Agent Greene obstructed justice by hiding this evidence."

"Make up your mind!" Screamed the prosecutor. "Either he didn't commit a crime and we made it up or he did and we hid the evidence. He can't have it both ways, your honor."

"I agree," said the judge. "I also think what Agent Greene did was wrong. That computer was not obtained legally and Agent Greene should be investigated for, and may well be guilty of, obstruction of justice in the state case against Mr. Tate. I am pained to feel this way. But the law is the law. I have no doubt Gage Tate had such videos on his computer. I have no reason to believe that the FBI has manufactured this evidence. But I also don't believe it was handled by the code of law.

Agent Greene, you acted hastily to avoid sharing information with the local police due to a lack of confidence in those detectives to maintain a level of professionalism required to proceed with this case. I don't believe it had anything to do with terrorism. As a result of your lack of faith in state government and your failure to communicate, an innocent man went to prison and Mr. Tate's rights have been violated."

"Your honor," said the prosecutor, "We would also like to argue inevitable discovery. This computer was in possession of law enforcement. The items on the computer would have been seen regardless."

"Regardless of the law, you mean? Whether or not they would have been found legally had you left them alone, they weren't. This is why the people we call terrorists stay a step ahead of us. If the federal and local governments can't trust each other, they won't ever be able to effectively work together. And then who wins?

I rule that the computer itself is out. However, I will allow you to prosecute Mr. Tate and any co-defendants that may be added using the information learned on the computer. You may not, however, charge Mr. Tate or any other co-defendants with charges relating to the specific contents of the computer."

What a blow. I was almost in shock. Could this get much worse? I didn't think so. Without that computer, how could they make any case stick? I wasn't a lawyer, however, and there were other ways to make this case. But at the time, I didn't see any of those ways. Turns out, Gage can still be prosecuted on the raping of the children, just not the possession of the videos depicting the rapes. Obviously, the rapes themselves were the crime most in need of prosecution. Still, at that very moment, I did not know this and I was sick.

"As to suppression, that is all from the defense, your honor."

"Same for us, your honor. However, we do have a motion to submit. We'd like to move to revoke Mr. Tate's bond and have him remanded to federal custody on the grounds that he has violated his bond by ordering threats toward Brayden Cooper."

"Your honor," Gage's attorney said, "None of these threats can be substantiated beyond speculation. None of them can be tied directly to my client nor did he make any threats himself."

"The threats were called into the FBI by a man we believe to be connected to Mr. Tate."

"My client has too been threatened, your honor. He is in danger just by association in this case. He has his own safety concerns and is not in any way involved with these threats."

"Unless you have something more..." the judge said to the prosecutor, "I can't see the level of proof here. Any threat Mr. Tate is receiving is not due to any "association" sir, he is the case. And might I remind you, if he had no involvement in this case, threats shouldn't be coming in. This case is sealed as are its proceedings. I will not revoke Mr. Tate's bond today, but please, Mr. Tate, give me the slightest reason and I will."

"Your honor," Gage's attorney said, "We would like to file a motion to give up the right to a jury trial and motion for a bench trial."

"Mr. Tate, do you understand what your attorney is asking for?"

"Yes," Gage said.

"Mr. Tate, do you understand that if you have a bench trial, and I find you guilty of these crimes, you do not have the right to appeal?"

"Yes," Gage said.

"Does the prosecution object?"

"No, your honor," said the prosecutor.

"Ok, well I see no reason why not. Motion for a bench trial is granted."

I would later find out there weren't but a couple of reasons why Gage's attorney would request a bench trial. Either the defense wanted to be positioned to bargain for a better plea, or the defense wants to go to trial and likes the chances with a judge more than with a jury.

A jury will often time convict on emotion. When they see pictures and videos that show Gage Tate having sex with a child, they would convict for that alone. The law aside, legalities aside, they would convict him just knowing what he has done. By going with a bench trial, you take that emotion out. A judge may sentence harsher on emotion, but will convict or acquit based on the law.

Feeling rather defeated, I was returned to LAC. I wondered how bad this was and what it all meant. My TV was there now and I wanted to just crawl in my bunk and watch TV. My mom had sent me a box of clothes. All we could have was sweat pants and shirts, t-shirts and underwear. But that was plenty good for me. It was nice to relax in something other than those stiff khakis and watch my own TV.

As a feeling of emptiness and aloneness took over, it was hard to imagine me getting out and being free while Gage could sit and rot in a jail. He was so cocky, and I couldn't imagine how a person could be, facing charges as serious as child murder. I was developing a twitch in my left eye that bothered me often. Several nervous ticks, what I liked to call my insanity, began to show their head. This was truly driving me crazy, in every sense of the word.

Chapter 17

The Promise Was A Lie, Wkcc, And The Sex Offenders.

Often times at LAC, inmates watch TV with other inmates. Sometimes it was because one of them didn't have a TV, but mostly it was for company. I remember the night before my transfer, sitting and watching the Discovery Channel. They were talking about a murder case, one of those reality crime shows. I had seen the previews and settled in just before it came on.

"Hey, are you going to watch that story tonight on Discovery?" asked Whitey, a nickname given to our laundry man. He was inmate serving a life sentence and he hates going outside, giving him quite a pasty look, hence the nickname Whitey.

"Yea, planned on it," I said.

"Cool, can I join you?"

"Sure," I said.

The story told of a man who was married to a woman for fifteen years and he suspected she was cheating on him. He came home at a couple random times trying to catch her to no success. But one day, he came home from work early and found another car in the driveway. He went in the house to find his wife in bed with another man. As you can imagine, he was quite outraged. Turns out, the guy was a co-worker of his who was familiar with his schedule and that's how they timed their rendezvous.

The man then took a shotgun from the closet and shot them both dead in the bed. He set the house on fire and walked outside to sit on the porch to have a cigarette. After his smoke, the house was beginning to smoke up heavily. He called 911 and told them he had just killed his wife and her lover. He told them to send the fire department too because the house was also burning down. He waited on the police and when they arrived, he gave a full confession. He never attempted to get away with it.

So, just another man mad at his spouse for cheating and he kills her. We've seen this story before. What made this one important to me is the man I called Whitey, the man sitting on the bed next to me, was the man this story was about. He was sentenced to life without parole. And he was serving his time at LAC, right next to me.

When the show ended, he said, "What do you think?"

"Well, I didn't know that," I said, really thinking I was at a loss for words.

"Do I scare you now?"

"No," I said. "Should I be scared?"

After a purposely timed pause, he said, "Nope. What do you think about that story?"

"That bitch shouldn't have cheated on you," I said, hoping to stay in his good graces.

After another pause, he said, "That bitch was my wife."

"Yea, sorry, I just meant she shouldn't have been cheating on you."

"She was a bitch. And now she's dead, right?" He said with a chuckle.

With a chuckle myself, I said, "Yea, guess she is."

"You laughing at my dead wife dude?"

"No, just, well you were laughing too."

"Ha ha, all you fish are the same. Never know what to think of me. I could kill you while you sleep tonight, but I like you."

"Well good, and I like you too, but if you try to kill me in my sleep, we might have a problem continuing down the friendly road. I didn't screw your wife. And don't act like that's not funny, cuz it ain't gonna work this time."

He laughed, thank God.

"Mr. Cooper, I need you to follow me," said a guard when walking by me for count.

"Ok... am I in trouble?" I asked.

"No, you are transferring."

I was excited. I was finally going to Blackburn and be closer to my family. I followed him down the aisle and into the office for the caseworker. He looked over his copy of the transfer order and gave me two large plastic bags.

"Put all your clothes in one bag, everything else in the other bag. Your TV you can just carry with the bags, you don't have to put that in a bag. Do you have any questions?"

"Nope, don't think so. I am ready to get back close to my family."

"That's great. Are you from Paducah?"

"No, I'm from Lexington. Blackburn is in Lexington."

"Right... but the transfer says WKCC, which is Western Kentucky Correctional Complex and that is in Fredonia, KY, which is close to Paducah."

"What? Are you sure? My classification worker said he got me approved to go to Blackburn."

"Sorry, must have been some mistake. But now you gotta go to WKCC."

"Is there someone I can talk to, like check this out so I can maybe wait to go to Blackburn? The caseworker said I got approval from Frankfort to go to Blackburn."

"No, sorry. We do transfers at night and there is no way out of it now. Once D.O.C. says transfer, you have to go. Maybe they can get you to Blackburn."

"So, the guy just lied to me about getting closer to home and instead, I'm going to go 200 miles farther away!?"

"I guess so, kid. Pack your stuff; you need to be done in twenty minutes."

I was totally dejected. I felt like a complete idiot. I had trusted Gage, and he betrayed me. I had trusted the police, and they lied about me. I had trusted my lawyer, and he failed me. I'm not sure what made me think these people were any different, and clearly, they were not different. It was becoming more and more transparent how incredibly screwed up this system is.

As I bagged up my stuff, another inmate approached me. He was a tall guy, about 6'1" with salt and pepper hair and several tattoos. He was thin and you could tell by his demeanor that he had been in prison for a while. He was calm and knew the steps. He knew what to expect and when to expect it, clearly an advantage in this system.

"You going to WKCC too?" he asked.

"Yea, I was supposed to go to Blackburn, but they lied about that I guess."

"Ha, yea, lying is something these guys are good at. I'm Junior," he said, offering a handshake.

"I'm Brayden, but everyone around here calls me Bobby."

"Yea heard about that. You are a dead ringer for Bobby Hill. Well listen Bobby Hill, we got a long drive together, just me and you it looks like, so get your shit together and let's go get some chow."

At least it appeared I would have an ally. I thought to myself, 'this will be different.' I decided to proceed more cautiously than ever in this 'friendship' after misguided trust had gotten me nowhere thus far. By this point, trust was something I had mostly lost, along with faith in mankind as a whole. I did finish packing my shit and I did go down to have chow with Junior. After about an hour of waiting, we were called to leave. They took us out and loaded us on a van. Ironically, we had to travel right through Lexington to get to Fredonia. I had never heard of that city, but we were in for almost six hours of travel, in cuffs and a black box.

"So what's your story?" I asked Junior, whose real name was Clifton Glass.

"Long roads of disappointments. I've been stupid in the past, mellowed out now. I was crazy back in the day. Be lucky you met me now, cuz back then I wasn't so kind to the fish."

"You don't seem crazy. I guess this isn't your first bit?"

"Nope. My first bit I was in on a low felony possession charge. Got five years in prison, served seven flat to get out because I caught a case inside."

"Damn! Went in with five and served seven? What happened?"

"I ran a store. This guy got some stuff from me and didn't pay me for it. I confronted him and he said he'd steal all my shit and I couldn't touch him cuz one of his brothers was a guard there. So, I waited till he went to sleep, I put my lock in a sock and beat him half to death. I got five more years for that, run consecutive. Seven years served out the ten years."

"Wow, that's insane."

"Yea, it was insane. Like I said I'm mellow now. Just couldn't shake my dope habit on the street. I ended up catching another thirteen years on a trafficking case."

"Whoa, they hand out a lot of time for drugs."

"Yea they do. Well look man; don't do anything stupid down here on the yard. This place is prison. Lee County is crack compared to Western. We can look out for each other."

I got the feeling what he meant to say was, 'hey fish, don't get me killed if we hang together.' Nonetheless, he seemed cool. I was going to miss my cubie Craig, but at least I have someone who knows what I came from and is experienced in the system to help me along the way. He said he most likely knew people here from the last incarceration. He also said his mystique and reputation had likely followed him. He knew it would be an interesting transition. Not that it was common practice, but if you are perfectly willing to double your sentence to nearly kill someone who owes you money, people tend to have a better payment percentage.

As we pulled into WKCC, it truly did look like a prison. It seemed like much tighter security on the grounds than at LAC. The warden didn't appear on the van to welcome us, instead, some snot nosed twenty year old guard told us we'd sit there and wait until *he* was ready to unshackle us and we'd like it. He wasn't sympathetic to our six hour van ride with no food, bathroom and a black box on our wrists.

After we did finally get off the bus, our shackles were removed. These guys were pushier than other guards and they didn't care about being friendly. They went through all of our belongings and most of it we were allowed to keep. They matched up the inmate ID numbers on our TVs to our inmate badges, to make sure we didn't steal a TV just before the transfer. I wondered if people actually tried such things, but then I remembered this is prison. After all our stuff was accounted for and verified to be ours, we were instructed to sit in a waiting area. After a few minutes, a Sergeant with a clipboard came in.

"Ok guys, we have a bit of a miscommunication. Apparently the numbers were off by one. We don't have room in the camp for you both. Cooper, you'll stay behind the fence until another opening comes up and then you'll be at the top of the list. Glass, you'll go on out."

"Sir," Junior interrupted, "Let me stay back here, send him out."

"Well isn't that just precious, why?"

"I've been in before; he's just a fish, not supposed to be behind the fence."

"Commendable for a crook, but no. Cooper stays, you go."

My gratefulness for Junior aside, I was fuming. I had been promised a transfer to Blackburn and instead been sent down further from home and *now* I have to go back behind the fence because of a paperwork screw up. This whole going to prison thing was not working out for me at all. And no one cared about that.

I was escorted behind that building where a narrow corridor led to a long row of dorms. I was told which dorm to look for and sent out on the yard, alone. I remember wondering what would happen if I got lost. The buildings seemed reasonably marked with big letters. After about ten minutes of searching, I found the dorm I was supposed to be in. I went in the front door and noticed a guard in the hallway.

"What the fuck are you doing here right now?" he screamed at me.

"I am supposed to be reporting to this dorm, sir," I said.

"During count? Who sent you over here?"

"I'm not sure, some guy in the office over there; do you want me to go back?"

"No, just give me your paperwork."

He swiftly examined all the chicken scratch and pushed me towards the correct door. I was told my bunk would be halfway down on the left side. On my way to my bunk, an inmate was walking very close behind me and started yelling "Boss! Boss!" and I turned and looked at him.

"What you looking at faggot?"

"I thought you might have been talking to me, since that was my head you were yelling at."

"Is your name Boss, mother fucker?"

Already irritated at my situation, I said, "No, *mother fucker*, that's not my name. But it was my head you spit on the back of. So seriously, back up."

"What fish? You wanna get stuck or something?"

I continued walking and ignored him. I felt mostly retarded, and a little amazed, that I had just said that to a random guy who pissed me off. My aggression had grown and I was at a boiling point. I wasn't scared, more like anxious. I felt like I had ten Red Bulls in me and about six shots of tequila. Pumped up, half crazy, and unpredictable. That basically described my mindset.

As I made my bed, I noticed a few guys staring at me. I didn't think much of it, but as I finished, I noticed mostly the whole dorm was staring at me. I climbed my rack and lay down with a book that I stole from LAC. Hey, I was freaking bored as hell and I was in the middle of a good book. What are they gonna do, arrest me?

The guy who slept on the bottom bunk under me stood up and said, "Hey fish. You better watch your back. I couldn't give a fuck what you said to that nigger, but he's got friends and he might stick you for real dude."

"If I was worried about it, I wouldn't have said it," I said casually.

He sat back down. If I had learned anything through my time, consistency was important. Perhaps I acted hastily and was unprepared to hold up this 'tough guy' image, but once it was started, backing off would be a deadly move. I had moved to the second choice of being left alone; make everyone think you are crazy. At this point, for the first time, I thought I could pull off crazy.

I didn't sleep well that night, but no one tried anything. I missed my TV, as they didn't give it to me yet. They had to process all my stuff and it could be two or three days before I got much else. The next morning, after I made my bed, I sat up reading my book. I noticed that the guys on the top bunks on the left and right of me were having a conversation over my bunk. From the bunk on the left, passed my bunk and to the bunk on the right was no more than twenty feet, so they weren't yelling. I could, however, hear their conversation.

"Yea I had this one boy, man he was so hot. I loved his little smooth hole... Mmhmm."

"Man, I preferred the girls; they liked to be more vocal. Boys try to be all tough, girls are more 'ahh I'm a victim' and that's what I like."

Overhearing this, I was getting heated. Not only because of the situation I found myself, but the horrific things they were discussing was beginning to push me over the edge. I jumped down from my bunk and stormed off. I headed straight to caseworkers office. As I approached the door, the lady out front told me I couldn't go in there without an appointment and I think the look on my face gave the impression I might hurt the nice little caseworker.

As I waltzed in, I said, "I'm not supposed to be behind the fence. I am sitting in my bunk and listening to two pedophiles describe how they raped children on the street. Now, here's what is going to happen. You are going to find a bed for me outside, at the camp, or I'm going to kill one of those guys. And I know right now, there are more pedophiles in there than there are normal people. They will likely gang up on me, and when they kill me, have fun explaining to my family's attorney and the FBI how you fucked up!"

"Hey buddy, you don't just come in here and make demands!"

"I will too. I demand I be taken out of level three housing and put in level two. I am classified level two. If I sleep here tonight, I will have attorneys and feds in Frankfort and I'll be helping choose the guy that will be replacing you. Get this right, or you will find out who calls the shots!"

I left as quickly as I had entered. I knew I would likely go to the hole for what I had done. But, even in retrospect, it would have been worth it to get away from those guys. I went back to my dorm and as I approached my bunk, I could hear them continuing their conversation. When I got to my bunk, I put the rest of my stuff back in the bag I had taken it out of. I tied up the bag and laid it on my bed. It got quiet around me and I turned to face the man on the top left bunk.

"You sick fucker," I said as I shoved him off the bunk and onto the floor on the opposite side. I then walked over to the other bunk on the right side and repeated the process.

By this time, the guy on the left had gotten up and headed toward me. I punched him in the face and he fell straight to the floor. Behind me I heard a thud. When I turned around, the man I had yelled at on my walk in had a broken wooden handle from what used to be a broom and had hit the guy over the head. He walked up to me and stood toe to toe. After a second of silence, he moved to the other guy and whacked him in the face too. I was completely confused.

Guards quickly rushed in and told everyone to get down. As he handcuffed us all, he asked what was going on. The man with the broom handle answered.

"These pedo freaks shoved dude here out of the bed. I came over and whacked 'em with a broom stick."

He totally lied and covered for me. After what I had said to him on the way in the door, I couldn't imagine why he had done this, unless he just hated those guys already. To this day, I don't know his name or why he did what he did. On the way out of the dorm, in cuffs and still under investigation for the fight, I saw the caseworker.

"I guess you *don't* play well with others," he said.

"He didn't do it," the guard said. "That guy did it. Bloodied those guys up with a broom stick."

"Ok, Mr. Cooper. I have a bed for you outside. Take his cuffs off and let him go pack. Do it now, Mr. Cooper."

That caseworker seriously thought I had orchestrated that whole thing. I have no idea how he thought I could do that, but he seemed to believe it. Either way, no matter what, in the end, I got my outside placement at the camp. I was actually looking forward to meeting up with Junior again. And, I was happy with the new 'crazy' persona. To me, it felt more natural at this point than being the guy everyone liked.

I had truly begun to be this unstable guy who people looked at funny. My friends, at this point, would not have recognized me. While I looked the same, I was a different person. This sort of chain of events changes a person and I knew that. But this was first time I could look in the mirror and say, 'hey, I'm really a different person.' I wasn't afraid to push to the edges, play the kind of goofy, kind of psycho guy because that is exactly what I felt like all the time. Twenty four hours a day I was seconds from tears, laughter or insanity, all at the same time. And my horrid ordeal was only just now getting revved up...

Chapter 18

The FBI, Secret Service And CIA, Oh My, A Task Force!

"Cooper, you are needed at the front gate," I was told by a guard.

I was just getting used to the camp portion of WKCC. So far it was ok, but the people were a bit crazy. Good thing I was too! The front gate was a good distance from the camp, almost a mile, and you walked up there alongside the fence and unaccompanied by anyone. I wasn't sure what they wanted but I was pretty sure I wasn't in trouble. I was abnormally relaxed about it. I tended to generally have a jumpy attitude about everything, but anymore it seemed more natural for me. Noticing myself saying certain things or doing certain things, I sometimes caught myself wondering if I *was* truly going nuts. On my mental checklist of things to do later in life, get a therapist had been added.

"I was called to the front gate," I said to the gate guard.

"I need your name and institution number please, and I also need to see your ID."

I showed her my institution ID, which had all the information she had asked for, including a picture. I didn't say anything to her, believing she could read the info she wanted from me off the ID badge.

"Sir! I need your name, your institution number, give it to me!"

"It's on the badge, lady, damn. Brayden, B R A Y D E N, Cooper, C O O P E R, number is 201220."

"Listen ass hole, I don't need your attitude. Go through those doors behind me and ask the receptionist for Stacy. And lose the fucking attitude!"

Except for losing the attitude, which by this point I felt truly righteous in the development of that attitude, I did as I was told. I went a few doors down and noticed a small name tag outside a door that read "Stacy" on one line and underneath read "Sex Offender Registration." This is when my heart skipped a beat. I tapped on the door and she motioned me in.

"Mr. Cooper?" she asked.

"Yes."

"I need to talk to you about your upcoming parole hearing. We have to get a few things ready, just in case you make parole so we can get you out of here as soon as possible."

"Soon is good, but what do I need to do with sex offender registration? I don't have to register as a sex offender."

"Yes you do," she said.

"*No*, I don't," I said.

"Look, there is no reason to battle with this. I have the order right here and I have reviewed your charges, they do require registration."

"Listen lady, you don't understand. I was convicted just before those laws changed. I talked to my lawyer about this at the time. The judge never said anything about registration. This is a mistake."

"Well you gotta take that up with Frankfort. In the meantime, we have to do this. If it is a mistake, we just wasted a little time here, no harm. If it isn't a mistake, and we don't do it, you will be delayed 2 – 3 months getting out."

"Ok, whatever you say, but I will contact Frankfort today."

"That's fine; I can give you the office to contact there, if you like. Now, I have a few questions for you. I just need you to answer them as honestly as possible, ok?"

"Ok."

"How long had you been looking at child pornography before your arrest?"

"I never looked at it. Not before my arrest or ever. I'm not guilty."

"Right... Ok, so are you attracted to boys or girls under the age of 18? Do they make you excited?"

"No lady, I told you, I'm not guilty and I don't have any attraction to that stuff."

"I can document that in your report, but I can tell you, it won't help you at the parole board and it won't help your sex offender level if you get out. Are you sure you want me to do that?"

"I'm sorry, I misunderstood. I thought you said for me to be honest with you."

"I did, and I do want you to be honest. Why did you take a plea deal if you weren't guilty?"

"I was pressured. If I went to trial, my misdemeanors in this case would have turned into felonies because the law was changing right then. I could have faced 60 years in prison. My lawyer was an incompetent douche bag and I wasn't given any other options. I didn't *choose* to take a deal, I wasn't given an alternative. It was 'take a deal or do 60 years' and I took the deal. Now if that's all you want to ask me about, you are going to get nowhere."

"How did they find child porn on your computer and you didn't put it there?"

"My codefendant, Gage Tate, he put it there. It was all a setup. I was his scapegoat to get probation in the case because he knew I was already on probation."

"That's a convenient excuse, can you prove this?"

"Well I couldn't prove it in time to matter. And beyond that, I am not at liberty to discuss it per federal gag order."

"Ha ha, yea, you have a lot of convenient answers, Mr. Cooper."

"And like most everyone else in the system," I began sarcastically, "you are an incompetent bitch. Anymore questions?"

"You have a smart mouth. Open it up so I can get a DNA swab."

She took a cotton swab and ran in it on the lining of my cheeks and then placed it in a bag. She then took a picture of me and took another set of fingerprints. She put everything into a file folder with my name on it. Then she sent me back to my housing unit.

I left her office so mad I couldn't see straight. I couldn't wait to call my mom and get her to call Frankfort to straighten this out. I just knew this was all one big mistake. I passed the receptionist and went back out to the guard at the front gate. I tapped on the cage and told her I was all done.

"I wish. I'd like to send you on back, but I can't. You have some people here to see you. You need to go through the chow hall and look for the building with S.H.U. on the outside and see the guard just inside the door. He is expecting you and will direct you from there."

S.H.U., often pronounced 'shoe' was also known as segregation or the hole, and with an attitude I said, "Damn, you're sending me to the hole over that?"

"If I could I would, ass hole. No, I said some people are here to see you and they are in that building. That's also where they hold attorney visits."

Attorney visit? I knew this wasn't an attorney visit. The F.B.I. had returned, I thought, surely that must be the people here to see me. As I was told, I went through the chow hall and over to the segregation unit. I approached the guard inside and told him who I was.

"Damn, from the camp that was really fast," he said.

"Well you are assuming I wasn't already here. I had something I was taking care of in the administrative offices. When I was done, they told me to come over here. What's going on?"

"You have some federal agents waiting on you in the next room. They seem to be pretty serious, hope you aren't in trouble with them."

"No, helping them, not in trouble with them."

"That's good, just down the hall and the door marked "Special Visit" is the one you want. Just go on in, they are expecting you."

As I entered the room, there were two men sitting at the table and two men standing, one in each corner facing me. The man standing on the left side wore a polo shirt with the U.S. Marshal's logo, clearly identifying him. The other men wore suits. None of the men looked familiar, Agent Greene was not there.

"Mr. Cooper," the man sitting on the left at the table said, as he stood, "I am Special Agent Earl Brown with the F.B.I. You have been working with Agent Greene, is that correct?"

"Yes. What is it with the feds having colors for last names?"

"Agent Greene is no longer assigned to this case. A task force has now been formed to complete this investigation and we are the task force. We are here to do some follow up."

I noticed he didn't answer my question.

"So who are these other guys?"

He pointed to the man on the right side of the room standing in the corner and said, "He is our Secret Service consultant on this case."

"Secret Service?" I asked. "Like protecting the President type of Secret Service?"

"That's not all they do. They assist and consult in terrorism cases. The man on this side is with the U.S. Marshal's office, as you may have guessed by the shirt. And the man next to me here is our consultant from the C.I.A."

"Wow, is there something I've missed here? All I ever knew

was F.B.I. being involved; did something happen to need a step up in security?"

"I'm not at liberty to discuss our process. You just need to know this is serious. Listen, there are sixteen unsolved homicides of minors associated to or related to this case. There is an investigation of child trafficking that spans 22 states and at least 7 countries and involves thousands of children. Mr. Tate's involvement with this branch may help lead us to the core. The two countries we are most focused on in this case are both countries Tate has visited in the past and had planned to return and those are the Czech Republic and Thailand. We have information that suggests the ring is being run on an international level by a Thai and Chinese organization led by Pham Thi Thoa.

Pham Thi Thoa was arrested last year on suspicion of leading a child trafficking ring, but later released because the Chinese government was unable to make a case. Since then, we believe he has expanded his market into the Czech Republic. There have been several murders that were thought to be gang murders that the C.I.A. now believes was related to territory battles between Thoa and Czech Republic child traffickers.

Pham Thi Thoa connects with a contact in southeast Florida to make contact with U.S. citizens interested in children for adoption, sex or whatever. So, how does all this bring us back to Gage Tate? Well the man in Florida who is believed to be leading the contact in the trade has a right hand man, believed to be his closest ally, named Jason Hammond. Mr. Hammond does a bit of traveling, including to Kentucky. Based on travel records and his appearance, we believe Mr. Hammonds was the camera man in the video you watched of Mr. Tate and Lindsey.

We have found Lindsey's body and we have a DNA sample from a strand of hair. We believe we can match that DNA to Jason Hammond. He has already been arrested and is being held without charges as a terror suspect. After we confirm his DNA, we will charge him with murder. Lindsey's bodily evidence points to arsenic poisoning as a cause of death, which would explain what was put into her mouth before she died. We believe Mr.

Hammonds gave Lindsey a potent dose of LSD laced with a ton of arsenic. It would have killed her almost immediately.

Her body was stuffed in the duffle bag and dumped in the Ohio River. It was recovered two weeks ago. I notice you are breathing a little heavy. I am throwing a lot of information at you, and I know it is tough, are you ok?"

"I just... I just need a minute," I said.

I had to catch my breath and let sink in what was being said to me. Digesting this information was difficult. I knew, and had known for a couple months now, that this situation was serious and Gage was in a lot of trouble. It was now, however, that the true realization of what was going on had sunk in. I felt sick all over again.

"What does all this mean for me?" I asked.

"Well it means we are digging deep in this investigation and we need your help still. We have some items in pictures that we want you to look at and see if they belonged to Tate or if you have ever seen them before."

"How can these people do this? I don't understand how this is a big business. How can people sleep at night? I can't sleep at night just knowing what they have done and seeing the leftovers. I just don't get it at all!"

"It's hard to process, I know. I have been doing this for ten years and I don't get it either. I have talked with Gage and he says he was forced into it. I don't buy that, based on what we know. But maybe sometimes people are forced into it. Most people, however, pay for it. For as little as $600, you can purchase a non-virgin girl, an average age of 7, a median age of 9, and keep her in your hotel for up to three days to do whatever you wish. Virgins go for around $1,500 and boys are a bit more expensive, upwards of $2 – 5,000. Americans go overseas for 'vacation' and spend $50,000 in two or three weeks on these children. That's how it is so big."

"But in this country, it is big here too; I just think we should be hearing more about it on the news or something."

"American children are greatly desired. I've seen cases where

American boys, virgins as young as 9 have been sold for as much as $30,000 an hour. And they pay for it, no problem."

"So they take them overseas, that's why we don't hear about it here?"

"Well they are kidnapped from this country very often. And sometimes parents sell them into the trade for a hefty sum, I have seen that too. An average of 2,000 children enters the child trafficking or child prostitution business every year in Kentucky and Ohio alone. This is a big deal, Brayden."

"So what do you have that you think I can help with?"

"Ok, look, here's the deal. We are having a hard time building a murder case against Tate. We don't have enough evidence to take to trial. We know he knew some of these children, he raped them and made videos of them, but we can't prove he killed them. In fact, we believe Mr. Hammond is the hit man. Tate's attorney is saying they will turn over the entire operation to us. They will give us everything on a silver platter. Times, dates, addresses, names, phone numbers, everything. But the deal is, he wants immunity."

"Don't tell me you are considering this!"

"We consider everything that comes our way. But we are not going to let him go free with no punishment. Don't worry about that. That's why we need help proving our case so we don't have to. Take a look at this photo. There are several things in here that we are trying to identify to whom they belonged."

Tears came to my eyes almost immediately. The picture showed two small girls, no older than six or eight. They were crouched down together, holding hands, with a look of devilish fear. They were locked in cat carrier being used as a cage to hold them. They barely fit inside. They were dirty and naked. The picture, I was told, was found on Gage's external hard drive removed from his house. The feds believed that hard drive belonged to Jason Hammond.

The cage had newspaper on the bottom. You could make out the "Lex" in Lexington Herald Leader. It was the front page of a paper, though you couldn't tell the date. A red bandana was tied being used as a lock for the door. Nothing, however, looked familiar.

"I'm sorry," I said, "nothing looks familiar to me."

"Ok, look at this one. We found this knife inside a panel of Jason Hammond's car. There are traces of blood on the blade but it had been mostly cleaned."

I looked very close and was sure I recognized this knife. It was a silver oversized pocket knife with a black dragon on it, very much like one Gage carried with him almost always.

"Yes, this is Gage's. I'm almost positive. He carried this with him everywhere he went. I've seen it dozens of times, I've held it myself. That dragon is unique; I don't think it is some kind of standard order knife."

"No it isn't, it was special ordered. Very good. We are going to get that from evidence and get it to you so you can see it up close. If we had it in person, do you think you could identify it more certainly?"

"I will sure try," I said.

Agent Brown showed me several more pictures that contained nothing I recognized. I always felt like I should help more or should know more. I felt a personal responsibility to help get him convicted, not just for what he had done to me, but for what he had done these poor children. It was unimaginable that this was possible before now.

Chapter 19

Physically and Emotionally Broken.

Most of the people that are housed at WKCC, in the camp, work for the farm that is in on site. They grow many crops, raise animals for milk, eggs and slaughter and then sell it in the community. The proceeds went to pay for inmate salaries, usually about $1 a day and to help with housing costs. Most prisons in Kentucky are required to develop some sort of inmate activity that helps generate money for the institution because the state doesn't have the money to completely support it.

I got really lucky to find a good job, not on the farm. I found an opening shortly after my arrival at the warehouse by the front gate. The warehouse was the central location for everything coming in and going out of the prison, except for inmate letters. However, inmate boxes did come through the warehouse, as well as officer uniforms, institution supplies and food and anything else ordered by the institution. There was some manual labor in unloading trucks, stocking freezers and passing out supplies to the entire prison grounds. There was also a great deal of paperwork that had to be done to keep inventory straight and to make sure no one was stealing anything.

Lucky for me, and largely because I was one of a few who actually had a brain among the housed inmates, I got to do paperwork. The job was open because of inmates stealing items from the warehouse, imagine that. The turnover was high at the warehouse because inmates didn't like to do the paperwork and often messed it up because it could get a bit complicated. Most of these guys had never done this type of work before now and had no interest in starting. This led to conflicts with the two ladies who ran the warehouse and was also the reason they interviewed for these positions. When I interviewed, they loved me.

There was one more position that was open at the warehouse, too. Normally, a fully staffed warehouse was three men. When I arrived, there was only one because the other two had been fired. I talked to Mrs. Hurley, the head of the warehouse, and asked her about a friend of mine, Clifton Glass, AKA Junior working there too. She agreed to talk to him. He had been working on the farm and absolutely hated it. When I told him of the opening, he was happy.

After about three weeks working with the three of us, the other inmate was transferred to a halfway house. Junior and I convinced the ladies to not hire anyone else. We wanted to have it for ourselves to help keep us busy. We didn't mind working a little harder to get some alone time where it was quiet and we didn't despise the person we were with. And we made a great team. I did all the paperwork, which Junior hated doing, and he led the manual labor.

We both unloaded the trucks and loaded up freezers with the food because this needed to be done quickly. The dock at the warehouse had a very steep grade for the truck to back down and the bumpers on the end of the dock prevented the truck from resting flush against it. The ramp, that came out of the truck and over to the dock, acted like a bridge. Most of the pallets we moved with the pallet jack weighed over 600 pounds and were stacked a couple of feet higher than my head. When the pallet jack was in place and locked, we'd lift up the pallet. Then we had to unlock the pallet and back down the steep grade, all the time a 600 pound pallet chasing us. As risky as it sounds, we usually didn't have problems with it.

"One left," I said to Junior.

"All yours," he said. We usually took turns getting the pallets off the truck because they were so heavy and hard to deal with.

"I can't get the lock to come unstuck. It's like it got jammed. It usually pulls up real easy and now it's stuck."

"Try to kick it up; I've had to do that before."

I did kick it up and knew immediately that I would regret it. I was on one foot and off balance as soon as the pallet jack began moving towards me. I quickly spun around and got a firm grip on the handles and tried to stop it, but by this time it had too much speed built up. It completely shoved me backwards and I moonwalked as fast as I could.

"Right! Right! Go right!" Junior screamed because I wasn't going to hit the ramp.

And I didn't hit the ramp evenly. I heard Junior yell at the ladies to get out of the way because he knew the pallet jack was going to fly off the truck in their direction. My right foot hit the ramp but my left foot went straight down in the hole between the truck and the dock. My right side quickly followed but my left arm got stuck on the dock. When I began to fall, I jerked on the pallet jack handles and it veered closer to me. The front wheels ran straight over my exposed left shoulder and you could hear the popping sound clearly. The ladies thought it hit my head and it only actually missed by a couple of inches.

I remember them screaming for someone to call the warden and medical. The warehouse dock was directly across the street from the front gate guard. Junior ran over there to tell them what happened. Within a minute or two, a deputy warden and two nurses ran over.

"Are you ok?" asked the deputy warden.

"I think so," I said. "I'm just stuck here, my shoulder is messed up pretty bad, and it hurts."

The nurse told the warden that it was broken and they shuffled to get something they could put under my legs for me to stand on. After about twenty minutes, they finally braced me well enough to move the truck out and get me on a stretcher. I was put on an ambulance and taken to Eddyville where they have a Department of Corrections hospital inside the Kentucky State Penitentiary. It is a fully staffed hospital and looks very similar to a small version of a real hospital. It is necessary because this is where death row inmates and violent criminals are held. It is a maximum security prison and no one gets transferred to outside facilities for any reason.

The results of an MRI proved what everyone had expected and a bit more. I had three broken ribs and a broken shoulder. The doctor told me the shoulder was a clean break and should heal in 4 - 6 weeks. They put a cast on me and sent me back to WKCC. When I arrived back, medical looked at my paperwork and sighed.

"Do you want your meds?" the nurse asked me.

"Uh, yea, I guess so."

"Thing is, they prescribed Percocet for you and I can't let you take that at the camp. We can transfer you behind the fence and give it to you or you can take some over the counter meds."

"What can you give me?"

"Ibuprofen, and a lot of it, but that's all. It is nothing compared to Percocet. Can you handle that?"

"If I can't, can I change my mind later?"

"Yes, that's fine. We will try the ibuprofen."

Back in my dorm, Junior was waiting to razz me for getting beat up by a pallet of inanimate objects. But he was also genuinely concerned. I was out of work for about a week and then I went back. The ibuprofen was enough to kill most of the pain and I found that the broken ribs were by far more uncomfortable than the shoulder.

After two days back at work, the feds returned. Agent Brown was back again, only without his entourage in toe. A look of concern came over him as soon as I entered the room.

"Are you ok? What happened to you?"

"I got ran over by a pallet jack."

"A pallet jack? Do I want to know how that happened?"

"No, and I don't care to share. But I'm fine, thanks."

"Glad you are ok. I brought the knife," he said, as he pulled out a zip lock bag with the knife in it. "Is this the knife that you think belonged to Mr. Tate?"

I carefully examined the knife and was certain it was Gage's. Gage had larger hands than I did and he carried this knife often. He also opened and closed it while relaxing and his thumb had worn a spot on the side of the knife. I remember having held my hand to that spot in the past and laughing about the difference in where my thumb was and his wear and tear appeared. It was just like I had remembered.

"Yes, that is Gage's knife."

"And you can testify against him to that effect?"

"Absolutely, I'm positive." I said and proceeded to explain my reasons for positivity. "So, what are you trying to prove with this knife?"

"Well we are trying to connect Tate to a homicide. We have found another body of an eight year old girl. Her blood is on this knife. And now we know for sure it is Tate's knife. If he and the knife were relatively inseparable, as you say, then that's a lot right there in connecting the two."

"You better not let him get away with this. I swear, he better go to prison."

"He will," Agent Brown assured me, "And by the way, we got that whole registering as a sex offender thing cleared up for you. I know your mom has called about it a few times, just wanted to let you know it is not a problem if you can make parole."

"Great. Speaking of parole, this is coming up pretty soon. Any chance I can get you to write a letter to the Board for me?"

"I'll see what I can do. We caught Tate buying marijuana on surveillance last night. He is one brazen guy."

"Wow, did you arrest him?"

"No, we don't care about a misdemeanor weed conviction; we have bigger things in mind. He just isn't leading us to anyone. He has gotten a bit cocky about things. In fact, his lawyer said if we don't take the immunity deal, he will go to trial for sure. He swears he was forced into this and that they can prove that."

"That has to be a crock of shit."

"Yes, we think it is. He didn't have to get on your computer and do anything, he didn't have to trade stash with others online when he was in his room by himself. None of that fits with him being *forced*."

"So just to make sure, you aren't going to give him immunity are you?"

"Not a chance. We will go to trial first. You need to be concerned with getting healthy and getting your head straight for the Parole Board. His evidentiary hearing is the first week of February, and we are going to need you to testify regardless of how your parole hearing goes. I hope you can get out, but if you can't, this will still continue. I want you, and your family, to prepare for that possibility."

"We *can't*. I tell my mom that every time I talk to her. I tell her that I may not make parole, that I probably won't make it. I tell her not to get her hopes up. I know logically it is unlikely I will make it the first time. I can tell that to everyone around me and I can tell you I know that to be true. That doesn't mean I'm ready to hear them tell me I have to stay in any longer."

"I get that. Just try to keep your head focused on the bigger picture here. That's all I ask"

"What is the bigger picture again?" I asked.

"You know what it is. Children out there are being tortured and killed. Stopping that, in the long run, is more important than anything else. I know that you know that."

"I know that you are paid to know that is the most important thing. I know I have nightmares every night and cry almost every day because of things I know and have seen in relation to this case. I know that sometimes I feel like this is never going to end. It might sound selfish of me, but I can't help but want my going home to be the most important thing to me. I don't want anything bad to happen to any children. But at the same time, I want to go home so bad that sometimes that overshadows my desire to care about anything or anyone else. That sounds horrible, doesn't it?"

"It sounds selfish. I know this is hard. But overall, you don't have it that bad. You aren't going to have to deal with this in any time but a temporary inconvenience compared to children who lost their innocence and their lives. As hard as it may be, Brayden, don't look beyond our objectives. That is insulting to me, to this investigation and to all the victimized children."

"You know," I began, "I don't think I feel anymore. I don't how to feel 'bad.' I am numb on the inside. I do not remember what empathy feels like. Every time I feel 'bad' about something, some horrible bit of information gets shoved into my head. Once you hit rock bottom, you can't go down any more. I am at rock bottom. I am sorry for those kids, but at this point, I have to be honest with you, I'm in survival mode. And fuck you if that's not ok. I've been slammed with guilt trips from day one. If you want my help, don't you ever do it again."

I was angry and hurt, though at the time I was having a hard time distinguishing between the two. I stood and left the room, telling the guard I was ready to return to my unit. Agent Brown didn't say anything as I left.

Thanksgiving had just passed two weeks before and Christmas was on the way. I didn't feel the Christmas spirit. It was the first Christmas I had ever spent away from my family. My family was sad and I felt completely alone. I wasn't sure how to cope with all I had bottled up and crammed into tiny boxes labeled 'for therapy' and stuffed away in the back of my head.

You can't imagine how alone you can feel unless you have felt it. I don't mean alone like at night when you wish someone was with you to keep you company or to cuddle with in bed. I felt like I was completely cut off from the entire world. I was hundreds of miles from home, away from my family all because of lies told by my ex-best friend who is at his home enjoying Christmas with his family. On Christmas Day, I barely convinced myself that getting out of my bunk was worth it. I decided later that the phone calls made to family that day made it worth it.

Chapter 20

THE PAROLE BOARD: JANUARY 18, 2007.

The day began much like any other day. The sun came up, people grumbled around to get ready for work. Guards yelled for count and everyone was there as normal. I was not looking forward to my meeting with the Board but I was hopeful. The likelihood of me getting to go home was slim, but given the opportunity to argue the point to help my chances, I was as optimistic as humanly possible. I got dressed up in my nicest set of khaki pants and long sleeve shirt combination and headed for the guard station. In reality, I looked the same today as I did every day, but today I felt sharp. I was alert and aware, ready to put my best foot forward and valiantly argue my case before the Board members.

I had never done this before, so I wasn't sure of the process. Everyone was a bit intrigued by my case in the offices because the Board had asked to interview me on Class D charges. In years of service with DOC, none of these caseworkers, wardens or guards had ever seen the Parole Board ask to see a Class D offender that was scheduled to be file reviewed. Normally, Class D non-violent offenders, such as myself, were reviewed by a group of Parole Board members via a meeting where they looked over my file in detail and then took a vote. The fact that they didn't want to do that with me had my stomach churning and flopping around like

Jell-O in an earthquake. I wasn't sure why they wanted to see me, but I took it for the only thing I could process at the time; a chance to be heard.

All those meeting the Board were sat in a hallway outside the room where the hearings were conducted. We were told that inside the room, a Board member would be sitting across the table and another member would be on the monitor, joining the hearing remotely from Frankfort. Also in the room would be a Parole Officer assigned to our institution for the purposes of the Board meetings. No one from the institution was allowed to attend the meeting, but just in case I went crazy and began to get physical, there were two guards just outside and the hearing was taped.

We were told that the Board would ask us a few questions to verify our identity and then would read our charges in a list. After that, they would ask us more questions before giving us a chance to speak openly to the board members. Once the hearing was finished, we would be asked to step out for a few minutes while the Board made its decision. This seemed like a simple process. I felt like I had an advantage because I was well spoken, educated and I had a young face. The young face, hopefully, would send the message that I was just a young guy that got caught up in a bad situation and now that it's over, they can let me go home. My family and some friends wrote letters for me to the Board asking them to release me.

As my turn came to enter the room, my legs were wobbly like noodles. I baby stepped to the door and entered the room. A heavyset black man sat across the room and a much younger white woman was on the camera. I sat down and was told that the man in the room would be asking all the questions. After the door was closed, the Parole Officer asked me if I was ready to begin. When I said I was, the Board member across the table began.

"State your name please," he said.

"Brayden Cooper."

"Inmate number."

"201220."

"Are you of sound mind and free of any drugs or alcohol at this hearing today, Mr. Cooper?"

"Yes sir," I said.

"You are here facing the Parole Board for the first time. You are serving two five year sentences, run concurrently. Count one was arson in the 3rd degree. Do you accept responsibility for this crime, Mr. Cooper?"

"Yes sir."

"Why would I have reason to believe that you will not commit this crime again?"

"I had a bad time in my life then, and one mistake led to this charge. I assure you, I am no longer a threat to anyone and will not be back in jail, ever."

"Your other charges all stem from a second case involving child pornography. According to the plea agreement, there was a confession in the case. Is that correct?"

"No," I said, "that's not correct. I never confessed to anyone. I didn't know I had child pornography on my computer."

"But you did plead guilty to the crime?"

"Yes sir, but..."

"And you were found guilty thereafter by a judge, correct?"

"Yes, sir, but..."

"The police report says you told a detective that you gave child pornography images to your co-defendant. Is that correct?"

"No sir, I never said that. I..."

Again he interrupted, "Were you forced into taking a plea deal or were you under the influence of drugs or alcohol?"

"I was forced, by my attorney. He told me I had no other options. He said he wouldn't go to trial."

"But he didn't really force you, did he? No one held a gun to your head, Mr. Cooper. You need to tell the truth here, sir."

"I'm telling you the truth. I didn't download any child porn.

Gage Tate downloaded child porn on my computer. He is the one who told the police where to find it and when they did, they didn't believe me and then lied in their reports to have me charged."

"So," he continued, "The entire system was one big conspiracy to put you in jail?"

"I believe the Commonwealth's Attorney wanted to see to it that I went to jail. We didn't get along."

"I don't think we are being clear here, Mr. Cooper. If you can't take responsibility for your crime, I can't let you go home. If you are attracted to children, I am not going to let you go so you can rape some child and them come back to me wondering why I let you out."

"Is that all you care about? What people will think of *you* letting me out? What about the poor child? I would never hurt a child and everyone that *knows* me knows that."

"I know you, sir, and I don't know that. Why does the Commonwealth's Attorney in Lexington dislike you so much? He wrote us a letter opposing your release."

"I used to work in his office as a contractor. When I was arrested on the arson charge, I was still working in his office. I got probation on that charge and he wanted me to go to prison. I think this was his chance to send me in and keep me here."

"I think he just wants to keep a pedophile off the streets. That's what I think. We are going to deny you parole today. You will be deferred for 12 months, in which time I suggest you think long and hard about your responsibility in this case. Good day, Mr. Cooper."

It wasn't a good day. Not at all. As prepared as I was for this result, I truly wasn't prepared at all. I wanted to go home so bad and it was clear at that moment I had let myself get worked up with hope. I immediately regretted that. Hope did not exist, I thought, not anymore and not in this place. I hated to harvest such complete negativity, but our system is an awfully negative place. I decided that day to do whatever I could to change the system. I vowed to at least fight the system, considering the smallest change to be a bonus.

As I returned to the dorm, I was taking deep breaths trying to stop myself from shaking. I checked back in at the guard station and re-entered my dorm room. Junior, I noticed, was packing his belongings into a plastic bag. I went over to see him.

"What's going on?" I asked.

"They are sending me to a halfway house. I'm going to Louisville. Parole didn't go well?"

"No. You are my only friend here. And I didn't make parole. Yup, this day sucks."

"You'll be fine man. As soon as they process your deferment they will shoot you out to a halfway house too. I mean, if you want, I'll go stab one of these mother fuckers in here and stay. I don't care man, you're my boy."

"Well it's the thought that counts, I guess," I said with a chuckle.

"I'll do it, you know I'm crazy."

"Oh I know you would do it, which is why you should go and enjoy the halfway house. You've earned that, at least. Maybe I'll see you there sometime."

"Yea, you just might."

That was the last time I would speak to him before he left. He was my buddy. He hung out a lot and we worked together. It was an oddity for prisoners to work and live as close together as we did and not have issues. But Junior and I never had issues.

I couldn't wait to get out of WKCC. It was like a big jungle gym with a bunch of crazy people running the show. I was living in an insane asylum, a rehab center, the middle of Drug Town, USA, and surrounded by a bunch of control freaks that couldn't cut it as real cops. While most of the guards were decent to you if you are decent to them, some are in a constant state of ass hole because they couldn't be the mall cop they always wanted.

In less than two weeks, the feds came back. Joy, I should have added arrogant ass holes who think they know everything to the list...

Chapter 21

Cross Me and Lie, TESTIFY!

"Ok, Brayden. We are prepared to transport you to court. We will be here to get you on Thursday. The U.S. District Attorney will be here tomorrow to discuss your testimony and everything you need to know. Does that sound ok?" asked Agent Brown.

"Do you know what Thursday is?"

"February 1st?"

"Well very good smart ass. No, I was referring to the two week anniversary of my 12 month deferment from the parole board that you never wrote a letter to and you didn't even ask me about. I know your case is important, but would it be so hard to ask if I was ok?"

"It doesn't matter if you are ok. I can see you are still here, still alive and breathing, and that's more than the victims in this case. You are going to testify even if you are a bit heartbroken."

"Heartbroken? My high school girlfriend didn't dump me. I was told by a group of people who thought I was the lowest form of scum that I couldn't go home for at least another year."

"Well you're gay, so the whole girlfriend thing wouldn't happen and besides, you knew you were unlikely to make parole."

"You are a pretentious bastard. You are no better than me. Just because you wear a suit and talk down to me, at the end of the day, it is I whom you ask for help. Please don't you dare think you have ever won a battle over me or that you've convinced me to do anything. I assure you, Agent Brown, that I wouldn't piss on your burning corpse. If this case wasn't so much more important than you, I'd flush it down the toilet like the vomit I flush after having to spend time in the same room as you. When that attorney is ready, tell him or her that you don't wish to come. Goodbye."

I turned and left the room. As I exited, I heard him say my name, but I didn't respond. I hoped that he wouldn't tell the guards to stop me. At this point, I had decided that I loathed every inch of that man. It truly made me sick to my stomach that he cared so little for the collateral damage that this case created.

I tried to understand the process a person investigating such crimes must go through. Desensitization and a healthy distance from all emotional feeling must be part of it. I wondered if all people that hunt child molesters for a living become so dissocialized that they appear cold and callous to the average person. I knew by my line of thinking that I myself was becoming more desensitized to my surroundings. I cared less and less what people thought of me and my self-esteem was fading, fast.

The next day, as promised, the D.A. arrived to discuss my testimony. At my suggestion, or so I like to think, Agent Brown was not present.

"Mr. Cooper, it is nice to meet you," he said as he offered a handshake. He mentioned his name, but I do not recall what it was. "I want to talk about this knife, is that ok?"

"Yes," I said.

"I understand you are pretty sure this knife belonged to Gage, is that correct?"

"Yes. It did at one point belong to him."

"You say at one point, did at one point it not belong to him anymore?"

"Not to my knowledge. As far as I knew, it was always his and still is."

"Ok. I know you haven't really done this before, so I'm going to give you some insight into how this works. First, don't add any details that have not been asked for. For example, don't say 'at one point' unless you know that at another point the fact you are stating was different. I want you to be comfortable up there with me but Gage's attorney is going to go tough on you. Are you ready for that?"

"No," I said. "But then again, does anyone ever say yes to that question?"

"No they don't," he said, with a laugh. "I can't imagine what you are going through and I am doing everything in my power to see to it that it ends as soon as possible. Now, how can you be sure the knife belongs to Gage?"

I proceeded to explain to him my reasoning, as I had told it to Agent Brown. He went on to explain that, other than the knife, they would be asking me questions about his character and personality. He explained that the D.A. needed to prove that Gage fit the profile of a pedophile and just as importantly that I was credible to comment one way or the other. After our discussion, I was suddenly nervous about testifying.

Gage's attorney would no doubt fly into me. I wondered how I would react. I pondered ways to get close to Gage again. I believed the feds would step in and help me out if I had an outburst and assaulted him in court. And even if they didn't, I wasn't sure it wouldn't be worth it. When I punched him on the sidewalk after our meeting at Fazoli's, it felt really good. I thought it would feel even better knowing what new things I knew.

The hearing was at 8:30AM, so my ride to Lexington from Fredonia would leave at 2AM just to insure I had time to arrive before the start time. After my testimony, I would be returned. I was promised breakfast and lunch at a restaurant, likely fast food but still a welcomed change in pace to prison food. I wondered if my stomach would be tied in knots, making the consumption of food nearly impossible.

The ride there was quiet. I actually napped a bit in the van after my 'escorts' decided I didn't need to be handcuffed. We arrived in

Lexington in time to stop at McDonald's and get me two sausage, egg and cheese biscuits, some hash browns and a large OJ. I had to eat in the van so no one at court would know they bought me breakfast. That was fine with me, anything for a taste of real food.

Much like before at court, we pulled into this personal garage space and I was taken into the hallway and another door led straight into the courtroom. Gage and his attorney were sitting in their usual spot, the right side of the room from the judge's view. Unlike the last time we shared a room, I was sat on the other side, far away from him. After all, I wouldn't want him to feel uncomfortable.

The District Attorney spoke to me and I acknowledged with a wave. Agent Brown sat directly in front of me and I saw Agent Greene sitting in the back of the courtroom. I also recognized the other men who were introduced to me as part of the task force, including the CIA agent and the man from the Secret Service. I was still a little uneasy about those agencies being involved and the fact that neither of their men was fond of talking didn't help much.

The judge entered the courtroom and we all stood as usual. After a few minutes of hellos and getting some procedural items out of the way, the judge said I would be the first to testify since I had a long way back to the prison. Their goal was to get me back there as soon as possible. By this point, I was seven hours in to this trip and court was just now getting started. I was tired and nervous, but ready to get this done.

I was taken to the front and asked to sit in the witness stand. I got a good look in Gage's eyes sitting to my right. I stared at him for as long as I could. I wanted him to feel what I have felt and I wanted him to be scared, if only for a moment. I didn't know if he was, his poker face was great.

"Mr. Cooper? Are you paying attention?" asked the judge.

"I'm sorry, what was the question?"

"There was no question; the bailiff is trying to swear you in.

Don't make me tell you again to stop staring at Mr. Tate and pay attention to what's going on."

"Yes, your honor."

"Mr. Cooper," began the bailiff, "Raise your right hand and place your left hand on the bible. Mr. Cooper, do you swear to tell the truth, the whole truth, and nothing but the truth, so help you God?"

"I do," I said.

"Do you understand that you are hereby under oath and if you lie before the court while under oath you could face perjury charges?"

"I do."

And just like that, I was sworn in. The District Attorney would begin with me. He picked up his notepad and stepped to the podium. He got a drink of water and asked the judge if he could begin. The judge told him to begin.

"Mr. Cooper, I'd like to start by asking you to identify the defendant, the man sitting right over there," he said, as he pointed out Gage.

"That is Gage Tate."

"And how do you know Mr. Tate?"

"We were friends. We met in school and have since worked together and had become friends."

"To your knowledge, Mr. Cooper, prior to this case, were you aware that Mr. Tate was a pedophile?"

"Objection!" screamed Gage's attorney.

"Sustained, no name calling please," the judge said.

"Let me rephrase. Mr. Cooper, did you ever think that Mr. Tate had an attraction to anyone under the age of 18?"

"Only when he was too underage."

"Can you be more specific?"

"Well, I mean, in high school he liked girls his own age. They were all underage then."

"But after high school and after Mr. Tate turned 18, you didn't know of any attraction he had to anyone under 18?"

"No," I said.

"What did Mr. Tate like to do for fun?"

"Lots of things. He liked playing pool, going out. Normal stuff for a guy his age I guess."

"Did he have any hobbies?"

"Sure. He collected knifes and swords and liked video games."

"Did you ever know Mr. Tate to use any of those knives or swords for any purpose other than collection?"

"Other than stabbing me in the back?" I said as I glared at him.

"Your honor!" screamed Gage's attorney.

"Mr. Cooper," the judge said, "Leave out your editorial opinion. Stick only to the facts."

"He carried one knife most everywhere and, yes, he used it regularly for whatever he may have needed. He used it at work to open boxes and bags and really anything he needed a knife for. Some of his collection was just for that, but most of the knives he would carry at one time or another. I never knew a time he wasn't carrying a knife, he always had one on him."

"This is a knife that the police recovered from another suspect's car that they believe belongs to Mr. Tate," he said as he held up a baggie with the knife in it. "Do you recognize this knife?"

I took the bag from him and said, "Yes. This was Gage's knife."

"How can you be sure?"

"I've held it before. I've seen it up close, it was his favorite knife. His thumb wore the finish off the side right here," I said as I pointed out the worn spot. "I have held my hand up to it to compare the difference in our size hands. This worn spot is identical to the spot I have put my hand next to."

"And you have never known Mr. Tate to use a knife in a threatening way?"

"Yes. We were confronted outside a pool hall in our neighborhood once by some guys that were angry about a confrontation inside. Gage pulled the knife on them and they left us alone. He also pulled the knife on me after he was released on bond and I confronted him about making a statement to the police that was inaccurate about me."

"Objection! Where is the police report, your honor?"

"Mr. Cooper, did you contact the police about this matter?" the judge asked.

"No. But Detective Hailey knew about it."

"How did he know?" the judge asked.

"I broke Gage's nose that night and he asked me about it the night he arrested me. Neither of us was charged."

"Fine, I'll allow it, overruled."

"Other than those times, Mr. Cooper, did you suspect him to have used it in any violent way in another circumstance?" asked the District Attorney.

"Not to my knowledge."

"Did you ever see blood on the knife or any evidence that it had been used in an odd way?"

"No," I said.

"No further questions at this time, your honor."

"Cross?" the judge asked Gage's attorney.

"Yes, your honor. Mr. Cooper, you and Gage are best friends, isn't that right?"

"Were. We were best friends."

"Right and you both worked together, correct?"

"Yes."

"While you claim total innocence in this whole mess, isn't it true that you gave my client child pornography on a laptop?"

"No that's not true. Not at all true."

"Really? Because you told Detective Hailey that, didn't you?"

"No, I did not. Gage told Hailey that, not me."

"But in the police report, Detective Hailey said you told him that you gave those images to Mr. Tate."

"He's lying. I did no such thing nor did I tell him that."

"So you expect me to take your word over a decorated police officer?"

"I don't care what you believe. I did not tell Hailey that. Gage Tate told the lies and Detective Hailey also told lies. That's how I ended up here."

"So if you are so innocent here, Mr. Cooper, please explain why my client would benefit involving you."

"He got probation. That's what he wanted at the time. He didn't care who he hurt."

"So," the attorney began, "He just made a bunch of stuff up from nowhere? I mean it seems odd that he could be accurate and had just made it up."

"Your wife is a whore, counselor," I said to him.

"Excuse me?!" he said quickly.

"Mr. Cooper, you are on thin ice," the judge warned me.

"You see," I said, "I just told a completely made up lie and look at all the ruckus I caused. Whether or not your wife is or is not a whore, everyone in here had that thought for a moment. The things Gage Tate said about me are just as unfounded and fake as that statement. Not even knowing your wife, she either is or is not a whore, so I have a 50% chance of being right. Had I slept with her last night, I would know she was. Gage didn't just make up wild statements about me; he planted the stuff so he knew they would find it."

"Mr. Cooper, you need to keep your comments 'G' rated, do you understand?" asked the judge.

"Yes, your honor, I'm sorry but sometimes it is hard to make a point."

"Please continue, counselor," the judge said to Gage's attorney.

"Let me ask about that knife that you are so sure belonged to Gage. His fingers are longer than yours, and that is how you knew where the worn spot was, correct?"

"Yes."

"My fingers are longer than yours. That could be my knife, how do you know for sure it is Gage Tate's knife instead of say, my knife."

"First of all, the knife is unique. You can't just buy it anywhere. Gage had special ordered it. Secondly, Gage is the one on trial for murder, not you. Seems more logical that it would be his."

"Thin ice, Mr. Cooper! I will hold you in contempt if you don't control your comments," the judge warned.

"I'd like to hold the system in contempt, your honor."

"That's enough," the judge said. And I agreed. I had made my point.

This had seemed like a pointless waste of time but in the end, the judge ruled that there was enough evidence to suggest that the knife did in fact belong to Gage. That was a step in the right direction for the case, at least.

My day was over after less than an hour in the courtroom. As I was escorted out, I gave Gage a good glare, forcing his eyes back to the floor. He knew at this point, I thought, that he was in big trouble. I was hoping he was having trouble sleeping and agonizing over a fear of being someone's prison bitch. He deserved at least that, though I wasn't hopeful that was the case. Gage didn't seem to care what happened. He was caught and 'that was that' seemed to accurately describe his attitude.

I was transported back to WKCC, a place that I had learned to despise. For the next few days, I tried to digest what had happened. I wondered if it had made any difference. I often felt depressed after these hearings, regardless of the outcome. I still missed the Gage Tate that I knew. I didn't know the monster that he really was. It was still so incredibly difficult to digest the idea that he was some kind of evil person. I still held on to the idea that this was just a bad dream and I was going to wake up eventually.

Thankfully, I was still on the list to get transferred to a halfway house, which would be much better than where I was living. If I can't wake up from the dream in my own bed, I wanted to at least wake up closer to home in a more comfortable bed. That night, like so many others, I cried myself to sleep hoping to awake to something positive.

Chapter 22

Halfway Home.

"Hey Brayden, come in here for a second," Mrs. Hurley, the warehouse manager instructed.

"What's up?" I asked.

"You can't tell anyone, no one, that I told you this, but I am pretty sure you are on the list to be transferred to a halfway house tomorrow. I'd like you to train the other guys on the things that you completely handle so they know what's going on. Do you think you can do that?"

"Yes ma'am! That's great news. I've enjoyed working here so much. It has been a great distraction from the otherwise bad situation around me here. I'm not a fan of this place, but you've made it better."

"I'm glad we could, we've loved having you work here."

"Do you know where they are sending me?"

"I think it is Louisville."

"Great, I'm so excited. My family will be too. That is so much closer to home; they can actually come see me!"

"I know you are looking forward to that," she said.

And I *was* looking forward to that. I was stuck far away from home in a place that was horrible at best and I almost never got to see anyone in my family. I spent the rest of the day training the newer guys that joined the staff after Junior got transferred. When it was time to leave, I gave Mrs. Hurley a big hug and ran back to the unit to get my stuff ready. I had a hard time confirming from anyone else that I was part of the group scheduled to leave in the morning, but after an agonizing two hour wait, I was finally called to the front gate.

"Mr. Cooper, you are being transferred. You need to get all your belongings packed, including your TV and get all that stuff loaded onto the van in the next thirty minutes. Don't save anything except the things you have to have tonight. They will be leaving early, so we want to be all packed in tonight."

That was absolutely no problem. I was excited to be going closer to home and on the way to a place everyone at a penitentiary in Kentucky waits for, a halfway house. I got all my stuff packed up and loaded and then called my mom. It was Valentine's Day, so this was like a love story of emotions for me and my family. My mom was ecstatic and I vowed to call her as soon as I got to the halfway house. I remember at the time thinking that I talked with the guards about calling my family and how happy they were that I was coming closer to home. They didn't seem to mind that I told them about the transfer. At the jail, when I was told I was heading to prison, I almost got in big trouble for trying to call my mom and let her know that I was being transferred. The two systems worked differently in many ways. This was a changed I liked for the better.

The next morning, I was hyped up and ready to get on the road. We got on the road at about 7AM and I was ready to roll. The small group that was going to the same halfway house as me contained few recognizable faces. I knew of most of these guys, but I didn't have much of a relationship with or an opinion on any of them.

As we arrived in Louisville, we were taken to a place called the Diersen Center. It was a Dismas Charities owned Halfway House, or as DOC called it, a Community Corrections Center. Our first impression was not the best. It was bland on the inside and it would remind you of a homeless shelter in appearance. At WKCC, we had cable TV and a good commissary to buy food. Diersen had no cable and no commissary. You could only get food brought in by your family on visits and even that was highly restricted. The only food that was allowed was prepackaged, single serving, microwavable food that required no refrigeration. No fresh foods, no soda, no bags of chips. The only source of soda or junk food was two vending machines stationed in the cafeteria.

I'm not a huge junk food fan but I was hoping for a better source of food for me to cook instead of relying on what had been a questionable source of food when in the system. These things, I thought, were mild sacrifices to be closer to my family and in an environment more normal to me.

Most of the first few days involved orientations and get to know you type of sessions. Overall I learned that this place was extremely boring if you didn't get a job that allowed you to go out in public to work. Everyone had to get a job in house first and then after a short time, they would be given a chance to work outside the center. Inmates, or residents as they were called here, didn't get a choice as to what job they were assigned to, they simply went and did as they were told. If you hated a job and got taken off of it by your request, you would have a hard time getting another outside job. If you were fired from the job, most of the time you were transferred.

My first bunk mate was Phillip French, affectionately known as Frenchy. He was wild and crazy but a really good guy. He took the time to talk with me about how things were done around the center, who to avoid and with whom to friend. I became friends with several people in my dorm, which held 15 men. Much like society outside of prison, like it or not, your survival depends largely on the relationships that you forge with others. Luckily at the halfway house, I wasn't worrying about connections that could keep me alive in case of disaster. Here it was much more about eating better and passing time faster. But that was a big deal.

My time at Diersen was reasonably uneventful for the first eight or nine months. I played cards a lot through the summer. I got really good at Spades and Dirty Hearts, which is just a slightly modified version of Hearts. We gambled, though it was against the rules, and I became popular in my ability to win and take people's money. I learned that in prison there were two kinds of inmates, those who survive and those who don't. At Diersen, it was largely the same. The difference is, I didn't worry as much about getting shanked at night. Diersen was much more heavily divided than the penitentiary. The divisions here were not about race, as I had seen at LAC, but here it was just like being a free man, money is all that mattered.

You had money or you didn't. If you did, you controlled a great deal of things, helped people or hogged it all for yourself. If you did not have money, you hoped to find those that would help you along the way and mostly, you struggled to live a good life. My mom was able to provide nicely for me. She has this talent; a talent that I'm sure was lost on the families of many other inmates, for finding sales and using coupons. She can take a little money and stretch it into a lot of food. That food I could either eat or resell for a profit and make money. I also learned I could give it away.

I did a combination of things with my food and my gambling winnings. First things first, I had to make sure I had what I needed. We were allowed to order out to any restaurant that delivered on the weekends, Friday, Saturday and Sunday. So that was three dinners a week that I got good food. Our choices were mostly pizza, Chinese, and this burger joint named Toll Bridge that delivered amazing cheeseburgers and other assortments of sandwiches. Most of the time we could get a medium pizza for $5, most burgers were around the $5-6 range, and Chinese ran you about $7-8 for a meal. Unfortunately for the drivers, they didn't get much of a tip. No one there could really afford it.

We usually got together in a group and tried to order different stuff each weekend night so we could have some variety. In order to eat all three nights, and in all three places, you needed about $20. That was my first priority each week to set aside enough money to eat out on the weekends. Other than my sodas, there wasn't much else, besides an occasional snack out of the machine that I needed cash for. Before I went out on a daily basis, I spent an average of

$30 a week on everything I needed. My mom was able to bring everything else to me that I needed.

We usually played cards or dominoes for money at least two or three days a week. Most games were played for one dollar a game, maybe two. Rarer games might be five dollars and just a few times in my stay, we played for twenty or so a game. The staff there knew we gambled, but most didn't care. Like anywhere, we knew who would care and who wouldn't.

I met a guy named Dustin and he and I became good friends. He lived in the same dorm as I did and we were one hell of a Spades team. We didn't lose often. Dustin did not have money and no one ever came to see him. Mom was allowed to bring cooked food from home in on her Saturday visits and they became famous around the center. She would cook a lot and I would sneak the left overs in to have for later. Dustin was one guy I always made sure got a plate of food. We were partners in many money games and according to my note sheets; we won over $300 from different guys in a period of five or six months. That kind of money went a long way at a place like Diersen. I put up the money for the bet, in case we lost, and then I split the winnings with Dustin.

I also tended to buy him dinner from one of the 'eat out' spots on days we did well. Even though he was making his own money, nothing was available for free there except for toilet paper. If you needed soap, deodorant, clothes, toothpaste, tooth brush or anything other than toilet paper, you were on your own. When I first got there, they used to take people to Goodwill and help pick out some things if inmates had no money. Shortly after I got there, that stopped. In fact, many things changed around there during my stay, more on that later.

By July of 2007, I was a little concerned that I had not heard from the FBI. Dustin made parole that month and such ceased my winning and our great partnership. Also in July, I started school at the local Community College. I was so excited about this because it meant I could go to school, for free, and I could do that instead of working some horrible labor job that I didn't want to do. To me, it was a great situation. I could actually get educational value out of this incarceration on the state's dime.

On July 18, 2007, I was confronted at the school by the FBI. I was told they needed to talk to me and I was to come with them. They had already been to Diersen and that's how they tracked me to the school. They transported me to the FBI field office, which is just a few blocks from the campus.

"Gage Tate is in custody, for good. He is in the Fayette County Jail, bond revoked, and he is not getting another one," Agent Brown said.

"Wow," I said with a bit of a gasp. "I didn't think I would ever hear that. I also didn't know you were so close to getting him back in."

"Well," he began, "We weren't exactly trying to arrest him. And actually, we didn't arrest him. Detective Hailey did, again. Hailey received a tip and turns out he traded some other images on his dad's computer while on probation and during his bond. He even had some stuff that had been sent prior to his first arrest. We are picking up the case."

"So what does all this mean?"

"It means, Tate is in jail and he is not going home. And it also means he just picked up a new case. And what that means is we don't buy anything he's told us to this point about being forced. He is addicted, he is a pedophile."

"So what happens now?"

"Tate's attorney is already screaming for a deal. We won't have to go to trial most likely. I guess that's good for you. You won't have to testify."

"Wow. That is a lot to take in."

"Well the first thing we are going to do is try to quickly get a plea deal to Tate on these latest charges. These charges are not sealed, so we'd like to get them resolved as soon as possible. Essentially, he will be sentenced on the new charges before the old charges."

"What does this mean for me getting to go home?"

"Unfortunately nothing, at least not yet. When he gets sentenced on the sealed charges, we hope that things can go in motion then."

At least he is in jail, I thought. For some reason, I almost didn't care what else they had to say at that moment. I knew he was locked up for now and for a long time. I was so happy about that. I called my mom to talk to her about it and she immediately told me that Gage was on the news again because he had been rearrested. Good, I thought, good he has to go through what I did. It was about damn time.

As my semester wound down, I felt like I fit in well at Diersen. I was able to gamble and win money, I could help people with their write ups and certain case issues and I got to go to school. If I had to be locked up, this was the ideal situation. Home cooked meals every other week and some freedom meant everything to me at a time where I thought I was going crazy.

After my first semester, my mom brought my cell phone, which had not been disconnected, to the center. She snuck it in to me on visit and it meant saving a lot of money. No more paying a dollar for ten minutes to call from a pay phone, now we could talk more often, as long as I am careful. Cell phones, of course, were prohibited and if you were caught with one, you would be sent back to prison.

With my new toy, the cell phone, I was also able to make contact with Leala, Lyndee and Naomi, all of whom I missed dearly. It allowed me to stay in contact with them through a more affordable communication. It was the first time in nearly two years that I felt somewhat normal. I slit a tiny hole in the seam of my mattress with a broken razor and slid my phone up inside for hiding. It was a nice tool to have and so many others around the center had one. One mistake I would not make was charging for use. I learned from watching others that if you charge for use and someone needs it and has no money, they might tell on you out of spite. That sort of behavior was to be expected, not just there, but anywhere in the system. The best way to go would be hiding the phone from inmates as well. If no one knew you had it, you were far less likely to have any issues. Unfortunately, that was nearly impossible.

After Dustin left, another group of guys came in their place. Ethan was one of the new arrivals. He came in our dorm and took Dustin's spot. We hit it off almost immediately because we both figured out quickly that the other was capable of carrying on an intellectual conversation, a luxury not often found in such a setting. That friendship would build through the end of the year. Ethan got lucky to get out to school a little earlier than he would have normally been allowed. We began going to school together in August.

Going to school was nice, not just for the educational value, but for the freedom. The school was about 15 blocks from Diersen and we were allowed to check out an hour early and walk there on our own. We sometimes chose to take the bus, but whichever we decided; no one was directly supervising us. We felt free, if only for a few hours. At school, no one other than our contact there knew we were incarcerated and all the school officials preferred we keep it that way. No students or teachers had to know and this prevented any problems that might arise.

The FBI didn't return the rest of the year and I wondered often what was going on. I could look Gage up on the Fayette County Jail's Web site. His picture was there and it he was listed as being held on federal charges. That made me happy, but I would have been happier with details. I also knew that everything with the federal system took longer than in the state system. For some reason, they scheduled court dates six or eight months apart. In the state system, two months apart is a long gap for court dates.

In December, I was notified that the parole board would again request to see me in person. My parole date was scheduled for January 28, 2008. I strongly considered going into this hearing with a different attitude. Maybe I should just cave in and give my sorry speech and go the hell home. That would be easy enough. I had certainly tasted freedom and I remembered how much I loved it. However, when it came down to the time to make the decision, I told my mom and the rest of my family that wasn't something

I could do. My mom was torn by the decision, but she totally supported me. She respected the decision, though she knew I was likely signing my own deferment. The decision and the weeks leading up to the hearing were agonizing times. We struggled to keep it together and I found myself in a bit of a desperation mode. I was beginning to have a hard time dealing with my situation.

Freedom of school was nice, but it had tested me to the farthest point. Every time I left, I was finding it harder and harder to convince myself going back in was the right thing to do. I seriously considered escape on several occasions. This had truly been the hardest thing I'd ever been through...

Chapter 23

The Parole Board, 2, January 28, 2008.

As I was preparing to enter the room, the parole officer outside the door told me to get ready, I was next in line. I was nervous again, much like I was before. I had hoped that I would fall into the category of most other non-violent offenders I had seen meet the board. If they were flopped the first time up on five years, they typically made it after that. I also knew my situation was considerably different than those guilty men who would grovel at the feet of anyone who would consider letting them go home. I not only wasn't going to grovel, I wasn't planning to even admit guilt to a crime I didn't commit. That, however, seemed to be one requirement that was non-negotiable to ensure your release. You are to give a full confession and showing of remorse, followed, of course, by a promise to never do it again.

The process to make parole seemed like a game that was simply about learning the process and how to play it right. Though many of us during my time of incarceration wondered if there was ever a pattern, I argue that the process is less about pattern, more about ego. If they don't like you, you aren't going home. Not only do they need to like what they see, but they have very few requirements that are set in stone that control a yes or no vote. You must admit guilt, show remorse and make that promise to never do it again. If you do these things, you have scored enough points to go to level two of this game.

Level two was a mind game played between the offender and the board members. This often times was an unfair matchup. Not only were many of the guys not intelligent enough to play this game, they often didn't understand the importance of how they spoke and their choice of words. I understood these things and coached several guys before going to see the board. My problem was largely my refusal to play the game, rather than an inability to play it well. I refused to sit in a room and apologize for a crime I didn't commit and couldn't very well promise that I wouldn't do it again if I had never done it before.

As I entered the room, I saw a similar situation as WKCC's room. The biggest difference here was that both board members were on the monitor and none were present. I sat down and we went through the same process as before. I stated my name and institution number and we went through my list of charges and sentences. I was asked to explain the arson charge again, and again that part went smoothly. Things began to get rocky when we got to the next set of charges.

"Mr. Cooper, we see that you failed to take responsibility for the child pornography charges that you pled guilty to in 2006. Can you explain how you came to have these charges?"

"Yes," I began. "My co-defendant, Gage Tate, set me up to take a fall for him so he could get probation. He accessed my computer, with my permission, and put child pornography on it without my knowledge. I had no idea when I gave him permission to use it that he was using it for that. I was in no way involved with that at all."

"So," began the board member, "can you explain why you pled guilty in the case?"

"My attorney told me I had no other option. He virtually refused to take this to trial saying I had no case. I told him I wasn't guilty but he said it didn't matter if I was or not. He said if the jury saw the same things he had, I would surely be convicted."

"So, you expect us to believe that your attorney *bullied* you into taking a deal? That he didn't care if you were not guilty?"

"I am not expecting anything, ma'am. I am telling you what happened, the truth."

"You must understand why I have a hard time believing you," she said. "It is a tough justification for me to say I vote to let you be released based on your statement of innocence after you pled guilty. How can I be sure you aren't going to repeat this crime?"

"Well I can be positive I am not going to *repeat* this crime since I never did it to begin with. I can assure you also that I have no interest, not now or ever, in child pornography. I have no interest in children whatsoever and will never be in possession of anything even similar."

"You pled guilty, Mr. Cooper. There is nothing you can say that will change that. If you can't take responsibility for your crimes, which you did plead guilty to, then you have to give me some other reason to let you go home. I don't have a good reason at this moment."

"Please," I said, trying to hold my anger back, "please, just serve me out. I am not guilty of this crime. I am not going to say I am. So just stop wasting everyone's time and serve me out."

"Excuse me?" the parole board member asked.

"Just serve me out. We played this game last year. I haven't changed my tune on the truth from then and I'm not now. I refuse to be attacked any longer, so if what I have said or not said is not satisfactory, please, just serve me out so I can get along with my life."

"Well if you don't want to go home, Mr. Cooper..."

"YOU don't want me to go home! Don't patronize me lady. I am not an uneducated drug dealer you can run over. Let me go or serve me out so I can go on with my day!"

"Fine," she said, "Mr. Cooper, our decision is to deny your parole today. You are hereby served out, to serve the rest of your sentence handed down by the judge in your case. You are permanently denied parole. That is all, you are dismissed."

I stood and angrily left the room. I went into the hallway and used the pay phone to call my mom and tell her the news. As always, she was very supportive. She didn't like the results, but she completely understood why I had to do what I did. I knew, based on my time calculation that I only had about another year to serve out my time completely. This, I thought, wasn't ideal but it wasn't horrible either.

After the hearing, I went back to school to take my classes for the day. When class was over, I returned to the center where I ate my lunch and told my friends of my fate. Most of them were surprised I hadn't made parole, but they really didn't have the whole story. As I threw my lunch trash away, I noticed the two female parole officers that are in charge of our center walk through the door. This was a common theme on parole board day. If someone gets deferred longer than 18 months, they have to go back to prison. But this visit, shortly after their arrival, gave me a bad feeling.

"Mr. Cooper, come over here," said Mr. Thompson.

"Grab my phone if you can and mail it to my mom," I whispered to Ethan.

I went over and one of the officers said, "Turn around." She handcuffed me.

As we walked towards the door, she said, "Do you know where you're going?"

"Well I'm not positive, but based on the handcuffs, I'm guessing jail."

"Yes and do you know why?"

"No," I said, "That I do not know. I haven't done anything wrong."

"You were deferred today at your parole hearing, right?"

"Well I got served out," I said.

"Right, well apparently you did have more than 18 months to serve, so that's why we are locking you up."

"That's not right; I just got an updated time sheet from my counselor two days ago. I have less time than that right now," I insisted as she put me in the van.

"Well the paperwork we have says you do. Maybe you are mistaken."

"I am not mistaken. With all due respect, if I know anything about anything, I know how much time I have to serve."

"Nothing we can do about it, the paperwork..."

"Is fucking wrong," I said. "Can't you call someone and check again?"

"No we..." she began.

"Fine," interrupted the other officer. "But if you are wrong, you're going to regret that."

"I'm not wrong."

She made the phone call and there were two conflicting dates. Turns out, I was right, I did have less than 18 months to serve out. And the crazy thing is, the date they had on my paperwork, even though it was wrong, it only showed me having 18 months and 4 days left to serve.

"Are you sure we shouldn't take him to the jail for the four days?" she asked the person on the phone. "Here, she wants to talk to you," she said as she handed me the phone.

"Hello?"

"Mr. Cooper, legally I can't send you back to the center until I have paperwork that says you have less than 18 months to serve. But I do know it is a mistake. So, if I send you back today, are you going to run?"

"Ma'am," I said, "I've had a year to run from here and I haven't yet. If that's not good enough, I can't offer a more solid guarantee."

"Give the phone back to the officer."

'And take him back to the center' is what she told them. We were stopping a few blocks up the road to pick up another inmate. After that, I was told they would be taking me back to the center.

"She must like you, that's against the rules."

"You must hate me to want me to lose everything I've worked a year for over four days."

"I just follow rules, but I guess you don't know about that," she said sarcastically.

"You don't know me, so please don't pretend to. You have no idea what you're talking about and you have no right to judge me."

"You have a smart mouth."

"Well that makes two of us."

"Do you want to go back to the center or do you want to go to jail?"

I didn't respond. And she didn't take me to jail. A fair trade off, I thought.

When I arrived back at Diersen, Ms. Karen was shocked to see me at the door. She seemed hesitant to let me in when she saw me. She walked to the door and peered out to see if she could see the van. She also looked me over to make sure I didn't have my cuffs on. When she decided it was safe, she opened the door.

"What happened, Mr. Cooper?"

"I talked them out of taking me to jail. They were wrong about my time and they were trying to lock me up over four days. They are crazy. Can I go see Leach?"

"Sure," she said, "I'm glad you are back," she said with a smile.

Leach gave me the usual pep talk about how I was doing right and as long as I stayed on the right track, I was welcome there. He seemed genuinely happy that I had come back so quickly. At the time, I remember thinking it was at least a small victory on a day of disappointment.

Chapter 24

H.I.P. and Plea Deals Galore.

I was pissed off about the parole hearing. I was really pissed off. I found myself so unbelievably frustrated that I was back to my crazy mindset that I adopted at WKCC. There was no hope for this system and it seemed no hope for me either.

I was beginning my third year of incarceration and the effect it was having on my personality and my ability to function was growing. Tension around Diersen had grown. Our Director, who is the head of our center, was Gary Thompson. No one liked him in general. He was a sarcastic guy and very much a control freak. As an ex-military officer, he decided everything should be run in strict dictatorship fashion. And while sometimes that works with inmates, no one respected him. The assistant director, Richard Leach, was more popular. He gave off the 'I have no control over that, Thompson said no' image. And it worked, we liked him.

Leach had a sense of humor, which was hard to find. He wanted to be director more than anything and since no one liked Thompson, a plan arose to get rid of him. Leach respected my willingness to challenge policy and challenge authority, pushing the envelope while staying civil and within my rights as an inmate. One of the staff members, Ms. Adele, that no one liked, had gotten out of control.

When it is time for count, whoever is on duty goes around and calls count. Often times, there is only a female officer on duty. When that was the case, they never went into the restrooms or shower areas; they would just stand outside and scream at us that it was time for count. On the day of the 'incident,' Ms. Adele was announcing count time. Count time happens every two hours during the day. I had been there for over a year at this point and I knew the process well. About thirty minutes before count, I decided to take a shower, knowing I would have time to complete it before count.

After a few minutes in the shower, Ms. Adele entered the shower area to call count. I told her it was early and I was going to be just a minute. She left for a few minutes. I finished and exited the shower. While I was drying off and still undressed, Ms. Adele returned.

"It's count time!" she screamed a step just inside the door.

"And I'm naked. So, if you could get the hell out of here, I'd appreciate it."

"Don't you curse at me," she said as she took another step inside.

"Seriously," I said, louder, "You are not supposed to be in here with me! I don't give a shit what you write up, but right now I'm naked and you need to get the hell out!"

By this time she had stepped far enough inside that the door closed behind her.

"You have no respect for authority," she said.

"And you do?" I asked. "Seriously, if you want to do this cock watch shit, we can do it in Thompson's office! If you don't get out of here, I'm going to shove you out the door."

I can only assume it was the thought of me and my nakedness grabbing her and forcibly removing her that convinced her to leave. I was affectionately and commonly known around the center as the guy who could beat almost any write up because of the dirt I had, connections I had and my legal aid skills. This I would consider a challenge since I was truly personally offended by it. Ms. Adele might write me up, but I too would write her up.

As soon as count was cleared, I immediately requested a grievance form. I filled it out, describing the events and making an official sexual harassment claim against Ms. Adele. This would have been the 15th or 20th grievance I had filed to this point, so the office upstairs was not surprised to see my name on one of these forms. This grievance, however, would be handled differently. Since sexual harassment was a big deal and a lawsuit waiting to happen, and the video evidence completely backed up my story, my claims were taken very serious. Mr. Leach faxed the complaint to Frankfort, where DOC is headquartered, and he interviewed me to start the investigation.

A couple of days later, DOC sent a representative down to Diersen to interview me. I was told that this sparked great interest because grievances are never filed from this center and this was a serious accusation.

"Well, grievances are filed here all the time. I guess they are just not serious enough to come to you," I clarified. This clarification was part of Leach's plan to have Thompson removed.

"How many have been filed?"

"I have filed 15 or 20 myself and dozens of others that I know about."

Leach grabbed the file and presented it to the woman. The file contained over 50 grievances that never left the center. All grievances are supposed to be sent to Frankfort. The lady was quite upset and Leach, of course, put all the blame on Thompson. He said he had nothing to do with that process.

Two days later, Mr. Thompson's office was empty and he had been transferred. Leach, we would discover, would be our new director. This is something everyone was happy about. Leach and I had a great report and most were of the opinion that the center would be a better place with Leach as our director. Spirits were high for the first time since I had been there and many around the place regarded me as a game changer for things that I accomplished just like this. It was good to lead guys, who had previously felt hopeless, into an era of hopefulness.

The FBI finally returned in Mid-March of 2008. Agent Brown returned to talk about the finalization of Gage's cases. I was surprised at what I heard.

"We can't prove murder. If we went to trial, we would charge it and hope for the best. But there isn't going to be a trial. Since Tate's second arrest, he has now reached a deal in that case. He has agreed to plead guilty and receive 10 years in prison. He is scheduled for sentencing on April 25. In May, we plan to have him plead guilty to several serious charges in the sealed indictment. He will take a deal in that case for 60 years. It will finally be over in just a few months."

"Sixty years?" I asked. "He raped, tortured and murdered children and he can't get a life sentence?"

"This is the safest deal. Trial could mean a lot of things for both sides. And he wants to plead out. He's going to give us everyone he knows in the operation."

"How long will he serve on that?"

"You have to serve 85% of your time in the federal system. He'll serve 51 years on the 60 year sentence. He'll serve 8.5 years on the 10 year sentence. He'd be in his 80's before he could get out."

"But he could get out, right?"

"Not at a young enough age to do anything harmful to anyone else. And it's likely he won't live that long in prison, especially with his charges."

"Good. I don't believe in the death penalty, as a rule, but this is one case I wouldn't oppose it. Too bad that wasn't an option."

"He got a death sentence. He will have to sit in a cell for the rest of his life and he will die there. He just has a long awaited death full of suffering. He will get what he deserves."

I was thrilled, relieved and sad all in the same notion. I was going crazy and I had only served three years. I couldn't fathom a life sentence. But I know that is what he deserved. I was mostly glad that this entire nightmare was finally coming to an end.

I was told that he would be sentenced April 25th on the second case and I would not be invited to that court date. However, when dates were set for the guilty plea and sentencing on the other case, I would be welcome to come watch if I wanted. I wasn't sure I wanted to. That decision would weigh heavy on my mind over the next few months.

Laws change all the time and sometimes they change just in the nick of time to help someone. Those in charge of the Home Incarceration Program in Frankfort, commonly known as HIP, decided to offer nonviolent offenders who have been served out the opportunity to finish their incarceration from home, up to six months. I was visited by a counselor to discuss that as an option. The program was expensive; its cost was around $5 a day. At $150 a month, for a newly released inmate, you better have some money to take care of the costs prior to agreeing to go on this program.

The highlight features include, curfew, ankle bracelets, telephone check-ins and the constant threat of being sent back to prison. Though it didn't sound glamorous, what was so wonderful is you get to go home and sleep in your own bed and eat your own food. That was worth it to me, so I signed up for approval. I knew after this that I would finally be going home for sure in September of 2008, shortly after my birthday.

Finally, with the light at the end of the tunnel, I was going to be ok. But just to make it tough on me, things didn't go well with the transition of Leach into the director seat as all had hoped. Mr. Leach decided to flip his entire personality and his egomaniac side began to show. He was so much worse than Thompson that we all began to see that Thompson wasn't that bad.

Our state pay for our jobs became more and more scarce. At times, payments would come two and three months late. Leach stopped talking to anyone about problems and started screaming hysterically at those who tried. His sense of humor also left the building. His favorite saying soon became "I make too much money to talk to you." His salary was public, on their website. He made around $35,000 a year, hardly enough to get arrogant about it.

So, things weren't perfect, but my spirits were looking up. I had to get out of there and go home and I was finally going to get to. The FBI returned shortly after Gage's sentencing on the public case to tell me he had been sentenced. Sure enough, he got the full 10 years. For the first time, I was able to feel good about what I had done in cooperating with the FBI. I was given the dates of his future plea hearings, the first being the third week in May. He would finally plead guilty to the charges and give his account of what he had done. I was interested to hear his side of the story, but at the same time, I was concerned about the details he would reveal. I feared it may get worse than I ever knew.

Chapter 25

HOW DO YOU PLEAD? GUILTY.

Gage had been in jail for just about a year and I was happy just to know that. The feds work slowly and that means longer jail terms while they schedule distant court dates. Gage deserved to be in jail, so all did seem more right with the world. Ironically, his final arrest date was July 17 of 2007 and his court date to change his plea to guilty on the sealed indictment was July 17, 2008. I assume he will remember that date for a few years. Personally, I was just happy to be going to court and seeing Gage is the one that was uncomfortable.

The Diersen Center had become a magnet for drama and despair. I was no longer hailed as a hero for helping to dethrone Thompson. Now I was more commonly known as the guy who thought Leach would be better. Oops. My concerns were focused on Gage's court dates that were upcoming and my home incarceration. I may have been wrong about Leach being better, but ever since I caught him sleeping with what turned out to be a federal halfway house inmate, in his office, I didn't worry about getting in big trouble. Blackmail may be wrong, but it is oh so effective.

I would find out later that Gage had reached the deal in September of 2007 that he would plead guilty in 2008 after his conviction for the newest case. It was important that he be sentenced on the newer case first so as not to have increased levels, which determine the amount of time he could serve, on either case. Levels being increased in one case because of conviction in the other case could double his prison term. His attorney was still planning to ask the judge to consider a lighter sentence, which would be hopeless if his levels increased anymore.

I remember traveling to Gage's plea hearing. I had my mom bring me up some dress clothes so I could at least wear a tie instead of a jumpsuit. That was already an improvement. I was coming from the halfway house so I wasn't even cuffed. I was told on the way there that since I decided to wear dress clothes, they weren't going to even cuff me in court. After all, I was no threat to anyone but Gage, and at this point, no one cared much for him.

As I entered the courtroom, Gage's eyes grew huge. First, I don't think he expected to see me at all. Second, I don't think he knew what to think about me wearing normal clothes. You could see the look on his face and tell that the gerbil was running the wheel inside his head. He hadn't heard of me being released, but you could tell he thought I had been. I didn't want to tell him otherwise. I smiled at him on the way in and gave him a pleasant wink and nod. He didn't seem to appreciate it.

When we got settled, the judge called attention to the court. He seemed rushed or impatient; it was hard to tell which. He first asked the attorneys from both sides to approach. They discussed something briefly and then were returned. The judge asked if the two sides had reached a deal and both acknowledged they had. He instructed Gage to stand up.

"Mr. Tate," he began, "It is my understanding that your attorney has bargained for a deal on your behalf that you have agreed to accept. Is that correct?"

"Yes, your honor," Gage said.

"Do you understand that in federal court, when you change your plea to guilty, you cannot withdraw that plea and you cannot appeal the conviction?"

"Yes, your honor."

"Do you also understand that the deal you have formulated with the prosecutor does not bind me to any sentencing term? I can sentence you to more or less time than your deal stipulates and if I decide to sentence you to more time, you cannot change your plea back to not guilty and proceed to trial. Once you enter your guilty plea here, it is final, do you understand?"

"Yes, your honor."

"Good. I have in front of me the plea agreement. I will read off the charges you are facing and ask you how plead, Mr. Tate. If you plead guilty, you will then be asked to recount what you did to be guilty of the charge. Do you understand?"

"Yes, your honor."

"As to count one, Promoting the Sale of Material Depicting the Sexual Performance by a Minor, Gage Tate, how do you plead?"

"Guilty, your honor."

"And can you explain to the court what you did to be guilty of this crime?"

"Yes, your honor. I had a contact that I remained in contact with from the beginning of this stuff. He..."

"Objection," said the prosecutor, "He needs to be more specific. We don't want to hear 'stuff,' we want specifics."

"Be more specific, Mr. Tate," the judge instructed.

"I was involved in a child pornography family, as we called it. I had a contact in that family to whom I would locate and forward child pornography. In some cases it was new photographs and videos taken at the time of an encounter with a minor and myself. The purpose of forwarding such material was so it could be edited and distributed for sale on the black market and the internet."

"Counselor?" the judge said.

"We stipulate," the prosecutor said.

"Moving on to count two," the judge continued, "As to count two, Sexual Abuse in the 1st Degree, Gage Tate, how do you plead?"

"Guilty, your honor."

"And can you explain to the court what you did to be guilty of this crime?"

"Yes, your honor. During the time of my involvement with the child pornography family, I had several contact encounters with minors. On several occasions I was nude in the presence of a minor and forced the minor to touch my genitalia."

"Counselor?" the judge asked again.

"We stipulate," the prosecutor said.

"As to count three, Complicity to Traffick a Human Being Under the Age of 16, Gage Tate, how do you plead?"

"Guilty, your honor."

"And can you explain to the court what you did to be guilty of this crime?"

"Yes, your honor. I acted as a middle man in the trafficking process. I would be delivered a minor with the purpose of completing a certain job, most of the time a sexual act. Then I would send them with a carrier who transported the child through the rest of his or her process."

"Did you ever transport these children?" the judge asked.

"No, your honor. I was the middle man. It was my job to make movies and take pictures. Everyone had their own job."

"Counselor?" the judge asked again.

"We stipulate," the prosecutor said.

"As to count four, Promoting the Sexual Performance of a Minor, Gage Tate, how do you plead?"

"Guilty, your honor."

"And can you explain to the court what you did to be guilty of this crime?"

"Yes, your honor. I helped in sales in the family by making contacts online that may be interested in buying high end, never before seen child pornography. It was worth a lot of money and I helped make contacts to get the material sold."

"Isn't this how you were caught originally by the FBI? Selling some of this material to an undercover agent?" asked the judge.

"Yes, your honor."

"And how much do you think you sold or set up to be sold through contacts you personally made?" asked the judge.

"I don't know for sure but in the neighborhood of $80,000."

"And how did you get paid for these sales?"

"Cash, from my carrier," Gage said.

"And how did the buyer pay?"

"They were sometimes given an item on eBay that was worth a lot of money and told to do the 'Buy Now' feature and instead of the item, they would get what they ordered. Other times, they were just told to email credit card info to an address or mail a check or money order to a P.O. Box somewhere. I didn't really handle that, I just know a tiny bit about it. I never dealt with direct payments."

"Ok, counselor?" the judge asked.

"We stipulate, your honor, we just want to make the point that this falls under Promotion of a Sexual Performance because without the pressure type sales tactics and marketing of this material, the access would be more restricted and it wouldn't encourage those in this business to continue abducting children for this cause," the prosecutor said.

"Ok, as to count five, Sodomy in the 1st Degree, Gage Tate, how do you plead?"

"Guilty, your honor."

"And can you explain to the court what you did to be guilty of this crime?"

"Yes, your honor. I forced minors, some under the age of 14, to participate in oral sex with me for the purpose of making videos and taking photographs."

"Your honor," the prosecutor interrupted, "We object to the purpose. He was sodomizing minors for personal enjoyment as much as for work or whatever he calls it. We are going to need him to be specific about his intent."

"Mr. Tate?" the judge directed at Gage.

"Yea, so I enjoyed it. I'm not sure what you want me to say."

"I think that suffices, counselor," the judge said to the prosecutor.

"We stipulate," said the prosecutor.

"Good. Finally, Mr. Tate, as to count six, Rape in the 1st Degree, how do you plead?"

"Guilty, your honor."

"And can you explain to the court what you did to be guilty of this crime?"

"I raped minors, over a period of time, for the purpose of making videos and taking photographs for the family. And yes, I enjoyed it, because I'm sick," Gage said as he glared at the prosecutor.

"How many minors did you rape, Mr. Tate?" the judge asked.

"I lost count, your honor," Gage said.

"Can you take a guess? Was it more than 10? More than 20?"

"More than 20, sir," Gage said.

"Ok," said the judge. "Mr. Tate, I am satisfied, counselor?"

"We stipulate as to count six and all counts in this plea."

"Mr. Tate, as to count 1, this court finds you guilty. What is the sentencing recommendation from the District Attorney?"

"We recommend 60 months, your honor."

"Noted. As to count 2, Mr. Tate, this court finds you guilty. What is the sentencing recommendation from the District Attorney?"

"We recommend 60 months, to be run consecutively, your honor."

"Noted. As to count 3, Mr. Tate, this court finds you guilty.

What is the sentencing recommendation from the District Attorney?"

"We recommend 120 months, to be run consecutively with earlier counts."

"Noted. As to count 4, Mr. Tate, this court finds you guilty. What is the sentencing recommendation from the District Attorney?"

"We recommend 120 months, to be run consecutively with earlier counts."

"Noted. As to count 5, Mr. Tate, this court finds you guilty. What is the sentencing recommendation from the District Attorney?"

"We recommend 120 months, to be run consecutively with the earlier counts."

"Noted. As to count 6, Mr. Tate, this court finds you guilty. What is the sentencing recommendation from the District Attorney?"

"We recommend 240 months, to be run consecutively with the earlier counts. Our total comes to 720 months, your honor."

"That's the total I have. Mr. Tate, your sentencing will be scheduled for September 4 this year. Until that time, you are remanded. Do you have any questions?"

"No, your honor," Gage said.

And with that, it was nearly over. Gage had finally been found guilty of these horrible crimes. While it still seemed like 60 years was a light sentence, I was mostly just happy that there was some closure to the case. For the last two years, and this would make a third year, I was incarcerated on my birthday. This third year, however, would be different. Not only will I be going home just a few short weeks after it, but for my birthday this year, I will get to attend Gage Tate's sentencing. I couldn't have asked for a better birthday!

Chapter 26

Gage's Sentencing.

Finally the day had arrived. After literally years of waiting, I think I needed this more than anything. While the deal only called for sixty years, I knew deep down that the broken system did the best it could. At least he did not walk away a free man or slip through the gaping cracks in the system. Before entering the courtroom, I had a short talk with Agent Brown.

"How are you?" he asked.

"I'm ok," I said.

"Are you ready for this?"

"I've been waiting for this," I said, with confidence.

"I know this won't be easy on you, though. You may be ready on the outside, but inside, this is going to be somewhat traumatic. I'm glad you are going home soon. You are going to need to get some rest and some help. Promise me you'll seek out some sort of therapy."

"I'm not in a position to give maybes, let alone make promises. But I assure you, I'm ready for this. This is the day we've been waiting for all this time."

I thought, in that moment, that Agent Brown was not the brightest. This is exactly what I was waiting for and the only thing that would upset me is if something ridiculous happened, such as he gets probation. That would be impossible to deal with. That, too, was impossible because federal law prevented such a ruling.

Gage, just like the last time I saw him, wore his green jumpsuit from the Fayette County Jail and I dressed nicely. He sat looking forward with a straight face. He looked dead. I imagined it was tough on him as well, but deep down I tried to not care about that. Though we had been best friends, the haunting thoughts of his horrid actions still kept me up at night. My nightmares weren't fading and he shouldn't feel good about where he's at or what he's done.

The courtroom came to attention as the judge entered and sat in his place at the head of the room. He asked if the attorneys were ready to proceed and everyone affirmed their readiness. He announced that he was ready to sentence Gage and instructed him to rise. He took off his glasses and folded his hands together to rest his chin on them. He stared directly at Gage but didn't say a word. After several minutes of staring, Gage's attorney finally asked if he was ok. The judge told him to shut up. After that, he spoke for the first time.

"This case has haunted me. I have looked over the evidence against you, Mr. Tate. In looking at this evidence, I'm disappointed. I'm disappointed that murder charges were not filed against you. I'm disappointed that our system has been reduced to making a deal with a terrorist such as you to solve what might be a bigger problem.

I don't know if you are aware, Mr. Tate, but anyone convicted of terrorism charges are mandated with a minimum of a life sentence. I understand that you have not been charged with terrorism related charges, but Mr. Tate, you are the definition of a domestic terrorist. To prey on children the way you have, it is beyond me how you are able to stand and look me in the eye. Your life is not worth my time and if it were in my power to have you executed, I would, sir."

At this point in the courtroom, you could hear a few gasps and people opened their eyes a bit wider. This judge meant business and was going to make sure Gage got a thrashing before the sentencing.

"Fortunately for you, I do not have the authority to execute you. Aside from your child victims, you have told lies that have resulted in the incarceration of an innocent man. And not just any man, your best friend." He shifted his look toward me and said, "Mr. Cooper, it is good to see you have been released."

"I have not been your honor. I will not be released until September 30th," I said.

After another pause, he said, "Forgive me, son. I know you will be home soon and I know that is where you deserve to be."

"Thank you," I said. That meant so much to me, just to hear someone say it.

Back to Gage, he said, "Mr. Tate, do you have anything to say before I sentence you?"

"Would it do any good, your honor?" Gage asked.

"No it won't," the judge said. Gage did not say another word.

"The United States District Attorney, Eastern District has offered a deal to your attorney, Mr. Tate. You have agreed to that deal and you have been found guilty on six horrendous charges. The District Attorney's office has recommended a total of 720 months incarceration to be served consecutively with any other sentences before the United States Federal Court. You in turn agreed to the term of 720 months.

Though you agreed to that term, Mr. Tate, I did not. I did not enter into any agreement with you or the District Attorney. I am not obligated to uphold such an agreement. I am obligated to serve justice and that is what I plan to do today. Mr. Tate, I hereby sentence you to no less than 1,200 months, plus 1 day in federal prison. May you rot in hell, Mr. Tate. Bailiffs, please escort Mr. Tate out of my courtroom."

My heart sank. I don't know why, but I suppose I was in as much shock as Gage was in that moment. As he was escorted out of the courtroom, he looked back over his shoulder at me. A part of me wanted to smile big and wave. But I could not. Instead, I sat with tears streaming down my face. Part of my slight hysteria was the emotional crash I felt when it finally seemed to be over. This entire ordeal was over and though I thought it was going to feel liberating, I felt a heavier burden than ever. I was relieved from one set of feelings, only to just begin the process of grief over what had happened in my life the last few years.

I can equate this feeling to having lost a loved one, someone you cared greatly for, but then circumstances prevented you from taking the time grieve over that loss. Eventually the time would come when you crashed and were forced to deal with that grief. This was my time to deal with losing Gage Tate. This was my time to deal with what he had done to me and to my family. This was my time to cry.

One hundred years and a day is most assuredly a lifetime. Gage would never see the light of day again as a free man. And he would never be able to hurt anyone again. While those facts were pleasing to listen to, Gage Tate was my best friend. I wasn't sure I would ever trust anyone or anything again, not after this. A part of me and a part of everything I knew as a man in this world went to prison for life with Gage Tate.

May God look after those Gage Tate hurt. And may God look after those he brought down in the process. For God is the only one who can save anyone from such a wretched debacle. God bless you.

PTSD

We all know conspiracies are dumb;
But while your rational excuses explain away scum,
My life has passed along trapped in the cage,
And I have muffled all my rage.

Suspicion leads to lies,
And officials close their eyes,
To ensure personal deniability,
And to control system stability.

I have learned a few things
As the pendulum swings,
And I can see what others ignore,
A victim in our system is treated like a whore.

With false allegations and a cruel twisted word,
And replacing my words with what they never heard,
A life, my life, can be snatched out of thin air.
A life now in need of rescue and prayer.

And as I lay beaten and bruised,
Licking my wounds and feeling used,
I know it cannot get any worse,
I know this is a short road to traverse.

In gaining my second wind, a will to fight,
I know no matter how dark and cold it is at night,
I must battle this calamity with the loudest voice,
Until someone listened to my lack of choice.

But from the cage I was so cruelly forced in,
My patience and hope quickly wore thin.
As I was spun through the system like a damaged wheel,
I had to listen to the judge give me the bad guy spiel.

We all know conspiracies are dumb,
And whether right or wrong, this is what I have become.
And whether or not it did any good,
I have to believe it would.

Chapter 27

A HAPPY ENDING, IS TO BE CONTINUED...

CPSIA information can be obtained
at www.ICGtesting.com
Printed in the USA
BVHW07s2104210618
519632BV00001B/24/P

9 781456 764814